# Surfing and Social Theory

Surfing has emerged from ancient roots to become a twenty-first century phe-nomenon – an 'alternative' sport, lifestyle and art form now with a global profile and ever-increasing numbers of participants. Drawing on popular surf culture, academic literature and the analytical tools of social theory, this book is the first sustained commentary on the contemporary social and cultural meaning of surfing.

Core themes of mind and body, emotions and identity, aesthetics, style and sensory experience are explored through a variety of topics, including:

- evolving perceptions of the sea and the beach
- the narrative of surfing history, media and photography
- the globalization of surfing
- surfing as a subculture and lifestyle
- the embodiment and gendering of surfing
- the lived experience of surfing.

*Surfing and Social Theory* provides students and researchers in sport, sociology, culture and geography with a new combination of perspectives, and a new research agenda.

**Nick Ford** is Senior Lecturer in geography at the University of Exeter, UK. He is a lifelong surfer. **David Brown** is Lecturer in the sociology of sport and physical culture in the School of Sport and Health Sciences at the University of Exeter, UK. His research focuses on qualitative socio-cultural understandings of the body, the self and society.

D0294084

# Surfing and Social Theory

Experience, embodiment and narrative
of the dream glide

Nick Ford and David Brown

 Routledge
Taylor & Francis Group

LONDON AND NEW YORK

First published 2006
by Routledge
2 Park Square, Milton Park, Abingdon, Oxon OX14 4RN

Simultaneously published in the USA and Canada
by Routledge
270 Madison Ave, New York, NY 10016

*Routledge is an imprint of the Taylor & Francis Group*

© 2006 Nick Ford and David Brown

Typeset in Goudy by Keystroke, Jacaranda Lodge, Wolverhampton
Printed and bound in Great Britain by The Cromwell Press, Trowbridge, Wiltshire

*British Library Cataloguing in Publication Data*
A catalogue record for this book is available from the British Library

*Library of Congress Cataloging in Publication Data*
A catalog record for this book has been requested

ISBN10 0–415–33432–2    ISBN 9–78–0–415–33432–7 (Hbk)
ISBN10 0–415–33433–0    ISBN 9–78–0–415–33433–4 (Pbk)

# Contents

# List of illustrations

## Figures

## Plates

## Tables

# Preface

The writing of this book on surfing and social theory has involved a collaboration between researchers from the diverse backgrounds of human geography and sports sociology. Nick Ford's prior work has primarily been in culture, lifestyle and sexuality, and David Brown's main research interests have been in the body, identity and gender. However, both have core interests in embodi-ment, experience and the mind/body interface and the collaboration in writing emerged from a recognition of shared research aspirations and theoretical interests. In particular, both authors are concerned with seeking to develop forms of living knowledge that provide the potential to transcend the mind–body dualism that dominates the Western scholastic tradition. Nick's interest in writing about surfing stemmed from both more than 30 years' experience of surfing throughout Europe and the tropical world and an awareness, as external examiner of both of the UK's new Surf Science degrees, of the paucity (with some notable exceptions) of scholarship on the sociocultural and experiential aspects of surfing. Both authors recognized that the combination of surfing as embodied practice and cultural phenomenon provides a focus to explore numerous dimensions of the mind/body interface. In structuring and composing this book the authors have had necessarily to be selective in the choice of the themes finally included in the text. They have attempted to draw out numerous connections between wide-ranging bodies of theory, which afford the potential for future research to further explore and develop the understanding of surfing, and hopefully, for surfing-related research to impact back upon more general scholarship.

# Acknowledgements

Particular gratitude goes to the following colleagues for feedback both on the book's development and particular chapters: Malcolm Findlay, Brett Smith, Andrew Sparkes, Grace Davie and Kate Brace. We would also like to acknowledge the stimulation from the numerous students whom we have supervised over the years in surfing-related dissertations, their enthusiasm for their surfing studies encouraged us in this venture. We would also like to thank Clare Knapman for all her careful and timely typing of certain chapters, and David would like to express his thanks to Tamsin for her support.

# 1 Introduction

A sliding flight, explosive manoeuvres, moving walls, momentary green caverns, shocking whiteness of sun-lit foam, exquisite patterns forming and dissipating, thunderous roar, feathering peaks, translucent lips, transcendent highs, gliding along the edge of the two great realms of sea and sky – such are some of the vivid expressions which may be associated with the simple practice of surfing. An autotelic, non-instrumental glide along an ephemeral line of force expending its energy along the margins of our share-based world. An embodied experience with an addictive tendency which may connect with the seemingly endless search for some form of mythical perfection, the 'dream' of surfing. Such dreams inspire journeys, lifestyles and, in retrospect, shape and inform memories of personal significance. This book seeks to explore the encultured 'dream' and the embodied 'glide' of surfing in terms of a whole series of theoretical prisms, drawn mostly (but not entirely) from the interpretive or hermeneutic turn of the social sciences. This text is not an aesthetic evocation of surfing, but rather an attempt to show how our understanding of the nature of surfing may be informed by a wide range of (often theoretical) literatures. As such, this book seeks to draw upon the relatively small amount of systematic scholarship that has focused on surfing, and to provide a basis for the growing body of academic research into the sociocultural, psychological and geographical dimensions of the phenomenon. Although the disciplinary 'homes' of the authors are human geography and the sociology of sport, the tone of the book is primarily transdisciplinary, but hopefully contributing to the newly emerging field of scholarship of surfing studies. Indeed, in recent years the first Surf Science degree courses have been established (at the University of Plymouth and Cornwall College in the UK) and there has been a very rapid increase in the number of student dissertations (from a whole range of disciplines) addressed to surfing.

The timing of this writing, however, is not purely academic. At this juncture in the development of surfing, as the sport/lifestyle reaches a certain maturity, along with the nostalgia of a 'greying demographic', beyond traditional affinities with youth culture, growing numbers of surfers are attempting to make sense of the immense impact that this simple, non-instrumental aquatic pursuit has had on their life course and personal meanings and memory. An aesthetically and intellectually rich popular literature of surfing has been unfolding over the past four decades, chiefly in magazine format, but also increasingly in terms of a proliferation of celebrations and analyses of surfing history and culture (e.g. Carroll 1991; Young 1994; Warshaw 1997; Kampion and Brown 1998; George 2001). This book also engages with more general surfing literature but, rather than repeating its contents, seeks to contextualize and explore the patterns which are emerging, as surfing culture has sought to make itself intelligible. It is also important to stress that the focus is not so much on the celebrated heroes and stars of competitive surfing, but rather on the everyday experiences of thousands of surfers the world over.

It is clearly recognized that the growth of surfing, especially in the latter half of the twentieth century, is related to, and partially embedded within, the emergence of and growing participation in the proliferation of so-called alternative, extreme, lifestyle or 'whizz' sports (Midol and Broyer 1995; Rinehart 2000; Rinehart and Sydnor 2003). The practice, experience and culture of surfing has so many parallels with allied pursuits such as, for instance, snowboarding and skateboarding. Such parallels include an ambivalent or even oppositional stance to authority, a concern with a sense of authenticity, an individualist emphasis on a direct, unmediated experience, which is nevertheless expressively shared in relation to both an almost tribal communitas and a more competitive pursuit of subcultural capital. However, while acknowledging that surfing shares many of the defining qualities of such alternative or lifestyle sports, the aim of this book is to focus specifically on the particularities of the experience and culture of surfing. Furthermore, while again recognizing the extremely close connections between the various forms of surf-based aquatic pursuits (e.g. bodysurfing, boogie boarding, surf canoeing, surf skiing, windsurfing and so on) the focus of this book is primarily on what may be described as stand-up board surfing. This decision was primarily based on concerns to avoid superficiality of discussion and in relation to the limitations of space within a single text.

The 'dream' and 'glide' of the book's subtitle reflect its core themes of mind and body, and the attempt to at least point towards ways in which an understanding of surfing may transcend Western scholarship's pervasive mind–body split. This theme is variously addressed throughout the chapters in terms of, for instance, representation (of texts, media, photography and so on) and non-representation (as embodied practice/unmediated experience). Recurrent reference is made to the senses and emotions of surfing experience. One of the distinctive characteristics of surfing practice and culture, at least in relation to many other 'sports' has been the pervasiveness and richness of its inherent and associated aesthetic qualities. The representations and sensual expressions of surfing's aesthetic dimensions comprise a further core theme which is recurrently alluded to and explored in several chapters. The final section of this introductory chapter briefly outlines the structure of the following chapters in terms of their core generating questions and main contents.

There are innumerable ways of organizing a book such as this. The broad structuring finally adopted here moves through the historical, the subcultural, the gendered, the embodied and, finally, experiential dimensions of surfing. While there is considerable cross-referencing between chapters, each chapter has also been written to be able to stand alone, although it is hoped that a fuller picture will be derived from a reading of all of the chapters.

The sea and its energy is obviously inherently and intimately related to the practice, culture and experience of surfing. Thus, Chapter 2 addresses a whole series of questions which seek to embed and situate the 'rediscovery' and diffusion of surfing, chiefly during the twentieth century, within changing perceptions of the sea and coastscape. The main disciplinary prism of this review is the cultural geography perspective of the ways in which space and landscape (in this instance the sea and coastscape) are socially constructed. Chapter 2 seeks to answer the question of the historical origins and nature of the Western cultural imaginary of the sea, and how elements of this relate to both the initial Western reception of surfing and the character of contemporary surfing culture. The chapter outlines the changing representations of the sea over the course of history and the particular crystallization of sensibilities in relation to the raw power and energy of the sea, variously associated with the notion of the sublime and Romanticism. Reflecting the book's core concern with representation and non-representation, special reference is made to Corbin's (1994) work on the 'coenaesthetics' (the development of sensibilities through direct sensual experience) of the cultural relationship to the sea. Chapter 2 further explores contemporary evocations and analysis of the beach as the place of both a wider 'system of pleasures' (Shields 1991) and surfing culture (Fiske 1989). The binary oppositions of, for instance, nature and culture, the immediate and the mediated, which such analyses explore allow a further elaboration of the core theme of mind and body. This chapter also seeks to lay down the first elements of what may be termed 'the surfing gaze'.

As noted above, in recent decades there has been a growing trend of seeking to explore and document the history of surfing, both in terms of discovering its origins and explaining the current state of the art and culture of surfing. Chapter 3 explores the extent to which a general consensus exists concerning the story of surfing, as expressed and elaborated within the proliferating literature of surfing. Rather than repeating the rich detail of the contemporary accounts of surfing history and culture, Chapter 3 seeks to distil key elements and to explore the nature and bases of the selection of surfing culture's core themes. In particular, Chapter 3 applies the concepts of narrative history to surfing. To what extent has there been a 'laying claim to history' in the expressions of the surfing narrative? Specific themes which are discussed include mediatization and stardom, the aesthetics of surfing photography, and core tensions which shape the contemporary narrative of surfing. The history of surfing, especially within the latter half of the twentieth century, has been one of accelerating growth and global expansion. Thus, Chapter 3 also examines the narrative of surfing history and culture through the prisms of various lines of thinking concerning the globalization of sport and culture.

One of the most long-running and fraught questions, or rather debates, within the surfing media has been that of whether, and in what ways, the practice of waveriding is, variously, a sport, artform or lifestyle? Chapter 4 seeks to elaborate on this debate with particular reference to theory pertaining to subculture and consumption. The general theoretical context is sketched out by reference to both, general theory pertaining to subculture, taste and lifestyle, and the specific application of such theory within the field of sports studies. These lines of thinking are then applied to surfing with reference to a series of themes; notably the appeal and attraction of surfing is explored in relation to the narrative of surfing history, the ascription of its cultural connotations and their appropriation and dissemination, through film and fashion, to the wider world. The development of such expressive aspects of surfing subculture as fashion, argot and style are discussed as epiphenomena to the core activity of waveriding. This section explores the degree to which surfing as subculture may be considered oppositional, and its parallel concerns with authenticity and ambivalence and antipathy to commercialism.

The second core theme seeks to explore the ways in which individuals may become involved in, and socialized into, surfing. This section focuses in particular on senses of identity and expressions of emotions in relation to surfing. In particular, this section draws upon recent research which has identified some intriguing changes in individuals' orientation to and concepts of surfing culture with deepening involvement, with reference to the concept of a surfing 'career' (in the widest sense of the term). Such questions of dynamic involvement in/with surfing over time are further explored in terms of the appropriation and creation of surfing lifestyles, with their coherence and aesthetic relationship to the ocean. In a more practical sense, surfing lifestyles are discussed with reference to income and cost aspects of consumption behaviour.

The third core theme of Chapter 4 pertains to surfing's inherent scarcities and territoriality, these matters are explored with reference to the place of prestige or subcultural capital and surf etiquette in the informal regulation of access to waves. A key tension within surfing culture relates to the expressive, social recognition-seeking, informally competitive tendencies, and the more spiritual and individualist orientations towards surfing. This section also reviews research pertaining to crowding, localism and 'surf rage' and the stereotyping and 'othering' of other surfers. Chapter 4 seeks to further develop the social dimensions of the surfer's gaze.

Chapter 5 explores surfing from the point of view of the gender relations that are readily observable within this subcultural activity. It begins by reflecting on how, until quite recently, representations of surfing culture have been based on the unquestioned logic that the social development of surfing was a physically and symbolically 'male' activity, that in some circumstances women also participated and invested themselves into without issue. It points out that such representations are both often romanticized and problematic. The chapter then seeks to introduce some critical feminist perspectives to the subcultural study of surfing by applying a conceptual perspective that helps to position surfing culture within the complex web of patriarchal gender power relations. This perspective contains a number of elements. First, that gender in surfing is most usefully considered as an embodied, relational phenomenon where gender legitimacy and hierarchy are historically constructed though the binary opposition of beliefs about femininity and masculinity. Next, the chapter begins to explore how understandings of gender in surfing need to go beyond such oppositions in order to consider gender in surfing as a pluralized complex of masculinities and femininities. This perspective is then broadened to consider how the development of competitive, 'sport' surfing has presaged the interconnection of gender relations internal to surfing culture with those of a globalized practical and symbolic (world) gender order that is locally and globally networked. The discussion then focuses on the development of men and women's surfing as set in this context, and in so doing offers some insights into aspects of social change and reproduction in equal measure. The chapter concludes in an attempt to make some sense of these apparent contradictions. In so doing it suggests a perspective that considers changing gender relations in surfing as socioculturally located, rather than universal, dynamic rather than fixed, and contested rather than agreed. Nevertheless, in conclusion it is suggested that the gender order still remains very apparent in surfing culture and, while recent transformations in gender relations have been significant, it also suggests that the dominant masculine groups in surfing do not concede their power and privilege easily.

The main purpose of Chapter 6 is to draw attention to the lack of focus on the social body that has hitherto characterized the investigation of the surfing subcultures. It points out that, as with so many sports and physical activities (until quite recently), surfing bodies have been largely 'absent' and assumed in the study of surfing. In so doing it highlights the potential insights to be gleaned from a fully embodied analysis of the surfing body, that immediately shows how the body is both active and passive (hence the title – surfing and surfed bodies). In recent years the literature on the body in society has moved from a 'dearth' to a 'deluge' and this chapter knowingly adds to this proliferating cascade of views, perspectives and applications. Moreover, acknowledging the limitations of space to represent the possible range of perspectives in relation to surfing, choices have been made. These choices are based on the observation that some fundamental properties of the body are applicable to every setting, arguably these are:

1   the practical body
2   the interacting body
3   the storied body.

As such these represent the ingredients of some core propositions about the surfing body that emerge from the text more generally. However, the chapter endeavours to make clear that each of these perspectives on their own does not present a sufficiently complete picture. It is only when we bring such views together that the impact and importance of the surfing body begins to come into focus. Thus, while bodies are simultaneously practical, interacting and storied, they also result in *lived* and *emotional* bodies. To this end, the chapter concludes with a consideration of these perspectives of the body as the way forward for the study of the body in surfing.

Like Chapter 6, Chapter 7 is concerned with surfing as an embodied practice. However, Chapter 7 reviews a range of different methodological approaches to understanding the nature of the surfing experience. Particular questions that Chapter 7 seeks to address include: what are the parallels and divergences between surfing and dance? What insights and directions may be derived from dance studies for the enhancement of the nascent field of surfing studies? Such parallels are particularly useful in exploring the underdeveloped analysis of style in surfing. Following a brief note on physiological research into surfing, this chapter seeks to examine the experience of surfing in relation to more psychological studies of the motivations underlying surfing. Key questions that are addressed include: what do the main motivations for surfing and their contrasting relation to more formal sports tell us about the nature of the surfing experience?

One of the distinctive aspects of surfing, in contrast to more formal sports and many other leisure pursuits, is the frequent allusion to peak and ecstatic experience. Chapter 7 seeks to review the conceptual bases of the sports' literatures on peak and flow experience in relation to surfing. Given that the verbal expression of peak experiences is often conceived as seeking to express the inexpressible, the chapter concludes with an application of some of the tenets of non-representational theory to surfing as an embodied practice. In concluding the chapter such an approach returns to the core theme of the book of seeking to transcend the mind–body dualism of the dominant, Western, representation-based, scholastic tradition.

Chapter 8 draws together the key conclusions which have emerged from the book. This concluding chapter is structured in three sections: first a concise listing of a series of core propositions which may be viewed as comprising a tentative and provisional thesis on the nature of surfing. Reflecting the exploratory nature of the book, this is followed by an overview of some key directions for further research into surfing. The book finally concludes with some reflections on methodology and ontology of research into surfing as an embodied practice.

# 2 The enchanted sea

## The evolving perceptions of the sea, coastscape and beach

## Introduction

The sea is not merely the physical medium in which surfing is undertaken, but, along with the beach, it is a place and setting of enormous personal significance and meanings to surfers.[1] Furthermore the cultural representations which surround surfing for the wider society are also imbued with the almost archetypal images of the wave as a natural energy force and the seashore as margin or cultural periphery. This chapter seeks to situate surfing within the broad sweep of (primarily) Western culture's evolving perceptions and representations of the sea and beach.

Of course, the origins of surfing lie with the pre-modern Pacific island peoples of Hawaii or perhaps the Marquesas. However, the focus here is on the changing perceptions of the sea in Western culture, because it is in that context that surfing was 'rediscovered' and from which it has developed and diffused to its current, global appeal. Furthermore, it is notable that the earliest European impressions of the sight of surfing, as evidenced in the reports from the members of Captain Cook's visit to Hawaii in 1778/79 (e.g. Beaglehole 1967 in Finney and Houston 1996), were dominated by an almost overwhelming sense of surprise and awe. We may speculate that the reaction of surfing's first European observers suggests a resonance with certain evolving sensibilities and images of the sea already present or nascent within the Western imaginary.

Given that the core themes underlying this study of surfing are those of the interplays of mind and body, thought and emotion, and image and experience, the focus in this chapter is not only upon representations of the sea, but also Western culture's evolving sensibilities and physical encounter with the waters and waves. The interest here is not just in seabathing as such, but rather in the encounter with the energy, raw power and turbulence of the waves which is so central to surfing. Particular attention is given below to Corbin's (1994) use of 'coenaesthetics' (the development of sensibilities through the senses) in charting our changing relationship to the sea at the shores.

This chapter is structured in three main sections: first, providing a conceptual backdrop, cultural geography's perspectives of the social construction of space and landscape are applied to the coastscape; second, drawing on literary and historical sources, an attempt is made to provide a sweeping overview, from antiquity to the present, of changing representations and sensibilities towards the sea; and third, some more contemporary interpretations of the beach are explored, which provide a context for later discussions of notions of surf culture.

## Landscapes/coastscapes

The concern here is with the coastscape and beach as *generic* phenomena, while the characteristics of *particular* coastscapes or surfing localities provide an avenue for further research. Surfing takes place within the very specific milieu of the fluctuating, overlapping boundary of the two great elements of the land and the sea. This liminal zone (Shields 1991) has often been expressed in terms of the binary oppositions and the interpenetration of society and nature. An increasing corpus of theory is stressing that, rather than being separable, 'nature' is better conceptualized as socially constructed. Macnaghten and Urry (1998) argue, for instance, that nature should be viewed as a set of specific social practices, involving five constitutive principles, these being: discursively ordered (through language); embodied (sensed); spaced (with conflicting levels of the local, national and global); timed (implications for the future), and related to models of human activity, risk, agency and trust.

Similarly, although geographers have tended to emphasize the visual aspects of landscape, it is primarily recognized (as with space more generally) as structured by social, material and ideological practices. Brace (2004) stresses that landscapes are not passive. As Morin (2003) puts it, it is a matter of 'what landscape does, . . . how it is produced and how it works in social practice' (Morin 2003: 319).

Social theory has sought to understand the creation of types of landscapes in terms of two sets of shaping systems: first, social structures and ideologies (Mitchell 1994) and second, discourses and texts involved in the representation and interpretation of landscape (Cosgrove 1998; Morin 2003). With respect to the former, in *Social Formation and Symbolic Landscapes* (1984) Cosgrove sought to locate landscape within a broadly Marxian, critical historiography, developing the thesis that:

> Landscape constitutes a discourse through which identifiable social groups historically have framed themselves and their relations both with other social groups and the land.
>
> (Cosgrove 1998: xiv)

Interestingly, in the extended new introduction of the 1998 edition of the same book, Cosgrove argued for the primary concern with the 'transition to capitalism' to be superseded by a broader concern with scopic regimes in the development of modernity with *complex* connections to social and technical change (Jay 1992 in Cosgrove 1998). Such a broadening of perspectives further included greater concern with texts of gender, embodiment, emotion and aesthetics in landscape discourse. This return to concerns with the emotional and aesthetic dimensions of sense of place echoes the earlier humanistic 'Topophilian' geography of Yi Fu Tuan (1974).

Nash (1999) has discussed the ways in which geographers have used different metaphors to explain landscapes, as a way of seeing (Cosgrove 1985) or as a text that can be read (Duncan 1995). Such discourses of representation generally involve multiple interpretations and levels of meaning, which are socially inscribed and change over time (Morin 2003).

Advocating more embodied and sensual approaches (later echoed by Rodaway 1994) to understanding landscape and place, Shields has stressed that '[t]here is tremendous complicity between the body and the environment and the two interpenetrate each other' (Shields 1991: 14). Describing 'image' as memory of a scene (such as the beach), Shields highlights the need to distinguish between peoples' existential participation in their environment (here the direct physical encounter with the sea further developed in Chapter 7) and the culturally mediated reception of representations of place (here the coastscape as a cultural formation expressed, for instance, in art and literature). Cosgrove has noted that the refocus of attention on the aesthetic and emotional dimensions of landscape has entailed 'a revival of interest in the referential capacities of art, but with a much freer attitude towards references and iconographic meanings' (Cosgrove 1998: xxii).

This brief outline of some of the main threads of recent cultural geographical approaches to landscape has sought to identify the themes which inform the following exploration of the changing representations of the sea, coastscape and beach ('sites' which have been relatively neglected in landscape studies). Thus the landscape can be seen as shaped by social processes and represented in art and literature, but with the meanings ascribed shifting over time in relation to major (including technological) changes.

## Historically changing symbolisms and representations of the sea and coastscape

As Osborn (1977) has noted, throughout history the sea has served as a symbol eliciting deep response, characteristic of a great archetypal metaphor for various meanings. Often linked to spiritual and existential dimensions, this is symbol, as Theodore Roszak (1972) would argue, not as some form of corresponding 'cipher', but rather perhaps as something sacramental, inexhaustible and experiential. Meanings associated with the sea may often be referred to as 'timeless' but they are certainly not changeless, being transformed by epochal developments in human culture and circumstances. Reference is here made to some of those images and symbolisms, noting in particular changing representations from ancient traditions, through to the Renaissance, 'age of discovery', Burke's 'sublime' and Romanticism. While drawing upon a range of writings, a core source underlying this section is Alain Corbin's masterpiece (1994) The Lure of the Sea.

Several ancient traditions share an association of the seas with the origins of life, 'the deep, the face of the waters' in Genesis, the 'primal chaos' of the Greeks, and the 'sea of milk' of Hindu cosmology, which echo the modern scientific notion of the 'soup of life' (Capra 1976). Auden expresses this earliest symbolism of the sea as 'the primordial, undifferentiated flux . . . that state of barbaric vagueness and disorder out of which civilization has emerged (and into which, unless saved by the efforts of gods and men, it is always liable to relapse' (Auden 1951: 18). Indeed, with the exception of the Romans who enjoyed possibly the earliest seaside leisure culture (Lencek and Bosker 1998), ancient societies viewed the sea with foreboding. Corbin identifies a coherent cluster of early representations, revolving primarily around the Bible and the ancient literature of the Greeks, wherein the sea inspired a deep sense of fear and repulsion. In Greek literature every boundary zone is an area of danger with the activities of the gods, human beings and animals living in confused proximity. Thus, based on antiquity's codification of the sea's anger, the seashore was represented as a zone of evil-smelling rotting flesh, containing the possibilities of epidemics, invasion, pirates and monsters rising up from the deep. The sea's storms evoked a sense of mortal danger and associations with madness.

Renaissance perspectives, as expressed, for instance, in Shakespeare, are often viewed as providing a bridge between the primarily dark and negative classical and medieval attitudes to the sea and the later more positive perspectives. Shakespeare's handling of the symbolism of the seas shows ambivalence. There is a transition from the purely negative stormy sea of his earlier plays, to the sea and voyage as a setting for purgatorial suffering and as a cleansing, transforming force in his later plays, such as *The Winter's Tale* and *The Tempest* (Knight 1932). While in the writing of the Renaissance the sea was still not a realm people entered for pleasure, there were at least intimations of more positive connotations. To Raban, Shakespeare's 'silver sea, triumphant sea and boundless sea' has a quality of 'brilliant irrealism' (Raban 1992: 6).

Corbin (1994) identifies some of the first steps towards the admiration of the sea in the ephemeral allusions to the joys of the seashore and marine enchantment in the works of early seventeenth-century French baroque poets, such as Antoine-Girard de Saint-Amant, and later ideas of natural theology. Both viewed the sea as a magical realm of metaphor and metamorphosis. To the baroque poets the ever-changing reflections of sunlight on the waters fulfilled the expectations of people for whom the spectacle of nature was a game of illusions. Natural theology saw mysterious correspondences between the physical and the spiritual world, the human and the divine and the microcosmos/macrocosmos. In these the spectacle of nature, manifested in the beauty of the sea, testified to the power and bounty of God. Such perspectives, reflecting a shift in the vision of the deity from a terrible God to a reassuring sovereign, began to erase the prior fearful images, and replace them with an Eden–Arcadian code of appreciation of a divinely ordained harmony of the coastscape.

Beyond such intimations of new aesthetic sensibilities, scientific and technological advances were having a perhaps greater impact on prevailing perceptions of the sea, as explored by Cawley (1940) and Bourke (1954). Osborn traces these changes to major cultural forces in the Elizabethan era. Progress in the new science of oceanography was displacing ancient myths of monsters and mysteries of the sea with more rational understandings. Furthermore, there was a new confidence in maritime technology on the path to what Raban (1992) has referred to as 'the domestication of the seas'. These advances underlay Europe's 'Age of Discovery' as imperial expansion and state rivalries led to voyages to ever-more distant parts of the globe, fuelled by a sense of adventure, enchantment with and attraction to exotic shores in search of profit and glory.

Corbin argues convincingly that it is during the period from around 1750 to 1840 that contemporary sensibilities surrounding the seashore are crystallized, especially in the many guidebooks and travelogues which were written to assist the growing desire for travel to classical Italy. These books combined a knowledge of the classics and identification of itineraries with interpretations of the hallowed landscapes, which combined neo-classical aesthetics with the Picturesque, even codifying the kinds of emotions which the journey was expected to arouse.

The rise of Picturesque values and desire for escape from the negativities of urban life, fostered increasing sensibility to marine aesthetics. However, of greater significance for the eventual ascendance of surfing is obviously the well-documented increase in seabathing. With this bodily practice, originally encouraged for its curative properties, but soon more generally for the sheer pleasure of its sense of invigoration, we move from purely representational attractions to a more sensual coenaesthetic phase of the West's relationship to the seashore. Corbin highlights the especial appeal of the turbulence of the sea:

> Pleasure came from the whipping of the waves. The bather delighted in feeling the powerful forces of the immense ocean. Bathing among the waves was part of the aesthetics of the sublime: it involved facing the violent water, but without risk, enjoying the pretence that one could be swept under, and being struck by the full force of the waves but without losing one's footing.
> (Corbin 1994: 73)

Seabathing was thus conceived as not only curative or cleansing but as vigorous exercize involving a multitude of sensations, entailing a virile image even including a latent eroticism. Corbin notes the social class differences in the experience of seabathing, contrasting the air of playfulness and spontaneity of the common folk, with the self-conscious coenaesthetic attention and construction of an emotional strategy of enjoying the sea and beach on the part of the middle and upper class (Shields 1991).

One element of this emotional strategy of relating to the seashore followed from natural theology's enjoyment of what is variously alluded to as stunning stupefaction, exquisite horror and terrible joy, as a feeling contributing to the sense of exultation of the divine. The significance of Edmund Burke's concept of the sublime is that it elaborated and codified these feelings. The sense of the sublime seems to conjoin ancient images of the ocean's immensity and dangers with a vital sense of its power and energy, especially in the primal form of the seastorm. Burke detailed the feelings aroused by the observation of such a spectacle: astonishment, mental panic and momentary amazement, overwhelming reason and jolting the individual into the present living moment. The sublime sea was characterized by magnificence, a beauty tinged with terror (see Plate 1), such that as Raban notes 'watching waves break . . . became a genteel occupation' (Raban 1992: 11).

The sense of the sublime was one of the major elements feeding into the emerging Romantic vision. Romanticism, as a reaction to the Enlightenment's emphasis on science, order and reason, was especially drawn to the image of the coastscape. The sea, especially in its wild and stormy incarnation, appeared as a recurring symbol of wild nature beyond the stifling control of reason. Drawing on earlier models, the creative contribution of the Romantic movement was to propound a coherent discourse of the sea, which enhanced the emotional strategy of enjoying the seashore. Corbin notes that Romantics such as von Stolberg, Byron, Shelley and Chateaubriand propounded a broad system of representations, an emotional strategy and a set of practices which led to new itineraries for coastal reverie.

Auden (1951) summarizes the distinctive Romantic attitude to the sea as including the desire on the part of the man [sic] of honour and sensibility to leave the land and the city, to voyage on the sea as the true test of masculinity, the realm where the decisive events, the moments of eternal choice occur. To poets such as Byron (in *Child Harold*) the land was associated with corruption, the sea with purity: 'Man marks the earth with ruin – his control stops with the shore' (in Auden 1951: 25). Thus, through the Romantic imagination the sea becomes a realm of freedom, containing the possibility, through heroic action, of self-realization. Such notions underlie the narratives of surfing journeys in innumerable articles in the surfing media. To Bourke (1954) the two symbolic qualities engendering this sense of freedom, were the sea's seeming boundlessness and seeming irresistibility. As Raban (1992) notes, in Britain the sea was the only untamed wilderness, an uncontrolled realm of sublime elemental forces.

Auden's exploration of the Romantic iconography of the sea was as much concerned with its implications for the understanding of the Romantic imagination, as with tracing changing societal perceptions of the sea. Indeed, a recurring theme in literature of the sea is the way in which perspectives and images of the ocean serve as a mirror to humankind and the human condition. For example, Conrad's (1906) collection of maritime essays was titled 'The Mirror of the Sea'. The image of the sea, its reflection of human nature, or more commonly to the Romantics, the depths of the human unconscious, and the Romantic voyage into the unknown and exotic, also inform much of Baudelaire's poetry. In *Correspondences* he conceives of a mysterious relation between images of nature and mind, conjoined in an intuitive vision. Baudelaire's sense of Romantic aesthetics is applied to the sea thus in *Mon Coeur Mis à Nu*:

> Free man, you will always love the sea!
> The sea is your mirror, you contemplate your soul.
>
> (e.g. in Richardson 1975: 50)

Through the Romantics' appropriation and crystallization of existing symbols a powerful image of the ocean was expressed as a realm of immeasurable potentiality, profundity and freedom. While the 'Enlightenment project' inherited the world through the unfolding advance of science and technology, including the continuing 'domestication of the sea', the Romantic image of the sea endured through time, continuing to shape contemporary perceptions. Furthermore, in their wild state the oceans have never been, and perhaps never can be, fully 'domesticated' or 'made safe', thus the primordial sense of the seas as a dangerous realm also persists. The ancient association of the sea with mortal threat and danger has obviously been powerfully reinforced recently by the Indian Ocean tsunami disaster of December 2004.[2]

Corbin expounds upon the new wealth of emotions which Romanticism crystallized in relation to the sea and shore. These included the longing for pantheistic merging, to become one with the universe, to dream of ancient magical realms, regression into the primordial and an intense sexualization of the seashore as a borderland with perils and magic. Such emotions fostered the desire for a greater intimacy and closer contact with the elements of the shore, both in terms of the spiritually uplifting solitary walk and in the more energetic bathing in the sea. Within Romanticism bathing takes on a greater refinement in the sensing of the physical encounter, relaxing into reverie and experiencing the soothing rocking of the surface in calm conditions, diving and plunging into the elemental depths, and swimming vigorously in the waves, as expressed by Byron, an energetic masculinized fight with natural forces.

The Romantic sensibilities towards and practices at the seashore were generally couched in terms of solitary pleasures and almost mystical communion with wild nature. Nevertheless they served to crystallize a whole emotional strategy which in time contributed towards the growing social trend of tourism to the seaside, initially led by the fashionable set, but subsequently, linked to advances in transport technology and statutory holidays, to mass excursions and large-scale resort development (Shields 1991; Lencek and Bosker 1998).

The whole Romantic tendency has been variously discussed (Corbin 1994; Steinberg 1999a, 2001; Rundell 2001; Casarino 2002) in terms of an intellectual reaction to the Enlightenment project of reason and French political reform, longstanding tensions in the related capitalist appropriation of the ocean and the crisis named modernity.

Casarino (2002) has analysed the unfolding forms of the nineteenth-century sea narrative as overlapping, but shifting, residual archaic, dominant and emergent forms of artistic representation. The first form which Casarino terms the 'exotic picaresque', including the accounts of Cook's voyages and other travelogues, is viewed as an ancient form which can be traced back to the Renaissance and Homer's *Odyssey*. The 'exotic picaresque' expressed a sense of awe and wonder, and fascination and repulsion for faraway exotic shores. The second form, the 'Bildungsroman' developed upon the earlier sea adventure narrative, but placed primary emphasis on the (often young and innocent) hero's trials and tribulations as a rite of passage. Both of these forms of representation incorporate obviously Romantic elements and resonate powerfully with both the wanderlust and self-realization dimensions of surfing culture. Casarino's modern sea narrative is structured primarily around the voyage as the self-enclosed and autocratic world of the ship, exploring more modern preoccupations such as disciplinary mechanisms, social and ethnic conflicts and gender roles. Casarino argues that the ship becomes a representation in the examination of the turbulent transitions entailed in the epochal shifts from mercantile to industrial capitalism.

Similarly, Steinberg's (1999b) work on the geography of ocean space seeks to place changing representations of the sea, primarily within the modern era, in relation to an overarching political economy. Steinberg contends that by the close of the twentieth century, there were three main images of ocean space: as an empty void to be annihilated by hyper-mobile capital; as a resource space requiring sustainable development; and as a source of consumable (post-modern) spectacles (1999a). This third form (as a site of spectacle for instance as a setting for cinematic adventures, harbourside heritage developments and touristic attraction) resonates with the Romantic representation of a search for alternatives to modern terrestrial society, as an untamed nature, 'the sea as a wild other'. The key point is that in contemporary representations of the ocean space there is a range of images linked to different discourses within the same time period. However, the different discourses obviously function in relation to different operational remits. With respect to the seashore and coastscape as a zone of pleasure and recreation the dominant imaging is that of a nostalgic space, fulfilling a need for escape (Steinberg 1999a).

The final section of this chapter further develops some of these notions in relation to contemporary interpretations of the beach with particular focus upon surfing.

## Contemporary interpretations of the beach

It is no accident that much of the finest interpretation and analysis of the beach has been written by Australians (Dutton 1983; Fiske 1989; Booth 2001a). As Dutton (1983) has argued, although the tradition of the beach is not necessarily understood or accepted in intellectual circles, it is endorsed by the vast majority of Australians. In *Sun, Sea, Surf and Sand – the Myth of the Beach* Dutton has composed one of the most sensitive, nuanced and beautiful exploratory evocations of the human experience of the beach. In this work Dutton drew upon artists, authors and poets of Australia to illustrate how the beach has become the dominant tradition in Australian life.

This section on contemporary interpretations follows a structure reviewing evocations, cultural analyses revolving around binary categories, environmental orientations to beach development and commercialization, with concluding reference to some of the ways such conceptualizations may be related to surf culture.

There are certain resonances between Dutton's explorations of the beach experience with Corbin's historical analysis focusing on representations and coenaesthetics discussed earlier. Dutton traces the changes in artistic depictions of the beach from earlier (late nineteenth-century) preoccupations with the visual aspects of the long lines of the coastscape and water, through a growing focus on the place of humanity in the scene, to later recognition of the sensual and sensuous qualities of the human encounter with sand and sea. The sense of the natural and cultural pervades the thematic treatments of the beach running through, for instance, a 'legend of pleasure' going back to Aboriginal times, through to ecstasy, hedonism and sexuality by the sea, images of different kinds of beaches, and the solitary and tranquil pursuits of beachcombers. A core theme running through the chapters is that of freedom ranging from an almost aesthetic and spiritual sense, through bodily sensation in the water, to the progressive relaxation of social restrictions and reduction of clothing on the beach, culminating in the 'quivering mirage of sexuality' across the modern urban beach. Documenting the growth of surfbathing, surf lifesaving and surfing in Australia, Dutton contrasts the more genteel seabathing in Europe to the Australian experience of waves thumping, massaging and bracing the body and muscles. These themes are further addressed more theoretically and analytically in the works of Shields and Fiske.

In his analysis of marginal places, Shields (1991) discussed the beach within a wider system of pleasures (representations) as a leisure space characterized by liminality and carnival, drawing upon the anthropological studies of Turner (1974) and Van Gennep (1909/1960). The seashore is both a literal, physical limen (margin) of shifting nature between high and low tide, and a cultural margin in emotional space. By virtue of their (general) absence of incorporation into private property, Shields argued, beaches have been 'free zones', with their liminality fostering a socially unifying experience of communitas and the relaxation of customary social controls on dress and comportment.

Fiske's analysis seeks to read the beach semiotically as a text as 'a signifying construct of potential meanings' (1989: 43). Fiske's discussion of the beach as an 'anomalous category between land and sea' which gives 'it an excess of meaning potential' (1989: 43) echoes Shields' application of the beach as a liminal or liminoid space. Furthermore, both writers elaborate their analyses on the basis of binary cultural categories. For Shields, the key binaries include liminal and mundane, ludic and rational, central and marginal, while for Fiske a whole series (Figure 2.1) follows on from the fundamental binary of nature and culture, echoing human geography's long-standing interests in the nature/society dualism (Hanson 1999; Preston-Whyte 2002).

Fiske works from an idealized model and relates its zoning to a case study of Cottesloe beach in Western Australia. Running from culture to nature, Fiske outlines the series of typical zones of city, road, lawn, esplanade, beach, shallow water and deep water, which signify the progressive shift from civilization to the uncivilized raw nature. The urbanized culture extends its control over the meaning of the beach through a whole plethora of human interventions including, for instance, groynes, sharknets, lifeguards' towers and various prohibitory notices (for instance, excluding dogs, specific types of beach and water usage and unclothed sunbathing). Thus, from the roadside to the deep water, and outwards from the city centre to more outlying rural stretches of beach, there is a progressive relaxation of cultural control. Fiske's primary interest is with the ways in which these

*Figure 2.1* Nature–culture categories as applied to the use of the beach

| Nature | Culture |
|---|---|
| Body | Mind |
| Physical sensation | Conceptual construction |
| Signifier | Signified |
| Pleasure | Ideology |
| Linguistic disorder | Linguistic order |
| Anarchy | Control |
| Danger | Safety |
| Freedom | Control |
| Sea | Land |
| Naked | Clothed |
| Raw | Cultivated |
| Immediate | Mediated |
| | (adapted from Fiske 1989) |
| Erotic/ludic | Rational |
| Periphery | Centre |
| Liminal | Mundane |
| Carnivalesque | Social order |
| | (adapted from Shields 1991) |

Source: adapted from Fiske 1989 and Shields 1991)

zones and human interventions involve the contestation and establishment of different meanings over beach space. Just as the deep water ('outback') is the zone of the most intense and risky surfing, so the outlying beaches and, in particular, the boundary spaces between named beaches, are the zones for the more 'scandalous' and topless sunbathing. Both are connected to the bodily and sensual pole of the nature–culture binary, outlined in Figure 2.1.

Such patterns of meanings underlie both functional beach development typologies (Morgan 1999) and environmental perspectives on coastline infrastructure and facilities (such as parking and toilets). Morgan derived a five-category beach development typology ranging from beaches with no facilities, through those with a few, basic facilities, to those of small, medium and large-scale resorts. Environmental values have been widely conceptualized as fundamentally revolving around ecocentric–technocentric (O'Riordan 1981), and ecocentric–anthropocentric (Rolston III 1994a,1994b; Benson 2000) dichotomies. The ecocentric value orientation places strong emphasis on preserving nature for its own intrinsic value, whilst an anthropocentric rationale views the natural environment solely in terms of its utility for human usage.

Meredith (2003) examined environmental perspectives with reference to attitudes to the Surf Centre development at Fistral beach, Newquay, UK. Her analysis articulated the multiple meanings that beaches held for different subgroups and individuals. In particular, attitudes to beach development were found to vary according to whether the primary value was conferred on the beach attributes of natural power, beauty and tranquillity, or commodified, recreational and commercial needs. Rees (2003) examined the contested character of beach development within the village of St Agnes in Cornwall, within the general context of Steinberg's (2001) political economy of the social construction of the sea. Her work showed how different users' beach needs shaped environmental and developmental perspectives. A further values-based approach to environmental advocacies has been articulated in terms of 'harmony', 'stewardship' and 'exploitation/domination' approaches (White 1967; Black 1970). Rees analysed the environmental group Surfers Against Sewage (SAS, based in St Agnes) as an example of a surfing pressure group reflecting a broader social movement. Her study, which combined quantitative survey and qualitative interview methods, showed that many local surfers' views of the sea expressed a harmony ethos, but in terms of the practical response, Surfers Against Sewage present a stewardship approach of recognizing a human responsibility to protect and actively manage the marine environment.

As Shields has argued 'sites are never simply locations, rather they are sites for someone and of something' (1991: 6). Although the practice of surfing may be embedded within wider cultural tendencies in the human encounter with the seashore, it is, nevertheless, a highly specific practice, which would be expected to be associated with distinctive meanings and cognizance of the sea.

It is highly plausible to surmize that there is a 'surfers' gaze' on the sea and coastscape, which would both link with wider cultural tendencies (for instance regarding representations of the sea) but which would also be distinctive to other sea and beach users' gazes. Environmental elements of such a surfers' gaze could include interpretations of 'signs' as in Fiske's reading of the beach as text, and aesthetic considerations of the coast as landscape. More operationally such a gaze would include the broad sweep and minutiae of ever-changing surf conditions (Preston-Whyte 2002). The more social dimensions of the surfers' gaze are discussed in later chapters such as pertaining to identity formation (in Chapter 3), and performance, subcultural affiliation and status (in Chapter 4).

In terms of the system of binaries following from nature and culture, Fiske locates the meaning of surfing strongly with nature and its associations with body, physical sensation, pleasure, freedom, risk and danger. 'The wave is that text of bliss to the surfie, escape from the signified, potential re-entry into nature' (Fiske 1989: 76). Thus, in Fiske's reading of the beach, surfing exemplifies the associations with the raw, immediate, physical experience of sensations, although noting that surfing is 'clawed back into cultural centrality by business' (1989: 67).

Linking with Fiske's analysis, studies of motivations behind surfing (Farmer 1992) have shown that the primary drive is for the experience of vertigo, or the thrill and exhilaration of the experience (see Chapter 7). However, such studies also show that surfing motivations also place a much higher value on the aesthetics of the experience, than most other sports. Such aesthetic considerations revolve around a whole range of factors including, not only performance, media and the ephemera of fashion, but also, in 'Topophilian' terms (Tuan 1974) the landscape setting which comprises surfing's sports arena. Heap's (2003) analysis of surfers in

Croyde, North Devon, UK has broadly replicated Farmer's Australian findings but also shown how different surfers place different levels of emphasis on the aesthetics of coastscape. She quotes one primarily aesthetically motivated surfer: 'when I'm surfing the best feeling for me is being at one with, and completely immersed in, nature'. These themes, along with the links between landscape and identity (Brace 2004), will be further explored with regard to surfing lifestyles in Chapter 4 and the surfing experience in Chapter 7. Suffice it to note here that the aesthetic experience, as Maquet (1986) has shown, is fundamentally contemplative, being rooted in absorption and so-called peak experience.

Finally, as well as such abstract notions of oneness with nature and rarefied sensibilities, the surfer's gaze is also comprised of a wealth of practical knowledge and awareness pertaining directly to the changing quality of surf conditions. Obviously such sensory-derived knowledge (Preston-Whyte 2002) involves a grasp of the way different types of swells interact with changing wind directions and strengths, tides and beach topography (sandbank, reefs, points and so on) in particular locations to shape the breaking of waves. In this learning process visual observation is reinforced by physical interaction with the waves, with surfers as 'reflexive performers grappling with a material environment that is active rather than passive' (Preston-Whyte 2002: 311 after Cloke and Perkins 1998; Perkins and Thoms 2001). On the one hand, those relatively new to surfing can gain a basic awareness of the quality of waves (choppy, glassy, peeling, closing out and so on) fairly quickly, learning initially from the observations of more experienced surfers. On the other hand, this embodied awareness deepens with time and experience, and there is always a new learning process when a surfer encounters a surf break for the first time and comes to terms with the particularities of its waves. Preston-Whyte's survey in Durban demonstrated surfers' rich awareness of the varied nature of the waves (bowl waves, shorebreak waves, outside waves, mound waves and reef waves) along the Durban seafront. Indeed, often with merely a glimpse of the texture of the sea and waves breaking over some distant rock, an experienced surfer (knowing the tidal situation) will immediately have a sense of the size and quality of surf conditions at a range of nearby breaks. A further, more micro-level, almost obsessive, aspect of the surfers' gaze is the tendency, when looking at the sea and waves, for the eye to automatically focus on the 'pocket', the unfolding section as the wave (or even shore-side ripple) breaks, as if riding the wave in the imagination. In parallel there is also a surf lifesavers' gaze whereby, especially when conditions are dangerous, the eye automatically seeks to identify the pattern of rip currents, strength of drag and power of shorebreak as hazards to inexperienced bathers.

This chapter has sought to provide some context for the understanding of surfing by illustrating its connections with some major threads in Western cultural history of the encounter and representation of the sea and coastscape. A broad overview of the changing representations of the sea and coastscape has been outlined. Such representations were seen to overlap with related images of the ocean as space and the realm of voyages and shipping. Above all it has been shown that in terms of leisure and tourism the prevailing imaging has its provenance in the Romantic attitude to nature. The development of these representations has been discussed in terms of unfolding sensibilities and an emotional strategy of how people may encounter and enjoy the seashore and coastscape. Within this process, particular emphasis has been placed on the coenaesthetic, sensual encounter with the sea of the shore. These unfolding processes of representation and more spontaneous sensual pleasures have been elaborated in order to show how the social phenomenon of contemporary surfing is embedded within this broader network of cultural meanings and history. Furthermore, as will be further developed in later chapters, surfing as a cultural practice resonates especially powerfully with the Romantic tendency in Western cultural development. Throughout, particular emphasis has been placed on the interrelation of cultural representation and coenaesthetic sensual experience. The subsequent chapters will further develop these themes in relation to the twentieth-century spread of surfing, the aesthetic symbolisms of surfing and wave, and the nature of the subculture of surfing, which in turn shape the representations of this exuberant encounter with marine energy.

# 3 The narrative history and globalization of surfing

## Introduction

This chapter is, primarily, concerned with the processes by which surfing has developed from a practice undertaken within the pre-modern cultures of the Pacific Islands to become a globalized international sport and (sub) culture. Linked to a concern to explain (to themselves) how such a basic, non-instrumental and ephemeral action as sliding along a line of force in the water has had such profound personal and lifestyle implications, there has been a growing trend to explore the history of surfing, both in terms of its origins and to explain the current state of the art and culture. Thus, a second concern of this chapter is to examine the ways in which writers on surfing have sought to place pattern and meaning on the history of surfing.

In order to explore these aims this chapter engages with the two main bodies of thinking, narrative (history) and globalization process. The first part of this chapter is concerned with some general theoretical discussions of narrative and an outline of the emerging narrative histories of surfing technology, culture and performance. Narrative generally involves the interrelation of plot and characterization. In this analysis primary attention is given to the plot of the surfing story. A deliberate attempt is made here to minimize reference to the 'characters' of surfing history for two reasons; first, one of the main concerns of this book is to try to distil the core *processes* surrounding surfing and their links to wider theory; and second, there is already a large and proliferating literature (mainly in the surfing media) which presents and explores surfing heroes and characters (for instance Warshaw 1997; Kampion 2003). Although it is beyond the scope of this book, a particularly interesting avenue for narrative research would be to examine the recurring patterns in individual surfers' articulation of their life histories and their links to the various processes and values running through surfing culture. The narrative history of surfing is further examined here in terms of sections on the aesthetics of surf photography, mediatization and stardom, the tensions which shape the contemporary narrative, nostalgia and some potential directions for further research. The third section of the chapter examines the narrative of surfing culture and history through the lenses of various lines of thinking on the globalization of culture and sport.

# The narrative approach

The ubiquity of narrative or story in human cultures suggests that it is fundamentally related to human consciousness and communication. Scholarly expositions on the form, motivations and effects of narrative go back, at least, as far as Aristotle's *The Poetics*, 2300 years ago. The core of narrative is generally recognized as a plot (or storyline) running through a beginning and middle to an end or resolution (McKee 1998). Such a basic structure provides a framework upon which authors have elaborated, drawing on archetypal themes, to create an enormous range of plot forms. The major academic interest in narrative has, not surprisingly, been in literary studies within which there has been a diverse proliferation of narrative theories of fiction, ranging, for instance, from Russian formalist, reader-response to deconstructionist theories (Miller 1995). Such approaches could be applied to the analysis of surfing fiction, such as the novels of Kem Nunn (1998, 2004). However, more recently there has been an increasing recognition of the potential usefulness of narrative analysis for the social sciences and history. The interdisciplinary application of narratology has reflected the growing 'interpretive turn' in the social sciences (Reissman 1993).

Social scientific analyses of narrative have been framed in terms of varied definitions, ranging from more restrictive foci upon the unfolding of specific past events (Labov 1972), to much broader efforts to explore patterning in the recounting of biography or life histories. Most studies of narrative follow the traditional chronological sequence of a linear series of events (Young 1987), although Michaels (1981) has suggested the alternative of thematic sequencing. In both approaches the key theme is that events become meaningful because of their placement (in time and in relation to other events) in a narrative.

As will be discussed later, narrative methodology could be particularly useful in the analysis of individuals' involvement in surfing (for instance, initial attractions, socialization, changing levels of engagement and so on). However, with respect to this chapter's concern with the, perhaps, more macro-level of developments in surfing performance and culture, the use of narrative in historical studies is especially apposite.

The analysis of narrative has been codified in a number of approaches that seek to break down events into a series of dimensions. For instance the structural approaches of Labov (1972) and Burke (1945) are noted in Figure 3.1 to give some brief indication of the initial categorizing steps in such analyses.

A fundamental aspect of narrative creation is that it seeks to order and simplify the complex and crowded events of reality in order to create a pattern and distil meaning. As Miller (1995) has emphasized, the creation of narrative is both 'order-giving' and 'order-finding', in which we both investigate and invent the meaning of sociocultural phenomena, such as surfing. Miller talks of human beings as 'homo significans' the sense-making and fiction-making animal. The practice of narrative can be viewed as performative (in speech-act theory) in that it may not only reflect culture, but propose values and behaviours for a particular (e.g. sub) culture. These notions may be considered with reference to the debates

*Figure 3.1* Formal properties identified in structural analyses of narratives

| Labov |
| --- |
| 1   Abstract (summary of the substance) |
| 2   Orientation (time, place, situation, participants) |
| 3   Complicating action (sequence of events) |
| 4   Evaluation (significance and meaning of the action, attitude of the narrator) |
| 5   Resolution (what finally happened) |
| 6   Coda (returns the perspective to the present) |

| Burke's dramatism |
| --- |
| 1   Act – what was done |
| 2   Scene – when and where it was done |
| 3   Agent – who did it |
| 4   Agency – how they did it |
| 5   Purpose – why they did it |

Source: adapted from Reissman 1993

and crystallizations of values, style and behaviours in the mediatization of surfing, in terms of the expressions in the whole breadth of magazines, books, photographic and filmic media, music, fashion and so on. Indeed, Miller notes that an important characteristic of narrative within a specific culture is the repetition of the same stories (or variations on a theme) over and over again. Miller contends that this is related 'to the affirmative culture-making function of narrative' (1995: 70). Miller's suggestion that a further reason for narratives' repetition relates to their rhythmic and orderly properties, that it is 'natural for human beings to take pleasure in rhythmic forms' (1995: 68), may have a special resonance with surfing.

In his discussion of the place of narrative in historical studies, Cronon (1992) raises a whole series of themes which are highly pertinent to the following exploration of the narrative history of surfing. Cronon notes that the post-modern assault on narrative has led to a greater concern with the way the form and content of historical stories are shaped by the deeper purposes of underlying motivations. Furthermore, in the simplification and inherent selectivity involved in presenting a 'reality', narrative 'cannot avoid a covert exercise in power' (Cronon 1992: 1350). We may consider in what ways the growing narrativization of surfing (with its legends, myths, 'firsts' and record making) involves, for instance, a 'laying claim to history', drawing upon and reinforcing particular voices in articulating that history.

Key themes in the analysis of narrative history include: where does it begin and where does it go? The origins of surfing among the pre-modern Pacific Islanders may be thought of as surfing's aetiological myth. We may inquire into the ways in which these ancient origins are represented in the surfing narrative in terms of the values of contemporary surfing culture. Furthermore, in A *Grammar of Motives* Burke argued that stories are 'about the changing stage on which the drama plays itself out as much as the specific events taking place' (1945: 6–7). The stage, or scene, entailing in this case the broader cultural contexts and localities in which the story of surfing unfolds, needs to be considered as well as the actions and events which have taken place.

Cronon (1992) further notes that narrative histories can be examined in terms of their articulation of central agency (that which fundamentally shapes the causality of events), their simplicity and elegance, their inclusiveness (of different interests) and coherence (degree of tightness of linkages as against extraneous detail).

With respect to evaluations of the overall direction of, or even conclusion to, a narrative, Cronon notes that they can be progressive (positive, optimistic) or declensionist (a sense of decline or even collapse). Obviously, the current narrative of surfing has no final 'resolution', it necessarily concludes in the present, in the perspectival assessments of the state of the art and culture of surfing. Inquiry may be made into what factors shape positive or negative perspectives on the current 'state of surfing'. Finally, we may consider the narrative of surfing as the way a culture tells and creates itself. People tell unique stories, but these are created via broader historical and cultural stories. Exploring such stories makes it possible to see how people are shaped by cultural and historical contexts. The next sections of this chapter seek to examine the history of surfing in relation, first, to the concept of narrative, second, with reference to a series of core tensions running through surfing's narrative, and third, by interpreting the contemporary growth and geographical spread of surfing in terms of consideration of the globalization of sport.

## The narrative history of surfing

The aim here is not so much to present, yet another, history of surfing (many excellent accounts already exist), but rather to comment on the nature of these existing histories, which underlie the invention or creation of a surfing (sub) culture. This chapter draws extensively on a number of recent works on the history of surfing (e.g. Holmes 1991; Young 1994; Finney and Houston 1996; Kampion and Brown 1997, 2003; Booth 1999, 2001a and George 1999, 2001, Drummond 2002, Jaggard 2003). All of these authors are experienced surfers, two, Kampion (1968–71) and Holmes (1982–90), were editors of *Surfer Magazine*, Young was world surfing champion in 1966, and Booth is a sports historian. While there has been writing on surfing since the early years of the twentieth century (e.g. London 1911), there has been a, seemingly accelerating, proliferation of accounts of surfing's history and culture since the early 1990s. This section will explore these accounts in terms of *thinking* on reminiscence and nostalgia, the formal properties of narrative structural analysis of Labov and Burke, the delineanation of technological, cultural and performance histories of surfing, a further pared-down or skeletal narrative of surfing culture and its links to key values, myth-making and the 'laying claim to history' and a review of a series of major themes or tensions which make up surfing's narrative plot.

While there has long been writing on the origins and history of surfing, such a tendency has been especially pronounced in recent years. On the one hand, this may merely reflect the growing numbers who have participated in the sport and the related market demand for literature. On the other hand, it is notable that the bulk of the (recent) writing on the history and culture of surfing focuses on the last half-century and generally involves authors writing about their 'own' (lived) era. Thus it reflects, perhaps, more mature surfers looking back on times in their lives which they may consider especially meaningful and significant, and the desire of younger surfers to gain a sense of the historical context of their sport. This process of reflection or reminiscence is key to the ways by which people come to know and experience their culture. Questions of surfing identity and culture are elaborated upon below in Chapter 4, suffice it to note here that a sense of identity as surfer, will be one among a series of pluralistic and overlapping senses of affiliation that a person may hold. Kershaw (1993 in Rojek and Urry 1997) has explored the question of how history and heritage is remembered by people. He notes that there is a 'reminiscence peak' in the more elderly who enjoy enhanced long-term memory, and whose conceptions of the past become increasingly influential. Kershaw also stresses that there is a performativity to reminiscence by which memories are both stimulated and created, involving an element of selectivity and perhaps simplification. This selectivity will be further explored below with respect to surfing's mediatization and myth-making.

Along with the burgeoning surfing literature it should also be noted that there is a real sense of the cultural heritage of surfing today (Blackburn 2001; Colburn *et al.* 2002). This sense of heritage is expressed in temporary and perma-nent museum exhibitions, the increasing market value of 'classic' surfboards, in-depth articles in *The Surfer's Journal*, and the pleasure taken in the 'retro' aspects of surfing even among some younger surfers (Blackburn 2001; Severson 2004). The sight of certain photographs, and films, artefacts, the sound of certain music and the revisiting of particular localities of past exploits, can all 're-awaken repressed desires and thereby connect past and present' (Buck-Morse 1989 in Rojek and Urry 1997: 14).

The 'invention' of surfing history is often discussed in terms of nostalgia, but it is perhaps important to note that nostalgia is one particular type of remembrance. Jameson (1988: 104) has drawn attention to 'the appetite for images of the past, in the form of what might be called simulacra, the increasing production of such images of all kinds, in particular in that peculiar post-modern genre, the nostal-gic film, with its glossy evocation of the past as sheer consumable fashion and image' (see also Snyder 1991). Davis (1974) has highlighted the collective dimension in the ways in which symbolic objects have a highly public and widely shared character that can trigger nostalgic feelings among large numbers of people. Robertson (1992) has elaborated upon the 'nostalgic paradigm' in terms of the work of Turner, which discussed nostalgia as 'a fundamental condition of human estrangement' (Turner 1987: 150), involving four main presuppositions:

1 the idea of history as decline
2 the sense of a loss of wholeness
3 the feeling of a loss of expressivity and spontaneity
4 the sense of a loss of individual autonomy.

To what extent does the current vogue for exploring surfing history and culture (of which this book is a part!) reflect a sense of the loss of youth with its philosophical simplicity, optimism and freedom? Further elaborating upon the negative aspect of nostalgia, Baudrillard (1983) has argued:

> When the real is no longer what it used to be nostalgia assumes its full meaning. There is a proliferation of myths of origin and signs of reality; of second hand truth, objectivity and authenticity.
>
> (in Robertson 1992: 160)

It is highly plausible that the nostalgic visions of a surfing past are likely to be at variance with aspects of the lived experience they purport to celebrate.[1] With respect to the recreation of surfing tradition, things may not be as bleak as Baudrillard's reflections on nostalgia may suggest, as many of those reflecting on surf culture are still enjoying the direct, raw experience of catching waves.[2] There is certainly scope for more systematic audience research to explore the ways in which the surfing past is being created, represented and received. For instance, Anderson's (2004) careful study has explored the ways in which practices of memory interweave with recorded music use. Thus, memory is not something simply automatic and given, but rather 'contextual, embodied practices of remembering generate the symbolic content of memory' (Anderson 2004: 4). Such an approach to the analysis of the contemporary efflorescence of surfing culture and nostalgia, could gainfully focus on the complex interaction of representations with the embodied experience of the various senses.

## An outline application of structural analytical frameworks to the narrative history of surfing

As a first step in the analytical distillations of surfing's historical narrative, the frameworks of Labov and Burke are applied as examples in outline to provide an initial structure.

### The Labov structural approach

1 Abstract (origins, historical development, cultural images and values, key tensions running through the narrative).

2    Orientation

- time – going back several centuries but primarily a twentieth-century history phenomenon
- situation – in totality surf coasts everywhere, but primarily developments emanating from Hawaii, California and Australia
- participants – in totality all surfers, but primarily 'legendary surf heroes' (both performers and design innovators), and the media figures (editors, authors, photographers and film makers) who identify and label such stars in the firmament of surfing history

3    Complicating action – developments and tensions running through surfing history summarized in Figures 3.2–3.8.
4    Evaluation – the significance, meaning and values of the unfolding surf culture as expressed by the authors as narrative myth-makers and the wider world of other participants.
5    Resolution – the current state of the art, culture and sport of surfing in the early twenty-first century. No ultimate 'resolution' of the plot of surfing as such.
6    Coda – authors and other participants' experience of, and involvement in, the practice and culture of surfing in the present.

### Burke's dramatism

1    Act – the actions and events underlying the technological, cultural and performance histories of surfing summarized in Figures 3.2–3.8.
2    Scene – as above re: Labov 2. Orientation in time and situation.
3    Agent – as above re: Labov 2 Orientation – participants.
4    Agency – raises extremely complex questions of multiple, interacting agencies shaping the events. For instance, most narratives of surfing history allude to a complex and interactive interplay of cultural and technological, influencing and facilitating, factors. It would appear likely that a range of theorizations of agency will emerge to explain the development of surfing in terms of various interpretative perspectives, as academic study of surfing matures.
5    Purpose – there is probably a range of overlapping purposes underlying the drive to articulate the narrative of surfing including, for instance (in no order of priority): academic explanation, reminiscence, finding personal meaning, evocation or expressive exuberance, even financial remuneration.

## The technological, cultural and performance histories of surfing

One of the most striking aspects of any review of accounts of surfing history is the very high level of consensus concerning the milestones, broad phases and tensions which pervade the culture or sport. This commonly includes even the repetition of a range of iconic photographs and other artworks, for instance those of the earliest shots of surfing in Hawaii and Duke Kahanamoku (from the Bishop Museum, Honolulu), 'classic' 1950s Malibu, certain film posters, Miki Dora, Greg Noll with longboard looking out at massive Pipeline, Rick Griffin cartoon artwork and so on.[3]

In terms of narrative theory this broad consensus may be thought of as an overarching, meta-narrative, by which a culture has reflexively made sense of/to itself. Within the books and (many more) articles reflecting on surfing history and culture there are, of course, variations in emphasis and some (but relatively minor) disagreements on detail. Given the richness and eloquence of the already existing accounts of surfing history, in this chapter an attempt has been made to keep the repetition of the history to a bare minimum, through the presentation of summary Figures 3.2–3.8.

The history of surfing is here distilled in terms of the three (sub) narratives of surfing's technological, cultural and performance histories. The core of surfing is, obviously, the performance of the embodied experience of the ride, slide or dance along the wave, the cultural dimension pertains to the significations, images and motivations which comprise the epiphenomena surrounding surfing and also influence the style of performance, while the technology of surfboard design facilitates the possibilities of the dance. In reality, each of these three dimensions perpetually interact, but it is useful here to attempt to disentangle them for analytical purposes. Historical accounts go beyond mere chronologies to comment on agency, cause, or, less determinatively, primary influences. Booth (1999) has suggested that in the traditional popular accounts of surfing there has been an excessive technological determinism, which accounts for changes in surfriding style and performance in terms of surfboard design and materials. To redress this, Booth argues for the recovery of the cultural factors (philosophy of the wave) that influence surfing performance. However, reading the various recent accounts of surfing history indicates considerable recognition within the texts for cultural influences on surfing performance style. While a detailed analysis of agency in surfing history is beyond the scope of this particular review, there may well have been two phases of broad influences, with surfing being limited by technology in the early phase (up to 1950) but from then on, and especially following the shortboard revolution of the 1960s, with cultural, philosophical and stylistic factors becoming increasingly pertinent.

Continuing with the focus on the narrative qualities of the consensus account of surfing history, it is useful to comment on narrative's three basic elements of plot, characterization and style of expression and presentation. The 'plot' of surfing's narrative history (summarized in Figures 3.2–3.8), as with any other historical narrative, involves a fundamental process of simplification to identify an intelligible pattern, comprised of a series of landmarks, milestones, breakthroughs and heroic and explosive 'firsts' in performance. For instance, the popular writing on surfing history sometimes includes such statements as:

Wayne Lynch single-handedly redefined the lines that could be drawn on the face of a wave (Kampion and Brown 1997: 108).

(Referring to John Severson, founder of *Surfer Magazine*) The single most important voice in the creation of twentieth-century surf culture (Kampion 2003: 41).

Kelly Slater, the best surfer in the world (Kampion 2003: 157).

Phil Edwards, father of the classic or functional style of riding (Young 1994: 76).

The forenoted statements also pertain to the second aspect of narrative – characterization. Obviously the litany of firsts and breakthroughs in the narrative history of surfing are associated with particular individuals, who in turn become the heroes and 'legends' of surf culture. In order to recount any narrative it is necessary to reduce and simplify an otherwise, unimaginably vast reality. A further attempt to distil recurring facets of the narrative can be made by identifying values of surfing culture in relation to phases of the chronology.

*Figure 3.2* The technological history of surfing

| Period | Evolution of the surfboard |
| --- | --- |
| Pre-modern Hawaii | |
| Up to beginning of twentieth century | • Solid Olo 14½–18ft long (exclusively used by chiefs)<br>• Solid Alaia 7–13ft long<br>• Also smaller bodyboards<br>• Most shaped from the fine-grained Hawaiian hardwood Koa<br>• Some from lightwoods such as breadfruit and wiliwili |
| Early twentieth century | • Surfing's revival<br>• 9–10ft long, preferred material redwood<br>• Experimentation with new designs and materials in the search for lighter, faster, more manoeuvrable boards |
| 1920s | • e.g. Tom Blake experimented with hollow boards, and crossover design from paddleboards<br>• Plywood longboards |
| 1930s | • Experiments with pintails and 'v' bottoms, to improve turning<br>• The 'fin solution' (arguably Blake) |
| Late 1940s | • Lighter balsawood replaced redwood – 9–11ft long |
| Late 1950s | • Shortage of balsawood, the search for alternatives<br>• Bob Simmons (following wartime work on aircraft design) revolutionizes board technology with the use of fibreglass<br>• 1952 – the first surf shop – Velzy, Hermosa Beach, California |

*continued*

| Late 1950s (cont) | • Gordon Clarke – applied foam compounds to create the classic 'Malibu' board which dominated for a decade |
|---|---|
| Late 1960s | • The shortboard revolution' – Bob McTavish's designs<br>• Theoretical and technical insights from George Greenough's kneeboards (crossover)<br>• Adaptation of shortboards to steep Hawaiian waves, partly through the improvements of narrow-based, swept-back fins |
| 1968/69 | • Increasingly shorter boards → 6ft, then up to 6½–7ft<br>• Innovations and influences crossing between California and Australia |
| 1970s | • Advent of the twin fin for smaller to medium-sized waves |
| 1971 | • Introduction of the leash (or cord) preventing loss of board after wipe-out also 'democratizing' effect of the invention of the boogie board |
| 1981 | • Simon Anderson's three-fin thrusters lay the basis for what has become the basic, high performance surfboard up to the present – primarily 6–6½ft long<br>• Accompanied by the last two decades of fine tuning refinements for particular localities and types of waves |
| Early 1990s | • At the extreme end of surfing, the advent of 'tow-in' surfing (from jetskis) to ride giant, outer reef waves |

Note: Today there is a plurality of boards, as well as the basic thrusters, including the return of the 'mini-mal' (7½–8½ft long) and the longer Malibu or 'plank', for more relaxed surfing, especially for older surfers. Unlike the development of the windsurfing board, stand-up surfers and surfboard makers have overwhelmingly remained committed to the basic crafted foam-based, fibreglass board, rather than adopting innovations from recent technological advances in materials. (It almost goes without saying that along with advances in board design, technological advances in wetsuit development have also enormously enhanced surfing in the cooler waters of the world.)

It is important to stress from the outset that the phases and developments noted in Figures 3.3–3.8 are better viewed in an Eliasian (1978) sense, as continuous tendencies and changing emphases of surfing's 'culture', rather than abrupt changes of direction. Thus, the narrative of surfing's beginnings in the islands of the Pacific, is imbued with notions of a pantheistic spirituality, courage and harmony with nature, which resonated with Western Romantic sensibilities. The demise of surfing during the nineteenth century missionary period in Hawaii may well have contributed to surfing culture's anti-establishment ethos and suspicion of repressive social tendencies. Surfing's rebirth in the early twentieth century allowed the expression of such sentiments more positively, in terms of an association of surfing with fun, hedonism and freedom, beyond societal conventions.

*Figure 3.3* The cultural history of surfing (values, style and images associated with surfing) – early phase

| Period | Ancient Hawaiian origins |
| --- | --- |
| Ancient to end of nineteenth century | • Paradisal beginnings in a cultural context of a ritual pantheistic, spiritual harmony with nature<br>• Enormously rich surf- and sea-related vocabulary pervading the Hawaiian language. Today perceived as a 'simple' casual, relaxed, hedonistic way of life ('noble savage' romanticism). (A secondary thread acknowledged in the surfing literature of, perhaps more negative, associations of ancient Hawaiian surfing with proscriptions of social status, contests, gambling and ego.)<br>• The demise and decline of surfing in the wake of the devastating impacts of Western disease and missionary-based repression upon Hawaiian culture |

| 1920s–1950s | Parallel cultural development | |
| --- | --- | --- |
| | Hawaii/California | Australia |
| | • Casual beach culture<br>• Early surfing photography and films<br>• Malibu in California as the site of the creative edge of innovative surfing | • Early cultural development within the more disciplined confines of the Surf Life Saving Association. Values of willpower and fierce competition |
| | • In both the USA and Australia surfing expands on the back of increased mobility (surfaris) and post-war affluence<br>• Heroic image as surfers meet the challenge of riding ever-bigger waves | |

Sam George has argued that 'all the surf-as-a-lifestyle basic tenets were established in the first two decades [of the twentieth century] and the most prominent – and enduring – of these is romance', 'beautiful natural surroundings, danger, physical prowess, escapism' (1999: 149). During surfing's steady development through the mid-twentieth century such values were overlain with parallel images of a pioneering heroic (in relation to progress in big waveriding) and of 'cool' as style in which surfing became associated with youth culture fashion. In Australia, within the ambit of the Surf Life Saving Clubs (SLSC), surfing became associated with an ethos of self-discipline and competition (Booth 2001a).

With the late 1960s counter-culture, the 'soul surfing' tendency emphasized a reinterpretation of the values of spirituality, aesthetics and the quest for inner peace and authenticity. With the growth of surfing's popularity and concomitant business opportunity, in congruence with late capitalism, business packaged these very values of authenticity and distinctiveness. Furthermore the mediatization of surfing amplified these values in a wider cultural dissemination.

The competitive tendency in surfing was reinforced in the rise of the professional circuit. The key point here is that surfing culture has a core set of (quite

*Figure 3.4* The cultural history of surfing (values, style and images associated with surfing) – middle phase

| Period | Middle phase |
| --- | --- |
| Late 1950s | • Increasing numbers participating in surfing |
| Early 1960s | • Surfing captures the popular imagination via a whole concatenation of creative expression inspired by surfing, involving music, film and fashion, primarily emanating from Southern California |
| | • For instance, Hollywood beach/surf movies such as *Gidget* (1959) bring a caricature of surfing lifestyles to a wider audience, while *The Endless Summer* (1964) crystallizes the feel and dream of surfing from 'an insider's' perspective |
| | • The invention and creation of surfing's subcultural tradition is expressed not only in surfing films, but above all (and more discursively) through the arrival of Severson's *Surfer* (1960) and other subsequent magazines |
| | • The surfing media express similar values of exuberance, hedonism, escapism and 'the natural' as in the earlier 'golden age' of 1950s surfing, but infusing them with a rich sense of aesthetics and greater self-consciousness |
| | • Surf culture continues to express a core or gestalt-like coherence, but interpreted through the, often oppositional, *Zeitgeist* of the times (e.g. through 'Beatnik' affinities (1950s), Counter Culture (late 1960s) and punk (late 1970s) (Booth 1999) |

powerful) underlying values and images, which are recast and re-expressed in different forms in different decades, but viewed over the larger sweep of history show a surprisingly high degree of continuity. Furthermore, as is elaborated below, some of these values (such as harmony and competition) are in tension with one another and thus are perhaps best viewed as interacting in an interplay or dialectic. It is important also to stress that these are not simple binaries, in the social practice and perceptions of surfing questions of status, competition, soul surfing and a sense of harmony are rather complex, as will be further explored in Chapter 4.

Within surfing culture itself, and reflecting 'the hegemony of vision' (Rorty 1980) of modern Western culture, the dominant artforms are visual. Furthermore, the visual arts associated with surfing continue to flourish and proliferate (Congdon and King 2002). Such visual artforms include painting, ('moving') film and ('still') photography. Surfing-related painting of the highest quality is probably still especially concentrated within Southern California. A review of the diversity and vitality of surf-related painting is beyond the scope of this book, but has been exuberantly documented in the recent exhibition-based volume by Colburn *et al.* (2002), as well as being regularly reviewed in magazine articles such as those of *The Surfer's Journal* (e.g. Colburn 1992; Short 2002; Gunin 2004; Elesh 2004; Hulet 2004). Film is clearly the optimal medium for the most 'accurate' depiction

*Figure 3.5* The cultural history of surfing (values, style and images associated with surfing) – recent phase

| Period | Recent phase |
|---|---|
| 1970s to the present | • Recent surfing culture history is perhaps best understood in terms of a series of narrative tensions or unfolding (converging and diverging) tendencies including:<br>○ Counter-cultural, soul surfing – individualistic, ranging through various preoccupations with peak experiences or highs (whether through spirituality or psycho-active substances) and varying accommodations with, and distancing from, wider advanced capitalist/technological society<br>○ Concerns with 'authenticity' and 'purity' of surfing<br>○ The sportization of surfing through competition (earliest international contest at Makaha, Oahu in 1954)<br>○ Long recognized as a way to make surfing more 'respectable', the process set back by the 1970s soul surfing tendency<br>○ Codification of manoeuvres for scoring<br>○ Competitions providing an arena for cutting edge performance and national rivalries (primarily between the USA and Australia)<br>○ The rise of the World Surf Tour (IPS/ASP) and, with commercial support, the beginnings of a professional surfing lifestyle (for a select few)<br>• Business and the commercialization of surfing<br>○ Through a series of 'booms', increasing participation levels enable the expansion of surfing business from small numbers of craft factories and small outlets to larger numbers of small outlets and a few becoming multinational corporations<br>○ Surfing culture's preoccupation with authenticity ensures that these major companies grow out of existing 'insider' surfers' companies, rather than being appropriated from outside surfing culture<br>○ In terms of market turnover, the boutiquing of surf fashion becomes far more important than sales of equipment – a trend enormously amplified by surfing business expansions into the exploding cognate pursuits of skateboarding, windsurfing and snowboarding<br>○ On a wider societal level, the image and dream of surfing is appropriated in the advertising of numerous non-surfing products<br>• The enormous increase in the numbers participating in surfing leads to problems of crowding in many urban surfing areas. In some parts of the world, e.g. Jeffrey's Bay (South Africa), Byron Bay (Australia), the coast of south-west France, substantial settlement patterns develop due to their proximity to quality surf. The inherent scarcity of waves in crowded conditions leads to expressions of localism and even 'surf rage'. The crowding problem further stimulates surfers' international travel, linking with the culture's traditions of wanderlust, further expanding surfing geographically |

*Figure* 3.6 The history of surfing performance (the early period, largely technology-driven)

| Period | Boards | Performances |
|---|---|---|
| Ancient Hawaii | Long heavy boards | Straight along the wave, often not turning<br>Statue-like rigid stance<br>'Tricks' added – e.g. headstands, riding tandem |
| Early twentieth century 1930s | Continuing long heavy boards with addition of fins | Allowed 'tracking' along the wall and changing direction<br>Some development of graceful poses |
| Late 1950s | The Malibu | Great increase in manoeuvrability<br>'angling' in the curl of the wave,<br>'hot dog' surfing – stalling, walking to the nose<br>Further emphasis on graceful stance and pose |
| 1960s | Shortboards | Enormous increase in manoeuvrability<br>Much faster and more spectacular turns<br>'radical' cutbacks and 'off the lips' |

of surfing, which is, obviously, in motion. However within surfing culture it is the 'still' photograph that is the most hallowed and predominant medium of recording surfing. Given the primacy of the photograph within the mediatization of surfing culture, the following section seeks to touch upon some of the associated cultural and theoretical ramifications.

## Surf photography

This section examines the nature of the genre of surfing photography, exploring the question of why it has been so significant to surfing culture and touching upon some lines of theory that may assist in providing some form of context for potential further research into surfing photography. In particular it will discuss the audience reception of surf photography in terms of both immediate, aesthetic, contemplative, and meaning-ascribing, signifying, responses, which mirror this book's core theme of the senses (or body) and mind relationship.

When riding (especially the fastest and more powerful) waves, vision and reactions are totally instinctive, denying that momentary reflection which allows the possibility of imprinting an image upon the mind's eye. Furthermore, an observer of surfing sees only a flowing pattern or series of rapid manoeuvres. The shutter speed of the camera (Bilderbeck 2002), obviously, freezes the surfing action to depict a framed stasis of surfer and wave. Within the mediatization, which is so fundamental to the development of surfing culture, the photographic image has been paramount. Although the words of surfing magazines are important, what really drives the purchase of such material is their rich and evocative visual images.

Such photography, which by definition depicts a particular activity, within particular place settings, for a particular audience, and depicting its chosen action

*Figure 3.7* The history of surfing performance (the latter period increasingly culture-driven)

| Period | Surf culture | Performance |
| --- | --- | --- |
| Late 1960s early 1970s | Debate in the surfing media concerning the relative value of graceful and aggressive styles | Period of contrasting styles ranging from surfing as dance, harmony and relaxed creativity, as epitomized by top Hawaiian surfers and 'radical shredding and ripping/ domination of waves' epitomized by top Australians Also increased emphasis on surfing in the tube (partly assisted by the advent of the leash) |
| Late 1970s | Increased rigour in codification of moves in surfing competitions, e.g. the key criterion is to perform the most radical manoeuvres in the most critical part of the wave, – results in a string of Australian victories in international competitions | Americans adapt to the radical Australian style, which thence comes to typify the most impressive surfing as practised virtually throughout the world<br><br>Increasing emphasis on 'working the wave' as intensively as possible |
| Late 1980s 1990s | Crossover of experience from skateboarding and snowboarding manoeuvres | Introduction of 'airs' (or aerials) (see Plate 3) and 'floaters', and more frequent 360° turns to the range of radical surf manoeuvres |
| 1990s to present | Very small minority riding massive waves, mainly using surfski 'tow-in' technology | Incredible surfing of monster (e.g. outer reef) waves, with some increase in surfing fatalities |
| | On a broader level, a greying demographic, and return to 'mini-mals' and Malibus | More graceful and relaxed longboard surfing especially by older surfers (see Plate 7) |

in particular ways, is clearly a distinctive genre of photography. Over the decades of surf photography's development a small scale, but international, industry has evolved, conjoining media (especially photographers, editors, art directors) technology, production, audience and connoisseurship. There is scope for research to explore these social conditions and institutional networks which shape the surfing media/production/audience complex. The financial returns of surf photography are modest, but for a small minority their art has supported a surfing and travelling lifestyle. Their work is increasingly celebrated and explored through volumes of collected works (e.g. Divine 2000; Brewer 2001; Bolster 2002; Grambeau 2003; Severson 2004) and in retrospective reviews in surfing magazines.

The main substance of these texts, which accompany the photography, concerns narrative biographies that interweave personal history, and artistic development with phases and trends in surfing culture. Especial attention is given

*Figure 3.8* Phases of surfing history and surfing cultural values

| Time period | Phases | Associated values (in surfing narrative) |
|---|---|---|
| Ancient | 'Paradisal' beginnings | Spirituality, 'harmony with nature', courage |
| Nineteenth century | The 'fall' and suppression of surfing | Anti-establishment, suspicion of repressive social tendencies |
| Early twentieth century | Surfing's rebirth | Fun, hedonism, 'freedom', beyond social conventions<br>Healthy, outdoors, beach lifestyle |
| | Australian SLSA | Olympian ideals, discipline, competition |
| | Parallel developments | 'Mastery of nature' |
| 1930s, 1940s, 1950s | Steady development of surfing – big waves<br>'Malibu' and the later 'cultural crystallization' in ephemera of film, fashion, music, etc. | Continuing fun, hedonism, freedom |
| 1960s | The 'shortboard revolution'<br>Counter-culture and soul surfing | 'Radical' surfing, wildness<br>Spirituality, inner harmony<br>Non-materialistic, aesthetics, authenticity |
| Past few decades | Rise of surfing as big business and the professional circuit<br>Enormous growth in participation and crowding | Competition, Olympian ideals<br><br>Localism and wanderlust |

within such narratives to the spatio-temporal contexts or the places of the surf action. It is, above all, the work of these auteurs that has carried and elaborated the rich aesthetic pervading surfing culture and its connotations to the wider culture.

As with photography more generally, the reception of surf photography is bound up with the tensions between the idea of its capturing 'the real' or being primarily derived from artifice and craft. Bennett (2003) has discussed the variety of manipulations available to surfing photographers, the scope for which has become enormously enhanced with the advent of digital photography and computer programs such as Photoshop. Such digital manipulation is commonplace, or even the norm in surfing magazines, as throughout the mass media. The notion of photography as recording 'the real' may relate to Malraux's distinction between 'art by destination', which from the outset of its creation seeks to 'be art' and 'art by metamorphosis' wherein an image becomes art through discovery or interpretation (in Maquet 1986). Photographers of surfing may vary according to their intentions to be simply capturing 'the real' or rather creating aesthetic images. However, once the photographic products are submitted to the magazines, it is the aesthetic qualities that must become increasingly paramount. Magazines and photographers edit out extraneous material considered to detract from the coherence of the individual image. Such editing may seek to enhance the balance and proportion of the image of the surfer on the wave, for instance editing out another surfer 'dropping in' or 'pulling back' which may detract from the purity of the image.

The most fundamental aspect of the artistry of surf photography is, however, not manipulation of images, as much as their selection. As with other action photography, surf photography is primarily based on selecting from a whole series of sequence shots taken at rapid speed. Indeed, technological advance has facilitated the process of capturing the moment. Selection is undertaken on the basis of those shots that capture particular critical moments in surfing. Photographers are striving to find 'classic' images of waves and surfing. The selected waves are usually variations on the theme of perfection evoking beauty and power. Classic photographs depict particular spectacular moments of surfing, in particular the 'drop in' (catching the wave and going down the face) (see Plate 8), the bottom turn (see Plate 9), the 'off the lip', nestling within the tube, cutting swathes of patterned foam in 'cutbacks' and the apparently fluttering apex of an 'aerial' or 'air' (see Plate 3), when the board loses contact with the wave. Many of the more spectacular shots are, in fact, capturing the moment just before a 'wipe-out' (falling off) occurs. Further key elements include the overall composition of surfer in relation to the face of the wave, and the (very) precise bodily posture and the perspective of it, generally conveying both balance and elegance in classic surfing photographs (see Plate 2). There is scope for further research to explore the symmetry and aesthetics of bodily form in surf photography. Such work could gainfully consider the influence of classical notions of unity, symmetry and proportion which continue to inform perceptions of sport (Roberts 1975; Lowe 1977). Kenneth Clarke's (1956) observation of the 'rhythms of movement' within classical sculpture may well relate to the striking qualities of classic surf photographs. A further element in the development of surf photography has been the pursuit of novelty in terms of exploring different angles of shot, and working in various conditions of light.

Some examples of recurring classic surfing images may be found in the volume concerning the work of Jeff Divine (2000). A shot of Jeff Hakman (Divine 2000: 31) on a substantial wave at Sunset Beach, 1971, conveys an overwhelming sense of speed deriving from the almost cartoon-like figure in a crouching posture with left arm stretched ahead, and arcing trails of spray from the board, echoed in lesser lines of spray lining the face of the wave. Pictures of women surfers, Jericho Poppler (Divine 2000: 35) and Rell Sunn (Divine 2000: 93) in almost identical 'toes to the nose' (that is standing at the very front edge of the board) postures on similar medium-sized waves, capture an incredible sense of delicate balance and concentration, along with toned feminine elegance. Furthermore, in both shots the faces of the waves are patterned with the creamy texture of the foam left by a previous wave. A shot of Randy Pidd (Divine 2000: 43) in a seemingly languid arcing cutback (that is, turning back towards the breaking section of the wave) across the super glassy surface of a Californian kelp bed wave, evinces a timeless quality (see sketch in Figure 3.9). Again, it is the precise moment of the posture including relaxed, open arms that contributes, above all, to the aesthetic quality of the shot. In complete contrast is the classic picture of Larry 'Rubber Man' Bertleman (Divine 2000: 51) turning off the bottom at Ala Moana, 1976, seemingly coiled about to spring. The picture of Bertleman has a gauche quality about it, redolent of a whole style of radical explosive surfing pictures, as also expressed in the flying 'off the lip' (about to 'wipe out') shot of Rabbit Bartholomew (Divine 2000: 64) at Off the Wall, 1976. A shot of Richard Cram enacting a cutback at 'Off the Wall', 1983 (Divine 2000: 109) has a completely different feel to that of Randy Pidd's cutback noted above (see sketch in Figure 3.10). In the shot of Cram the sharpness of shadow and light on the posture contributes to a sense of strength, torque and total commitment. The combination of angularity of the surfer and board with the curves of the wave and explosive spray from the turn contributes to this picture's overwhelming sense of a moment of power.

In all of these cases and in the selection of photographs for publication the key elements involve the play of light defining the contours of the wave and the surfer's posture, along with the detail of the play of spray. Indeed, the smallest detail in the pictorial composition of the moment of posture captured in a shot can make the difference between a publishable photograph and a reject. Divine makes the importance of the momentary patterns of spray explicit when he notes, commenting on a shot of Brian Keaulana, at Makaha, 1981, 'of the three frames I shot in a single second, only this one captured the backwash display' (Divine 2000: 122).

A further recurrent iconographic surfing image is that of the seemingly diminutive surfer on a massive wave, as in the shot of Darrick Doerner at Sunset (Divine 2000: 99), at the bottom of the drop, with the shot framed looking into the enormous line of the wave, with a pack of surfers, to the far left of the picture, paddling over the peak, possibly trying to escape from the set of waves following behind that pictured. A considerable body of surf photography deals with just waves (see Plate 1), without human figures, as celebrated, for instance, in Kampion's (1989) *The Book of Waves: Form and Beauty on the Ocean*. Indeed, it is notable how little published surf photography gives any indication of the crowding and hassle that is so much a part of most surfers' surfing reality (see Plate 6). Furthermore, few shots show any signs of urban beachscapes, while tropical palm-fringed beachscapes are very common (see Plate 5). Clearly classic surf photography depicts the dreams of where we would like to be. The composition and framing of classic surf photographs is such that they can be fairly easily reduced to almost cartoon-like skeletal outlines (see Plate 2), which may further highlight the strength of the essential patterns around which they are structured. Such cartoon-like doodling of myriad teenage surfers as well as the sublime artwork of a Rich Griffin (Barilotti 2003) show the linkages between the daydreaming fantasies of surfing and pictorial depiction. Indeed, the Surrealists saw doodling as a path

*Figure 3.9* Elegant cutback, Randy Pidd, Saint Augustine, 1972 (Divine 2000: 43)

*Figure 3.10* Power cutback, Richard Cram, Off The Wall, Oahu, 1983 (Divine 2000: 109)

Notes: these two sketches seek to highlight the symmetry and compositional qualities, capturing moments of a certain perfection, that are often associated with memorable or 'classic' surfing photographs. The sketches also illustrate very different pictorial expressions of the same manoeuvre. The upper (Pidd) shot exudes a sense of almost languid, relaxed grace, in striking contrast to the tension and explosive power of the lower (Cram) shot. This partly relates to the contrast between the two waves; the super glass of a small Californian kelp-bed wave and the intense, concentrated energy of the North Shore (Oahu, Hawaii) wave. However, beyond the wave as medium, the two shots also express what Booth (2001) has called diverging 'philosophies of the wave'; the Pidd movement is redolent of a 'laid back', flowing ease, while the Cram posture is expressive of the Australian 'aggro' attacking style of surfing. Both images are fine examples of the facility for a 'picture to paint a thousand words', by tapping into a wealth of associations, feelings and sense perceptions.

into the subconscious. It is salutary to note that cartoon fantasies of yesteryear, dreaming up explosive manoeuvres and surfers on monster waves, are not entirely dissimilar to the realities of some surfing manoeuvres and giant wave surfing today.

There now follows a brief consideration of the visuality, or the ways in which the vision of surfing photography is constructed. Given the all-important process of selection (and later manipulation) of surfing shots, it is clear that the photographer is simultaneously creative artist and member of the audience. In particular, an attempt is made to explore the bases of both the aesthetic and symbolic dimensions of the visual apprehension of surf photography.

As with more general aesthetics there is a sense in which both the expert selectors of shots (magazine editors and surf photographers) and the audience of readers can instantly recognize a master photograph, or one that has the potential to be a classic. While some of the attributes of such pictures have been briefly outlined above (with respect to Divine's corpus of work) the concern here is to explore the nature of such aesthetic experience. It is the contention to be developed here that in the encounter with classic surfing photography the first, and foremost, impulse is simply to be lost in that aesthetic sense of wonder with the image. Maquet (1986) has summarized the following key features as pertaining to aesthetic perception:

1   It separates or 'frames apart' the object from its visual environment in order to favour the concentration of attention.
2   The context of the object (so important to the historian) is irrelevant to the aesthetic beholder.
3   A complete object is not broken down into an assemblage of parts.
4   The aesthetic experience is 'here and now', imbued with detachment and serenity.
5   Ideas and opinions are excluded so as not to interfere with the concentration.
6   It is concerned with the appearance of the object not its existence.
7   The state of aesthetic absorption involves a loss of the sense of time.

A crucial consideration in appreciating the nature of aesthetic perception is that 'if there is an attempt at analysis the specific perception recedes or disappears' (Maquet 1986: 33). The question is, what aspects of form in art (here surf photography) are aesthetically significant? In general the subject matter and the mastery in resemblance are not the crucial aspects that stimulate aesthetic experience. Rather (irrespective of whether the work is figurative or not) it is the complex of 'visual elements, outline and lines, shapes and colour, light and texture . . . which is aesthetically significant' (Maquet 1986: 41). Thus, part of the powerful aesthetic impact resides in the aesthetic qualities of the forms to which depictions of waves (see Plate 1) and surfing moves lend themselves, in almost abstract ways, which thence impact visually on human senses and consciousness. Beyond the visually aesthetic potential of surfing and waves as subject matter, comes the artistry of the photographer. The aesthetic quality is enhanced by the whole composition of the particular configuration of forms, which depicts a subject as a unified whole (thus the benefits of digitally manipulating photographic images to erase extraneous content). Both the science of visual psychology and the analysis of artistic composition draw on the design principles of geometry, with the former highlighting the ways in which it pertains to both our own natural history and the organic forms of nature. One suspects that although art directors and surf photographers are generally aware of such principles, in practice their day-to-day selection of shots of surfing are intuitive, based on their deep familiarity with aesthetic recognition.

A further dimension of aesthetic vision concerns a certain preparation of the mind. Maquet highlights that such 'preparation' is counter to the linguistic and conceptual knowledge of Western education, and rather the 'elimination of competing concerns accounts for the recognized importance of non-discursiveness and disinterestedness in the aesthetic experience' (1986: 44). This emphasis on the disinterestness, or freedom from self-interest and ego involvement, highlights the deep similarity between aesthetic experience and meditational experience. Buddhist and yogic sutras on meditational preparation emphasize the key importance of absorption, concentration, immersion in the moment, disinterestedness and the 'letting go' of discursive thinking. Furthermore, the various levels of meditative absorption, recognized for instance by Buddhists, could be paralleled by the different degrees of aesthetic awareness generated by various classics of surfing photography. The fundamental quality of both the aesthetic and meditative experiences is that of non-active contemplation.

Surfing photography's evocation of aesthetic or contemplative experience along with surfing's connotations of nature and freedom, resonate strongly with notions of Romanticism noted in Chapter 2. Within the Romantic movement the creative imagination 'became the way to unify [humankind's] psyche and by extension [humankind] with Nature, to return by the paths of self-consciousness, to a state of higher nature, to a state of the sublime where senses, mind and spirit elevate the world around them as they elevate themselves' (Engell 1981 in Rundell 2001: 22). The Romantic notion of self-elevation mirrors the sense of self-growth or self-realization which is concomitant to a deepening involvement in surfing and the sense of relationship with the ocean.

Beyond the wordless, contemplative encounter with a photograph 'in order to concretize that experience we must resort to discourse' (Sage 1998: 107). There are a number of approaches to analyzing and dissecting art, thus in order to explore the symbolic significations of surfing photography, approaches such as the psychology and sociology of art, traditional art history, iconography, semiotics (such as in the work of Flynn 1987; Fiske 1989) psychoanalysis and various narrative and linguistic themes may be employed (Maquet 1986; Roberts 1998; Sage 1998; Rose 2001). Such approaches variously highlight meanings intended by the artist (auteur theory), culturally-informed symbolic ciphers (iconography), and the polysemic signs related to broader systems of meaning of semiotics (Fiske 1989; Rose 2001).

While there is not the space to apply such theorizations within this book, it is perhaps worth noting that the kinds of meanings which a surfing audience may derive from surf photography will be multiple and dynamic. Furthermore, the 'wordless' aesthetic experience of such photography is far more to the fore than symbolic and discursive interpretation. Fiske's (1989) semiotic analysis of surfing culture (discussed in Chapter 2) with its emphasis on nature, direct experience, freedom and pleasure, for example, is one such expression, and resonates with the general exclusion of the signs of crowds and civilization from surf photography. Furthermore, some of the brief allusions made above with reference to classic photographs of Jeff Divine give a sense of the diverse meanings that may arise from surf photography.

A core theme in art interpretation is that of exploring meanings within the context of culture and discourse. Thus, a Foucauldian analysis could explore the meanings connoted by surf photography in terms of discourses ('as groups of statements which structure the way a thing is thought', Rose 2001: 136) of surfing culture. Such an approach would consider the ways in which meanings of images depend on the interplay of various pertinent texts. The location and time of surf photography is always of considerable interest to surfers, allowing the placing of the image in relation to the global geography of surfing. However, an emphasis on seeking the significations of surfing places and images perhaps begins to seem rather too textual and cerebral.

Taking a psychoanalytical approach to the appreciation of aesthetics, Pacteau has argued 'I am interested in the psychical apparatus to which the beholder's eye is attached. . . . Interested less in the contingent object of desire than the fantasy which shapes it' (1994: 15). Such a perspective allows the conjoining of the aesthetic experience of surfing photography with the nature of the appeal of or attractions to surf discussed in Chapter 4. Similarly Merleau-Ponty's approach to the understanding of pictorial representation provides a greater emphasis on the senses and the body than purely linguistic and textual approaches.

In a sense Merleau-Ponty's work allows an attempt to explore the nature of the aesthetic encounter as it is 'lived by our entire psycho-physiological system' (Roberts 1998: 130) revolving around perception, the visible and the body. From such a perspective the surfing photograph may be apprehended as constituted from 'various bodily libidinal, figural, gestural, and perceptual experiences . . . along with the picture's figurative elements' (Roberts 1998: 129) rather than as a static symbolic construct. Thus, the aesthetic experience is viewed in terms of 'non-rational forces – desires, drives, affectations, perceptions . . . [w]hich are not necessarily reducible to intelligible models' (Roberts 1998: 130). Such a perspective may have an especial resonance with surfers' (and yet-to-surf observers) experience of surf photography. The images tap into a complex of the surfer's repository of past embodied surfing experience, knowledge of surfing culture and places, as well as more general aesthetic sensibilities derived from evolutionary biology and socialization within the wider culture. Thus, the power of such surfing images is that they engage the body and senses with powerful mythologies (for instance, the search for the perfect wave, adventure and wanderlust).

As Maquet has argued aesthetic considerations can have a strong impact because 'art is more convincing than reality and because apprehension through art is more conducive to action than the direct apprehension of the outside world' (1986: 238). Certainly aesthetically framed surfing images will be a stronger stimulant to action (such as surf travel, the pursuit of surfing lifestyles and so on) than intellectual lines of argument. The main argument sketched out in this short section has been that the primacy of surf photography within the mediatization of surfing culture, rests on its propensity to elicit powerful aesthetic, contemplative experience. While an attempt has been made to avoid talking about the interpretation of surf photography in terms of static symbolic meanings, it has been tentatively suggested that much of the finest surf photography may engender action through tapping into, and expressing, embodied desires and (almost sacramental) mythologies of surfing culture. Furthermore, these themes of aesthetic experience, which pervade surfing culture, are further elaborated below in Chapter 7, with respect to peak performance, flow and non-representational theory pertaining to the surfing experience.

## Mediatization and stardom in surfing

Given the primacy of not only the visual but in particular the photographic in the mediatization of surfing, the history and significations of surfing are overwhelmingly expressed through pictures of surfing heroes or stars. There is an obvious, inherent complicity between photographer and 'star' surfer as performer. The visually captured moment of the surfer's slide (or dance) on the wave comprises a creative and created product for the photographer to exchange in the commodified media nexus. For the pictured surfer, their photograph appearing in a surfing magazine provides a celebration and recognition of their skill and artistry, primarily from their peer audience.

One of the significant aspects of the mediatization of surfing is the reduction of depictions of surfers in major surfing books to a core of named, 'star' surfers. Similar manoeuvres and moves as those of the 'stars' are being, and have been, performed by thousands of other skilled surfers all over the main surf coasts of the world. The same process of reduction also operates to a lesser degree through the variety of surfing magazines and there is probably scope for some interesting, more systematic research into the relationships between fame and celebrity in surfing photographers' selections of performers, editorial processes, and surfers' tacit propensities and orientations towards being photographed.

In a very real sense the media needs to both create and delimit the numbers of heroes to identify a cultural scarcity of excellence within any sporting or performance art culture. The very expansion in the numbers of highly skilled surfers worldwide militates against such identification of a corpus of elite heroes. In a telling (if hopefully ironic) caption to a photograph of five surfers on a substantial Waimea wave in the 1980s, Nat Young wrote 'in the '60s, Waimea was crowded with watermen. Now it's crowded with "wanna bes"' (1994: 209). Yet anybody, whatever the era, who takes off on a sizeable wave at Waimea is showing a certain nerve and accomplishment. Such a comment (which has, admittedly, been recognized and challenged in surfing magazines) revolves around the juxtaposition of the nostalgic canonization of surfing's pioneering heroes of the past and the denigration of the supposedly, fame-seeking, increased numbers 'swarming' around quality surfbreaks today.

Continuing with these notions of characterization within surfing's narrative history it is apposite to consider Kampion's approach in The *Way of the Surfer* (2003) which achieves an elegant interweaving of totemic themes of surfing culture with personalities who exemplify each theme. Different characters are thus employed to elaborate on core values underlying surfing culture (summarized in Figure 3.8). Thus Titus Kinimaka exemplifies 'the warrior' of surfing's Hawaiian roots; Richard Brewer, Gerry Lopez and Bill Hamilton are associated with the Oriental paths of Zen, the inner journey and the aesthetics and style of soul surfing; Nat Young exemplifies the complex interplay of professionalism, 'new era' aggressive surfing and a notion of a 'Renaissance surfer'; and Tom Curren and Kelly Slater are discussed in terms of surfer fame and celebrity. As he notes in his introduction, Kampion is only too well aware of the ultimate fallacy of such a reduction, stressing 'to represent surfing as the achievements of only its greatest practitioners on the most epic of waves is a misleading shorthand – a symbolic gesture in the direction of infinite truths residing deep in the oceanic reservoirs of our combined surfing experiences' (2003: 15). Kampion's writing epitomizes a further striking facet of the surfing media, the quality and expression of aesthetic considerations, blending with the photographic images.

Some of the most distinctive elements which pervade the surfing media, certainly in contrast to that of most other sports, are its self-reflexivity, its concerns with values (often spirituality) and the aesthetic qualities of the literature. This may partly reflect the aesthetic sensibilities of surfing media figures such as John Severson, the founding editor of *Surfer Magazine*, who came from, and continues to function within, an arts background. However, beyond such personality factors within the narrative of surfing culture, extensive reference is repeatedly made to what may be termed, surfing's cultural crystallization (Figure 3.3–3.5). It is certainly hard to deny that there was an incredible concatenation of cultural and aesthetic creativity around surfing in the early 1960s, primarily within parts of Southern California. It is important to note here, that for surfers the fundamental core is the embodied experience of sliding along the wave. Thus, the various facets of this cultural crystallization, as in the well-documented expressions of surf music (Blair 1978), Hollywood movies (Rutsky 1999), fashion and various other artworks, are in a sense epiphenomena of surfing. It is unlikely that any other sport has stimulated the development of such a rich corpus of cultural expressions. It is also important to note that while some of the creative artists of, for instance, surfing music, did surf, it was by no means an essential prerequisite. More usually, the images and significations of surfing resonated with and inspired the members and creators of a burgeoning youth culture, in turn linked to wider cultural threads (some of which have been discussed above in Chapter 2 and are further explored in Chapter 4).

Again it must be noted that the intention in this text is not to repeat the narrative of surfing's Californian cultural crystallization (noted in Figures 3.3

and 3.4) but rather to reflect upon it. As Californian surfer Sam George has put it:

> It was in California that the entire surfing scene was developed, to the point when it became hard to distinguish where surfing's culture left off and the State's indigenous culture began. The rest of the country – the world – looked on in wonder at this new, free-and-easy way of life. To them California became a place where life really was a beach, the summers were endless and the sunsets always golden.
>
> (George 1991: 67)

In considering surfing's powerful cultural appeal, in a sense the seductiveness of surfing, this gestalt-like quality of a whole set of interlinking expressive aesthetics, across music, photography, fashion-style and so on, and their embodiment and enactment in a particular place and time, was crucial. In a sense the artistic imaginary creations of a dream were given a tangible, reachable reality. The fact that, as George goes on to note, 'surfing in California bears little resemblance to its postcard promotion' (1991: 69), makes no difference, the point is that a whole web of connections could be drawn and richly expressed, creating a surprisingly enduring, surfing imaginary across Western cultures. Again, for the vast world beyond those who have already experienced surfing, it is the imaginative appeal of these epiphenomena of surfing that is culturally relevant.

A further point that needs to be made concerning this crystallization of surfing culture in Southern California, is not just that this was an appropriation of surfing imagery across music, art, fashion, photography, but the significance, for its seductiveness and posterity, of the sheer quality of what was being created around images of surfing in a particular locality. Amid the whole plethora of musicians and composers, artists and photographers, it may be argued with hindsight that some were clearly operating from genius. Furthermore, what is particularly striking is just how rapidly the quality of their artistic expressions evolved. This is readily apparent with respect to the surfing photography of Jeff Divine (Divine 2000) and Art Brewer (Brewer 2001), and also, for example in comparing Brian Wilson's fairly rudimentary *Surfin' Safari* in 1962 to his production of *Good Vibrations* in 1967 (Wise 1994; Granata 2003), and Rick Griffin's progress from the rather basic *Murphy* cartoon in early *Surfer Magazine* to the heights of his poster art for the film *Pacific Vibrations* in 1970 (Owen and Dickson 1999; Barilotti 2003). Obviously such artists were now creatively functioning in an international context (with Wilson for example responding competitively to the innovations of the Beatles). Creativity studies tend to downplay the notion of the solitary genius, working alone, and to emphasize the interactive social context of such work (Scott 2003; Mercer 2003), and here clearly surfing inspirations were being linked in social interaction to a vibrant and energetic youth culture within the locality of Southern California.

## Tensions within the surfing narrative

In contrast to the surfing imaginary of the non-surfing world, which comprises a warm, glowing dream of freedom, devoid of contradictions, the narrative of surfing history, and in particular its recent era, from the late 1960s onwards, is riven by a series of tensions. Such tensions, in themselves, further reinforce the strength of the narrativization of surfing history and culture. Just as there seems to be an inherent dialectical (at its simplest, negative follows positive, and vice versa) quality to the story – making propensities of human consciousness, so conflict and its capacity to enhance dramatic tension is integral to narrative plot. The very existence, strength and clarity of expression of these narrative tensions testify to an emerging maturity as well as vitality within surfing culture. As noted above, such tensions may also be considered, from a figurational sociological perspective, as unfolding, converging and diverging tendencies. It is also apposite to note that the narrativization of surfing history increasingly loses its clarity in the most recent decades culminating in the present.

Again the intention here is not to describe these tensions (which have been briefly summarized in Figure 3.5) in any detail, but to seek to make some comment on their interplay. While numerous permutations of core tensions running through surfing culture could be identified, these are here considered (reflecting the wider surfing literature) in terms of the interplay of four themes: soul surfing, competition, commercialization and crowding. While it is more useful to discuss competition and (professionalism) commercialization and crowding in the later section on the globalization of surfing, this section will consider elements of the critiques of such developments emanating from the soul surfing lifestyle and artform tradition.

One of the core values of surfing culture is that of non-conformity (e.g. George 1999) variously expressed in the surfing literature as anti-establishment, oppositional or counter-cultural. As Rutsky (1999) has argued with respect to the popularity of the (however caricatured) Hollywood forays into surf/beach movies, major elements of their powerful appeal to the wider public has been 'the attraction of a certain difference' (1999: 19).

Paul Holmes (1991) has argued that along with the invention of surfing style as a means of social differentiation, there was a strong sense of 'what was real and what was fake' (1991: 204). With the sharpening of surfing's anti-materialistic stance through the counter-culture came a deepening concern with authenticity and purity. In the late 1970s and 1980s there was a growing number of, often vehemently expressed, articles in surfing magazines attacking both the commercialization of the lifestyle and the competitive emphasis in the promotion of professionalism within the sport. The tensions between advocacies for a strong competitive and contest component to the sport, sponsored by a thriving surfing commercial sector, and soul surfing, counter-cultural tendencies, continue to pervade surfing culture. The commercial changes occurring in surfing companies are further explored in Chapter 6.

## Nostalgia and the surfing narrative

It is apparent from reviewing the structuring and composition of surfing histories that the narrativization of surfing increasingly loses its coherence and clarity, the closer it moves towards the present. In a sense there would appear to be a series of diverging sub-narratives underlying the world of surfing today. This could reflect a number of factors such as, first, the greater ease of placing coherent patterns on surfing when it was a smaller social phenomenon, and second, the greater facility to simplify and select salient details from further back in time, rather than sift through the complexity of the engulfing present. As noted above with respect to reminiscence, hindsight perceptions are not always wholly congruent with the original experience. If this is the case, then maybe in 30 years' time commentators will be distilling clearer assessments of trends in surfing culture at the beginning of the twenty-first century.

Rather than identifying any clear trend, other than a modest increase in contest surfing and measure (albeit at a low level compared to most other sports) of professionalism, the narrative of the past three decades tends to identify a 'mixed bag' of developments including the increasing emergence of women's surfing, a renewed emphasis (by a small minority) on riding massive waves (including 'jetski' tow-in surfing), the re-emergence of longboards, and increasing performance of explosive manoeuvres such as 'airs'. Such a combination of developments fails to illustrate any coherent pattern. Thus, it seems plausible to characterize the current phase of increasing levels of participation in surfing as one of a growing pluralism of surfing styles and lifestyles.

Notable features of narrative histories are their varying progressive and declensionist perspectives (Cronon 1992). With reference to the current period it would seem apposite to conclude that there are two main diverging narratives branching out from the surfing meta-narrative outlined above. The first, emerging from a soul surfing orientation, is declensionist in that it views recent trends as a fall from grace, from surfing's earlier golden age of innocence (less commercial, less contest-orientated), surfing as play and peak experience, in uncrowded, relaxed surfbreaks. Such a perspective resonates with Turner's (1987) discussion of nostalgia, in that it views surfing's development to be one of decline in terms of core value and expresses a sense of a loss of coherence and wholeness in the culture. In particular, the crowd-related phenomenon of 'surf rage' and fierce territorial 'localism' (Young 2001) are seen to be emblematic of surfing's cultural decline. Given that such a perspective is generally held by older surfers, it is perhaps pertinent to consider whether such a view involves idealization of one's youth and chagrin at the restrictions associated with adult lifepath developments and ageing. Furthermore, the identification of 'golden ages' in historical analyses is always fraught with imprecision and divergent viewpoints.

A second (positive) sub-narrative, which is more likely to be articulated by the surfing media-production complex, takes a more progressive perspective on surfing's condition. It can argue that more people, in more countries than ever before, are participating (and spending money!) in the sport, with business supporting a steady (if not exactly flourishing) international 'professional' circuit, with continuing innovations in cutting-edge performance, a greater range of surfing media (magazines, films), in a time when overseas travel to exotic surf coasts has never been easier nor less expensive (in real terms and in relation to disposable income in industrialized countries).

## Further research into the narratives of surfing

The previous section has sought to distil a meta-narrative in the writing on the culture and history of surfing. Narratology can gainfully be utilized in at least three other directions in the analysis of surfing.

1   Narrative analyses of the histories of surfing in localities other than the core areas of Hawaii, California and Australia could shed light on the global–local processes operating in the geographical expansion of surfing. It is striking (at least from a non-Californian, non-Australian perspective) how many accounts of 'non-core' surfing localities make especial reference to the visits and temporary residence of named 'famous' American and Australian surfers (e.g. Wilson 1991), rather than identifying significant local or indigenous surfers.

2   Narrative frameworks could usefully be applied to analyses of individual articles in surfing magazines, to examine the recurring themes and structuring which occur, with ongoing comparative studies being capable of providing a rich commentary on changing emphases over time and underlying orientations.

3   Anecdotally it is noticeable that the surfing meta-narrative is not merely textual or confined to the surfing media. Clearly there is a reciprocal interplay between surfing texts (which are after all generally produced by surfers) and the biographical patterns by which surfers seek to make sense of their own lives, surfing localities and motivations. Narrative analysis could be gainfully applied to explore the rationalizations of, and relationships between, surfing media accounts and personal histories, which should be at the core of research seeking to situate the practice and experience of surfing within a sociocultural context (Healey 1991).

## Surfing and the globalization of culture and sport

It is a statement of the obvious that surfing culture is a quintessentially globalized sociocultural phenomenon. It is also axiomatic in terms of globalization theory (e.g. Appadurai 1990) that global flows involve local responses and reformulations. The main task in this final section of this chapter is to consider some of the key themes of the surfing narrative through the lens of thinking on the globalization of culture and sport. This section provides something of a macro-level context for some of the later discussion of surfing subculture, identity and emotion explored in Chapter 4.

Along with the enormous increases in the numbers participating in surfing (especially during the past four decades) there has been a tremendous development of new surfing localities around the coasts of the world. This rapid geographical expansion has partly been fuelled by the mobility inherent to the wanderlust of some surfing lifestyles. Such worldwide expansion highlights the need to consider surfing in the light of some of the main lines of thinking on the globalization of culture and sport. Such thinking is here, first, outlined by reference to broad theoretical perspectives on globalization, and views of the nature of the relationship and agency between culture and structure (or economic base) underlying such thinking, themes (or binary logics) in the globalization of culture and notions of the flows and scapes in these processes. Second, further context is provided by noting some of the thinking on the globalization of sport, regarding for instance, notions of modernist and counter-cultural configurations, and the sociocultural impacts of tourism on developing world cultures.

The primary concern in research into the globalization of culture is with the trans-societal cultural processes in which the flows of people, products, information and knowledge take place. Of particular significance are the processes by which images and traditions are formed, communicated and reformulated. The specific meaning or connotation of the term 'globalization' refers to those processes that transcend the interactions of the apparatus of states (Robertson 1992). The globalizing processes are viewed as a form of time–space compression (Giddens 1991) involving the shrinking of space and speeding up of time.

A core theme of most of the traditional grand theories of the nature of globalization has been the notion of modernization, as Westernization or Americanization. Modernization theory generally views this process as a benign transformation involving the triumph of the West, with a progressive homogenization of global culture. By contrast, theories of cultural imperialism, dependency theory and world-systems theory (Wallerstein 1987) similarly place especial emphasis on the hegemony of the West (variously as culture or, more usually, capitalist economy), but view the globalizing tendencies as exploitive and destructive towards, in particular, developing world cultures. In considering surfing in the light of such overarching theories of globalization the first point to make is that the major part of surfing's expansion has been within the cultures of the advanced, industrialized, capitalist world. In this context, given the 'cultural crystallization' of surfing in early 1960s Southern California, it could be considered as a form of Americanization. However, it is clear from studies of the surfing culture of Australia (e.g. Booth 2001a) that surfing culture is re-expressed in terms of the receiving culture. As yet insufficient systematic research has been undertaken into comparative analysis of surfing cultures. The greatest cultural impacts of surfing, however, could be expected to occur where it is taken up in developing world cultures in the light of surf touristic travel. For instance, given the enormous surf tourism to the Indonesian archipelago, and the substantial numbers of young Indonesians taking up surfing, powerful questions of clashes with, or adaptions of, local values, may be hypothesized. Again, while some reference has been made to this indigenous growth of surfing and styles of surfing performance (e.g. Leuras and Leuras 1997), no systematic, theoretically informed research has yet examined the cultural ramifications. Such research could gainfully draw on the enormous bodies of empirical and theoretical literature on guest–host interaction in the transdisciplinary fields of tourism studies.

With reference to the agency of global cultural transformations there have been strong criticisms of the economism of, for instance, world-systems theory, which views culture as merely derivative or reactive to the economic structural base (Archer 1990; Boyne 1990). Similarly Rojek (1985) has argued that in understanding leisure relations, lifestyle is rather more than merely 'an epiphenomenon of class'.

The limitations of economistic theories such as world-systems theory for understanding surfing as a social practice are evident, given that surfing is primarily a cultural and lifestyle phenomenon. Economic factors are, however, of significance, but more as facilitating, rather than determining, the form of the expansion of surfing. Such economic factors include the relative affluence of the Western world, inexpensive international air travel and some touristic promotion. It should also be noted, however, that surfing is not, in Western capitalist terms, an especially expensive leisure pursuit, and that many 'hardcore' surfers are able to find cheap accommodation from which to spend extensive periods of time in 'exotic' surfing locations. Furthermore, because surfers, like backpackers, are perceived to be low-spending visitors, they are not generally a high priority target group in touristic advertising and promotion. The exceptions would be the small numbers of surf camps and charter boats which have grown up in some island locations in the tropics. It could also be countered that although surfers *are* generally, low-spending visitors, because they spend relatively long periods in surfing travel, the modest expenditure does amount up, and no doubt is a significant income to certain surf resort localities.

Featherstone (1990) has argued that much of the earlier work on globalization sought to comprehend the cultural changes taking place via the mutually exclusive binary logics of such terms as homogeneity–heterogeneity, integration–disintegration and unity–diversity. He continues that the post-modern turn has led to a substitution of the concept of globalization as a homogenizing process of a proto-universal culture based on Western economic and political domination, with greater emphasis on diversity, variety and richness of local discourses and practices.

Hannerz (1990) has highlighted the flows of meanings as well as flows of people and goods within a world-culture which is being created by the increasing interconnectedness of varied local cultures. In a sense this envisages a rich variety of subcultures within the wider whole. Within this context the distinction is drawn between the polarities of localism, which is territorially anchored or bounded cultures involving face-to-face relations among people with limited mobility, and cosmopolitanism, transnational cultural networks extended in space which encourage engagement with the other. One facet of such cultural flows is that transnational cultures are produced, which are genuine 'third cultures' that are oriented beyond national boundaries.

Hannerz' theoretical contribution clearly has resonance with surfing, particularly as the term 'localism' has a strong currency within debates on crowding and the inherent scarcity of surfing. In global terms, research could be gainfully directed to understanding the variations in the strength and expression of localism in different surfing localities. Anecdotally, for example, it appears to take particularly aggressive forms in some areas of Hawaii and California, but is rather more benign, for instance, in places such as the UK and Japan. The reasons are not simply a matter of the density of crowding, but probably reflect differences in the forms of social interaction in different cultures and other particularities of specific localities. The wholesale application of Hannerz' dichotomy is partly complicated by the fact that many surfers are likely to be localists, for example, at a 'home' break and cosmopolitans when travelling. In general, given its high mobility, surfing is an example of a highly cosmopolitan 'third culture' as a practice that transcends national boundaries. Such notions as localist/cosmopolitan may be usefully linked to the plurality of individuals' identities and affiliations within a globalizing world.

The influential work of Appadurai has sought to redress the arguments of an overarching homogenization (based on Americanization and commoditization) by emphasizing the need to consider the indigenous cultural response to such penetration, arguing that 'at least as rapidly as forces from various metropolises are brought into new societies they tend to become indigenized' (1990: 295). Appadurai proposes a framework of five scapes for exploring the 'fundamental disjunctures between economy, culture and politics' (1990: 296) within globalization. The suffix 'scape' is used to indicate that these are deeply perspectival constructs, inflected by the situatedness of different types of actors, and that many people live in 'imagined worlds', not just the imagined communities identified by Anderson (1983).

1   The ethnoscape – the landscape of flows of persons.
2   The technoscape – the global configuration of technology.
3   The finanscapes – fiscal and investment flows.
4   The mediascapes – both the distribution of the electronic capabilities to produce and disseminate information (magazines, TV stations, film studios, etc.) and the images created by these media.
5   The ideoscapes – also images, but often directly political, to do with state ideologies and counter-ideologies, including such concepts as freedom and welfare.

An outline operationalization of Appadurai's five scapes to surfing may take the following form:

1   The ethnoscape – mobility flows to surfing localities at a range of scales: local movements to beaches, and regional and international travel to surfing localities. Movements involve a wide range of time durations from daily, short

holiday and long journeys, to full migration. In some areas, for instance Jeffrey's Bay in South Africa, whole settlements have developed, purely due to the proximity of excellent surf.

2 The technoscape – as well as the whole range of transport and communications technology which facilitate all forms of flows, surfing is obviously influenced by the technological developments concerning surfboard (Figure 3.6) and wetsuit design and manufacture, as well as the increasing access to internet (including webcam) sources of wave forecasts (Banks 2004). Some surfers have lamented the demise of the higher level of chance that was involved in seeking and finding waves in previous eras. Improvements in forecasting have also substantially impacted on the crowding of surfspots. Surfing culture has also continued to express considerable ambivalence towards technological advance in surfboard construction. Noble (2004) has highlighted the ways in which the windsurfing community has enthusiastically and overwhelmingly embraced innovations in sailboard construction in contrast to surfing's 'stagnation' in its continuing reliance on foam blank/fibreglass craft methods established in the 1960s. In contrast to sailboards, which are constructed from the most advanced technologies available by a small number of very big companies, the making of surfboards is still a craft industry comprised of a vast number of small scale producers (Plate 4), as well as a few large companies. Major elements underlying surfing's preference for such craft methods include the counter-cultural values of intuition and 'feel' in craft, antipathy to big business and even science, and preferences for customizing for uniqueness.

3 The Finanscapes – the most substantial flows of investment in relation to surfing have undoubtedly related to the surf apparel section of the industry.

4 The mediascapes – alongside surfing's global expansion has been a growing proliferation of surfing books, magazines, websites and films. Surfing programmes and films are regularly shown on specialist TV channels such as *Extreme Sports*. Local, or rather, national surfing magazines have rapidly emerged in many surfing localities and are obviously now published in a wide range of languages rather than, as originally, only in English. The photography-based formats of most surfing magazines, however, are often very similar, following on from the early blueprints of the Californian *Surfer Magazine*. There is growing frustration among surfers with the increasingly high content of advertising in some surfing magazines (Hadersdorfer 2004). *The Surfer's Journal*, which is arguably the highest quality surfing magazine (although closely followed by *The Surfer's Path*), strives to keep pages of advertising restricted to a bare minimum, and to maximize direct reader subscription. The high cost per issue that such a strategy demands may well preclude purchase by many younger surfers; however, some of the content is, in any case, orientated towards a slightly more mature readership.

5 The ideoscapes – while the surfing media and culture does express a range of values (alluded to above) images of a directly political nature are comparatively rare. There has always been, however, a thread of ecological concern

running through the surf media, and the surfing world does contain some substantial ecologically orientated bodies, such as Surfers Against Sewerage in the UK and the Surfrider Foundation in the USA.

Interestingly, with respect to the mediascapes, Appadurai stresses the blurring of 'realistic' and 'fictional' landscapes in the ways audiences perceive the images, such that 'the further away these audiences are from the direct experiences of metropolitan life, the more likely they are to construct imagined worlds which are chimerical, aesthetic, even fantastic objects' (1990: 299). Furthermore the image-centred, narrative-based scripts from the mediascapes tend to be reduced to complex sets of metaphors (Lakoff and Johnson 1980), creating fantasies of possible lives that may influence consumption and mobility patterns. Such thinking could have implications for the ways that images of surfing are inter-preted by the wider audiences who reside away from the surf coasts. Appadurai's argument is that global flows occur in and through the growing disjunctures (or separations) between the five scapes. The different flows follow increasingly non-isomorphic paths, in which the flows of particular scapes predominate and show high levels of inequality in the exchanges between, for example, different countries.

Appadurai's notion of the non-isomorphic quality of flows is particularly interesting with respect to surfing. In historical terms it could be argued that much of the style and values underlying surf culture derived predominantly from the core geographical nexus of early 1960s Southern California. For many years, even as newly emerging surfing countries launched their own surfing magazines, the American (and to a lesser extent, Australian) magazines continued to sell particularly well internationally, benefiting from a perceived prestige. With regard to developments in surfboard design there is much evidence of very high interchange and cross-pollination between California and Australia. Developments in Hawaii were also important, but of lesser international impact as their distinctively powerful wave-forms are less typical of most other localities. Anecdotally it may appear that Australia has been more influential in board design innovation than California in recent decades. However, a major point is that significant innovations (and even 'fashions') in surfboard design have been disseminated with quite incredible speed across the surfing world, due not only to the ubiquity of the surfing media, but more importantly, as a result of 'hardcore' surfers' extreme levels of global mobility, and a correspondingly high degree of international interaction in the major high-performance arenas. Part of the surfer's gaze is to be acutely aware of fine surfing taking place in the vicinity, hence taking an interest in the details of board design, and often discussing apparent innovations.

Maguire (2000) has argued that the speed, scale and volume of sport devel-opment is interwoven with these broader flows conceptualized by Appadurai. However, before considering the globalization of sport, it is first useful, given its centrality to the debates, to make some reference to perspectives on moder-nity and sport, including the figurational sociology perspective, the modern competitive, Olympian ethos, counter-cultural reaction, the media–sport–production complex, and cultural markers of prestige and distinction.

The social development of modern sport is generally located, fairly directly, within the technological forces of urban, industrial society (Gruneau 1993). One of the main interpretations of the development of modern sport has derived from the application of Elias' figurational sociology (Elias 1978). The central concept of figuration is of 'a structure of mutually oriented and dependent people' (Elias 1978: 261), which was principally developed to overcome such traditional sociological dualisms as individual and society, and the reduction of social process to static categories. Elias' concept of human beings was that of 'homo aperti', as people bonded together by dynamic constellations of networks of, for instance, social learning, education and socialization. His fundamental focus was on the long-term civilizing process, which included the refinement of manners and social standards, and the shift from external to internal self-control. Thus, the development of modern sport was viewed as a cathartic, social control of violence and aggression.

The re-emergence of surfing in the early twentieth century, and its major development over the past half-century, is perhaps rather too short a time period for a strong application of Elias' notion of the 'civilizing process'. Indeed, it is an open question as to whether the social experience of sharing waves has progressively become any more 'civilized' with time. On the one hand, older surfers often reminisce concerning the more mellow, friendly and less selfish atmosphere of surfing before the beginnings of major expansions in participation from the mid-1960s. However, it is not only crowding that has changed the atmosphere in the water, but also the contemporary performance style in which each surfer wishes to be 'in the curl', increasingly precluding more than one surfer on a wave at a time, in contrast to surfriding in the earlier days of more relaxed longboarding. On the other hand, the surfing community is acutely conscious of the problems of crowding and annoyance, and has increasingly developed a sense of etiquette regarding the avoidance of 'dropping in' on another surfer and sharing waves. These matters are further explored in Chapter 4.

The term 'sportization' is used to refer to the process of the stricter definitions of rules, concepts of fairness, increased supervision of games, along with this wider process of greater self-control and self-discipline (Murphy, Sheard and Waddington 2000). Along with notions of fairness and stricter supervision of rules, 'the emergence of the idea of modernity was tied closely to a Promethean vision of human possibilities based on the necessity for constant growth and continual revolution of production' (Gruneau 1993: 88 based on Berman 1983). Similarly, Henning Eichberg has argued that the Olympian sports ideals are a reflection of Western industrial society (see Bale and Philo 1998). There would appear to be two possible tendencies in surfing related to such Olympian sports ideals. First, and obviously, the whole trend, especially from the 1980s onwards, towards increasing emphasis on the codification of competition and the steps taken to establish the international 'professional' circuit. Questions of ascribing value to style have a long history in surfing (e.g. Edwards 1964 in George 2001).

This codification sought to increase objectivity in judging competitive surfing, by scoring on the basis of clearly identified criteria which could command a wide consensus of respect.

The strengthening and greater visibility of surfing competition has presumably progressed high-performance surfing. As noted in the outline of the history of surfing performance (Figures 3.6 and 3.7) the codification of surfing competition and subsequent series of Australian surfers' victories in top international competitions led to the aggressive, explosive Australian style becoming the dominant form. In describing this approach, Australian world champion Nat Young is often quoted (e.g. in Kampion and Brown 1997; Booth 1999) 'the "new era" surfers were going for blatant changes of direction, radical manoeuvres, looking for the most intense areas of the wave, chasing the curl without too much thought for aesthetics' (Young 1994: 101). Booth (1999) has argued that this has led to the hegemony of this particular high-performance style of surfing, which top surfers from all countries have since felt it necessary to emulate in order to progress in competition. Alternatively, it could be argued that this style is simply the most skilful and intense form of surfing expression. Some of these questions of performance, experience and aesthetics are explored below in Chapter 7. A further outcome of this Olympian ethos of competition (which Booth 1999 traces back to the Australian Surf Life Saving Club tradition) is some development of a sense of national competition and rivalry. Statements of national surfing superiority, hegemony and domination have, in particular, been expressed by Australians in the surfing media. Given surfing's highly individualistic, non-conforming and aesthetic qualities, such nationalistic statements can seem somewhat incongruously bombastic, but probably just reflect Australian sporting culture's characteristics of intense competitiveness and a provocative sense of humour.

The second tendency, which could be seen as reflecting an Olympian ideal and Promethean vision of human possibilities, would be the incredible progress made in recent decades in surfing, never-before-ridden, monster waves, for instance on the outer reefs of Oahu, as pioneered by the likes of Laird Hamilton and Mike Bradshaw. Undoubtedly, this is a direction which entails the surpassing of both performance and perceptual barriers. In this form surfing is undeniably an extreme (as in life-threatening) sport. However, it is important to note that such surfing has developed outside any competitive contest circuit. Furthermore, the idea that it comprises an Olympian (and as such Western cultural) tendency can be easily questioned given that there is ample evidence that the drive to ride enormous (albeit not as large as those of today's 'tow-in' surfers) waves was clearly part of the ancient Hawaiian tradition.

Eichberg has further argued that Western or modernist domination in turn provokes resistance, which has taken the form of national cultural games, open air movements, expressive activities and meditative exercises. Gruneau (1993) also highlights the resistance to modernist Olympian sportization in the wave of counter-cultural critique which draws on notions of play (Huizinga 1949) as an alternative emancipatory aesthetic (Bale and Philo 1998). Such counter-cultural perspectives also entailed a critique of (authoritarian) bureaucratic rationality and complex social organization of sport. Within surfing culture, as discussed above in terms of tensions within the surfing narrative, the conflict between counter-cultural (soul surfing) and Olympian (contest-oriented, professionalism) perspectives has been particularly vehemently articulated. Critics of the 'contest/ professionalism' developments railed against the effect on surfing values, style and culture. For example, writing in *Surfer* in 1989, Dave Parmenter (pro surfer/ shaper) argued:

> Pro surfing has become the heaviest influence on kids today, only they can't see that a lot of it is just like the emperor's new clothes . . . they're growing up baited with all these crazy incentives so they can be brainwashed into being 'the next Tom Curren' . . . of doing it the way he did . . . In the mean-time they're missing out on surfing . . . surfing is not a material quest . . . it's a spiritual quest.
>
> (in George 2001: 122)

Similarly, advocates of the promotion of surfing's sports and commercial development were critical of what were felt to be negative characteristics of surfing's anti-social image. George (1999) has argued that two of surfing's most fundamental characteristics are non-conformity and a thrill-seeking, primal atavistic urge. Given such a combination it is not surprising that surfers have not always respected all aspects of the law, particularly in finding ways to support a 'hard core' surfing lifestyle. In surfing's narrative reference is often made to a few surfers' involvement in matters of illegal drugs (e.g. Kampion and Brown 1997), usually citing, for example, the Brotherhood of Light and biography of pro surfer Jeff Hakman (Jarratt 1997). Maybe the Brotherhood was the inspiration for the surfer gang in the film *Pointbreak*. However, anybody who has travelled on some of surfing's more remote fringes will have encountered a few surfing characters who sail fairly close to the wind. For instance, three Brazilian surfers were arrested in Jakarta in July 2004 for attempting to smuggle cocaine from Peru inside surfboards. This was despite the fact that one of their countrymen had been handed down the death penalty the previous month for a similar smuggling offence in Indonesia (Fidrus 2004).

The promoters of surfing's sportization and business development have been committed to fostering a more clean-living surfing image in order to gain wider respectability in society. Nick Carroll marshals some telling quotations from Shaun Tomson and Mark Richards (world champions from the late 1970s) that articulate such views. Shaun Tomson alluding to previous champion Michael Petersen's drug involvements, 'that guy held surfing back. He held sponsorship back from the sport' (from Tracks magazine, cited in Carroll 1991: 105) and Mark Richards 'I think the general impression that people had of surfers in those days was that they were drug addict dole bludgers' (in Carroll 1991: 106). Citing the contrasting positive image of Mark Warren, *Surfing World Annual* editors noted:

Always an outstanding ambassador for surfing, not only in Australia but worldwide, . . . Mark has been a pioneer in the development of professional surfing, as well as the presentation of our culture as a healthy and respectable activity.

(Channon and McLeod: 10)

The notions of sportization, the Olympian ideal and counter-cultural reactions, have been articulated in terms of both the development of sport within Western society and the diffusion of modern sport to other cultures (Elias and Dúnning 1986). The latter has been explored in relation to both colonial and post-colonial interactions, with Galtung (1982) stressing that modern sporting ideology is a carrier of deep culture and structure as a metaphor for Western cosmology.

Clearly, such cultural transmission is set within the material context of the global economy, with the capitalist marketplace threatening to commodify sport at every turn (Gruneau 1993: 92). Maguire (1993) has elaborated on the connections and flows of the creation and circulation of images, advertising and marketing of products and the development of sport in terms of the media–sport–production complex. Although those seeking to develop surfing's international professional contest circuit sought respectability for the sport to attract substantial funding from non-surfing business, surfing culture has been notoriously impervious to market penetration from non-surfing companies. As Paul Holmes has noted, for these surfing companies, established by the early 1960s, 'there was an incredible wave of commercial success to be ridden' (Holmes 1991: 204). Exploiting surfing culture's concerns with such notions as authenticity and purity, the initially small, surfer-founded, companies such as Quiksilver, Billabong and Ripcurl have grown their business base to become multinational giants, with their surf apparel stores now to be found in cities right across the world and often far from any surfbreak.

Taking a figurational perspective, Maguire has discussed the ways in which sports (as examples of tastes and conduct) act 'as signs of distinction, prestige and power' (2000: 262). Furthermore, and linking with Galtung's notion of sport as a carrier of deep structure, Maguire has noted that the 'shift toward competitive, rationalised and gendered bodily exertions of achievement sport', involved changes at the level of personality, body comportment and social interaction 'which are more important than the global movement of commercial products' (Maguire, 2000: 364).

This section has provided a very brief outline of some of the main lines of thinking on the globalization of culture and sport. Such thinking provides some context for the consideration of the processes underlying, and ramifications of, surfing's rapid global expansion. Surfing is clearly a transcultural social phenomenon, and lifestyle/alternative sports are sometimes discussed in terms of 'a transnational village, the peaceful brotherhood' (Rinehart and Sydnor 2003: 10). Chapter 4 on subculture and lifestyle further explores the extent to which surfing may be viewed in such benign terms. Surfing culture expresses the tensions between Olympian ideals of a sport and counter-cultural advocacies of play.

Furthermore, it is possible to discern a homogenization in surfing performance which may be related to ideas of sportization and hegemony.

## Conclusion

This chapter has examined the ways in which surfing culture has sought to make sense of itself through a reflexive awareness of its history and values. It has been argued that accounts of surfing history display a high level of consensus of phases of development, which in their form and repetition constitute a narrative structure. The major threads of this narrative were disentangled in terms of broad chronologies of surfing technology, culture, performance and values.

The process of the surfing culture's creation of this strong narrative was discussed in terms of its demographic expansion and maturation, and related reminiscence and nostalgia. Surfing's narrative was further discussed in terms of plot, characterization and style. The construction of surfing's historical narrative has necessarily entailed selection and simplification to identify a coherent pattern and celebrated heroes, (surfing's 'mediatization of stardom') in the process of myth-making and the laying claim to history which has taken place.

The unfolding expression of surfing culture was seen to involve the elaboration of a set of core values and orientations, which have unfolded in relation to developments in the wider sociocultural setting. In terms of agency, while economic structure forms an important facilitating context, surfing has developed primarily as an embodied performance, with a rich range of cultural and artistic epiphenomena, within the influencing sphere of culture and lifestyle.

Surfing's 'cultural crystallization' has been repeatedly identified with reference to a concatenation of artistic and youth cultural developments focused, in particular, within Southern California in the early 1960s. It is primarily through these expressions (which are probably more richly aesthetic than the cultural associations of any other 'sport') that values and symbolisms of a surfing imaginary have been conveyed to the wider non-surfing (or yet-to-surf) society. Aspects of such aesthetic and symbolic meanings – the charm and a certain seductiveness that are attributes of surfing – will be further explored in Chapter 4.

In terms of narrative structure it is possible to discern three broad stages, which nevertheless display continuing underlying consistencies in values and images of surfing. The early stages display considerable coherence, a second stage entailing surfing's major expansion and performance enhancement from the late 1960s involved the oppositional interplay of tensions within the culture, and the third, contemporary phase up to the present, entails something of a loss of narrative clarity, reflecting a growing pluralism in surfing practice and lifestyles. The tensions in surfing's narrative testify to the maturation and vitality of the culture, and represent the complicating forces which enhance dramatic tension in classic narrative composition of plot. Unlike narratives of much fiction, contemporary historical narratives, which reach into the present, do not usually entail the final phase of resolution or closure, but rather necessarily culminate in a sense of the openness of future alternative trends.

The tension running through surfing culture was seen to revolve primarily around the oppositional interplay of soul surfing and commercial/contest tendencies, the former associated with a declensionist narrative and counter-cultural surfing as lifestyle perspective, and the latter, within a progressive narrative, linked to an Olympian ethos of the sportization of surfing, but also seeking to market surfing as lifestyle.

A major source of this tension pervading surfing culture may be further understood with reference to Fiske's (1989) semiotic analysis of surfing culture as being associated with nature, risk and immediacy, and a correspondingly inherent suspicion of civilization (and associated commercialization). Thus, surfer-founded businesses have successfully developed lucrative, niche markets from small beginnings by articulating surfing's cultural values of authenticity (for instance Billabong's 'only a surfer knows the feeling').

Obviously transcultural, surfing may be viewed as a quintessentially globalized lifestyle and sporting phenomenon of the twenty-first century. The non-isomorphic qualities (after Appadurai 1990) of the technological, cultural and performance-shaping flows that constitute the sport/lifestyle were seen to be primarily structured by American (or Californian) and Australian sources. The especially high levels of international mobility along with the vibrance of the surfing media–sport complex, were seen to foster the very rapid cross-pollination of contemporary innovations, further enhancing coherence in the transcultural values of surfing. A particularly interesting area for further research was noted as theoretically informed, systematic comparative analysis of surf cultures of different surfing localities, which could explore the local responses to global flows. Major cultural impacts may be expected where surfing has been transplanted (via surf tourism) to communities in developing world cultures in the Tropics. Particular challenges to the idealization of surf culture as a 'peaceful brotherhood' may relate to the growing densities of crowding in what is an inherently scarce resource, at least with regard to what may be termed the optimal carrying capacities of surf line-ups. The macro-level themes of this chapter are further explored in terms of subculture, lifestyle and motivation theories, and recent empirical findings in Chapter 4.

# 4 Surfing as subculture and lifestyle

Within the surfing media there has been a long-running debate as to whether, or rather in what ways, the practice of waveriding is, variously, a sport, artform or lifestyle. However, there is a more general, less disputed, sense that surfing is a culture or subculture. The narrative history of surfing culture has been outlined in Chapter 3. This chapter seeks to connect understandings of surfing to lines of social thinking on subculture, lifestyle and consumption. At this stage in the book, rather than seeking to distil and defend a central thesis an attempt is made to provide an overview of a wide range of applications of relevant social theorizing to surfing.

The chapter is structured in terms of an introductory outline of some of the main lines of social theory in subculture, consumption and lifestyle, before relating such ideas to a series of core themes concerning the culture of surfing. These core themes include: surfing as a subcultural seduction (style and image), identity, socialization, emotion and lifestyle, status and the regulation of scarcity in surfing. A concluding summary draws the material together with respect to the notion of a surfing gaze.

## Introductory outline of subculture and social theory

As Thornton (1997a) has noted, the very process by which scholars portray social groups inevitably contributes to their construction, 'to label a social formation is to frame, shape and delineate it' (1997a: 1). Thus, scholarship on subculture interacts with discussions within the wider media, and with 'insider' and 'outsider' representations of collective perceptions of subcultures. With these considerations in mind this contextual section is structured in terms of definitional aspects of subculture, social theories and consumption, and development of subculture theory with reference to the Birmingham Centre for Contemporary Cultural Studies (CCCS), Bourdieu's notion of cultural capital, and the contemporary concept of lifestyle.

Jary and Jary (1995) have defined sport subcultures as 'any system(s) of beliefs, values and norms . . . shared and actively participated in by an appreciable minority of people within a particular culture' (in Donnelly 2000: 83). The prefix 'sub' primarily ascribes a secondary rank, referring to a group which is subordinate to, or beneath, but within, society or culture (Thornton 1997a). The 'sub' in subculture has also been described as pertaining to the level of analysis which is below the macro level, focusing on the everyday meanings, interpretations and interactions taking place at the intermediate level (Crossett and Beal 1997).

Subculture is differentiated from the term 'community' which indicates a more permanent population, generally aligned to some territory and constituted by collections of families. By contrast, subcultures connote people as separate from their families, and often in a state of relative transience in groupings which are often innately oppositional (Thornton 1997a), especially as expressed by the CCCS.

Recurrent definitional efforts have been made to explore the utility and precision of the concept of subculture in relation to related, but generally less commonly applied, concepts. For instance, Irwin (1970/1997 in Gelder and Thornton 1997) has explored subcultures as:

1   'social worlds' (after Shibutani, 1955) which are not tied to any particular collectivity or territory
2   'explicit lifestyle' or in folk parlance 'scene' which connotes a shared category and a commitment which may be potentially tentative and variable
3   an 'action system' in which a set of values and cultural meanings are conceived as making up a whole, with some measure of coherence.

Irwin has argued that subculture also shares with each of these concepts the sense that an individual may (and probably will) choose to, simultaneously or alternately, identify with more than one social 'world' or 'scene' among the range which is available to them.

Theories of subculture and lifestyle revolve around matters of personal consumption and associated meanings. It is important to note that social (and especially classical) theorists have traditionally displayed a productivist bias, leaving consumption relatively undertheorized (Ritzer, Goodman and Wiedenhoft 2001). The classical theorists tended to view consumption negatively, with the sociology of consumption being expressed in an 'unabashedly moral tone . . . of a moral condemnation of the hedonism that consumption is taken to incarnate . . . [being] . . . [p]rompted by such reprehensible motives as greed, pride and envy' (Ritzer, Goodman and Wiedenhoft 2001: 419).

Several strands of contemporary social theory have latterly contributed to a more balanced perspective on the processes of consumption. For instance, Featherstone has argued that 'styles of life (manifest in choice of clothes, leisure activities, consumer goods, bodily dispositions)' (1991: 83) are increasingly appropriated in ways which transcend traditional notions of fixed status classes. Similarly de Certeau (1984) has countered Marxist and neo-Marxian (such as the Frankfurt School theorists) ideas that consumers are controlled and culturally homogenized by market manipulation, to argue that consumers choose and use goods and services to suit their own needs.

Although operating within neo-Marxian (primarily Gramscian) frameworks, the CCCS, considered consumption, as a subcultural process of expression of style, to be artistic and political opposition to the mainstream, as discussed below. In contrast, Lipovetsky (1994) discussed consumption and fashion, not as a site of resistance, but as the setting of the expression of individuality.

A considerable body of research into consumption has explored the meanings of objects to consumers, an approach which could be applied to the purchase of surfing equipment. However, at least for affluent Western populations, the cost of surfing equipment, such as surfboards and wetsuits, is not especially great. It is more gainful to consider surfing in terms of the consumption of lifestyles, with reference to the choices made regarding work type and general expenditure to enable the, often extensive, time commitments involved in following the waves, as elaborated below.

The roots of subcultural theory are customarily ascribed to the Chicago School of Sociology whose analyses paid particular attention to the diversity of human behaviour in the American city, and to questions of the organizational and symbolic interactive aspects of groups of people with shared values and senses of identity. Such studies sought to develop a holistic and integrative appreciation of subcultures, which are viewed as responses emerging to address the problems faced by specific groups.

Concepts such as communitas (Turner 1972) and *bund* (Urry 2000) also resonate with the notion of subculture. As discussed by Jarrett-Kerr (2003), communitas, which acts as a social bond fostered through communication, communion, shared identities and comradeships, may be usefully related to subcultures such as that of windsurfing. Celsi (1991), for example, has highlighted the way in which the communitas of alternative or extreme sports groups is rooted in the high or flow state of the core action experience, but comprised of the shared or social expression of that experience. Similarly, Urry has discussed the relevance of the concept of 'the *bund*' as a 'community that is conscious and feeling related to an emotional satisfaction that they derive from common goals and shared social experiences' (Urry 2000: 143).

The primary focus on youth of the Birmingham CCCS highlighted the emphasis on consumption and leisure rather than production and work (Gelder 1997). Celebrating rather than denigrating consumer culture, analyses such as those of Hebdige (1979) discussed the specularity and style of youth subcultures as oppositional, adapting, dislocating and subverting established mainstream meanings of things in consumption. Hebdige further explored the narrative in which the style and 'look' of subcultures was in turn inevitably incorporated or diffused within the wider culture. Such incorporation occurred through the conversion of subcultural forms into mass-produced objects (the commodity form) and the labelling or redefinition of deviant behaviour by dominant groups (the ideological term) (Hebdige 1979). As Thornton has noted (Figure 4.1) the analysis of oppositional youth subculture had an especial appeal to academics operating within a particular critical, political agenda.

In time a wide range of powerful criticisms were levelled against the CCCS' work, including its one-dimensional view of resistance and incorporation, lack of attention to the variety and internal stratification within particular subcultures,

*Figure 4.1* Youth/academic parallel interests

| Youth | Academics |
| --- | --- |
| Celebrated the 'underground' | Venerated subcultures |
| Denounced the 'commercial' | Criticized hegemony |
| Lamented 'selling out' | Theorized incorporation |

Source: adapted from Thornton, 1995, in Gelder and Thornton 1997: 201

and its preoccupation with oppositional culture and resistance leading to a neglect of subcultural participation in commerce (Cohen 1980; Clarke 1981; Gelder 1997). Above all it has been argued that CCCS tended to view subculture in terms 'of a single over-determined response to particular conditions' (Gelder 1997: 146), in seeking to interpret youth style and leisure activities as responses to the broader structures of class and capitalism (Cohen 1980). Similarly, Thornton has attacked the CCCS analysis of youthful consumer choices as proto-artistic and/or proto-political acts (1997b: 201), in terms of opposition to the 'vague categories of parent culture and the wider culture'. Thus, later work on subculture has once again (returning in some ways to the Chicago School emphasis on interaction) sought to pay more attention to what members of subculture actually do and how they affirm identities.

Drawing on Bourdieu's (1984) discussion of taste, social structure and cultural capital in *Distinction*, Thornton has investigated social conflicts and competition within subculture (1995). Bourdieu defined cultural capital as knowledge accumulated through upbringing and education that confers social status, in a system of distinction in which refinement in cultural tastes is the foremost marker of status. Thornton has asserted that the chief difference between cultural and subcultural capital, is that the media is crucial to the definition, circulation and distribution of the latter. Through display, awareness of significations, various visual, aural and embodied self-representations, and sense of, 'hipness' and 'coolness', members of youth subcultures accumulate subcultural capital and distinguish themselves from the mainstream. Thornton has drawn attention to these 'micro structures of power', through which 'young people jockey for social power, . . . are both assigned social status and strive for a sense of self worth' (1997b: 208).

In a parallel discussion, Chaney (1996) has applied a similar set of ideas (although often drawing on different sources than Thornton) to explore the nature and character of lifestyle patterns and practices which transcend youth. Sobel defined lifestyle as 'any distinctive, and therefore recognizable, mode of living' (1981: 3). Drawing on Bayley's (1991) notion that taste is the new religion, Chaney discussed lifestyle groups as being defined by cultural style and sensibility as much as by more 'traditional', material, class factors. Central to the notion of sensibility underlying lifestyle is that it has a certain coherence, which is imbued with aesthetic or ethical significance, and, in turn, contributes to a sense of self-identity. Chaney has talked of lifestyles as 'interpretive resources' or forms of local knowledge, which, like Irwin's (1970/1997) notion of subcultures as social worlds, may have a certain transiency, into (and out of) which people may move at will. Following a brief note on subculture theory and sports studies, the remaining, and main, part of this chapter, will explore surfing in relation to these notions of subculture and lifestyle.

## Theoretical approaches applied to subculture and lifestyle in sports studies

It is very important that the developing corpus of research into surfing takes into account the widespread application of the forenoted bodies of theory pertaining to subculture and lifestyles within broader sport studies. In particular, analyses of surfing share many of the interests explored within the increasing numbers of studies of other, so-called, 'alternative', lifestyle or extreme, sports (Rinehart 2000; Rinehart and Sydnor 2003). Surfing shares with other lifestyle sports, for example, concerns with authenticity, sensation and thrill-seeking, mediatization, widespread social debate regarding the place of professionalism and competition, and especially high levels of involvement in the practice by 'hardcore' participants. It is important to re-emphasize at this point that the approach adopted in this book seeks to be theoretically and methodologically eclectic. Sports studies, of course, exhibit the whole range of qualitative and quantitative methodologies. However, the following areas of sports studies have especial potential for exploring the subcultural and lifestyle dimensions of surfing.

Interpretive approaches (Donnelly 2000) place their core emphasis on the understanding of sports behaviours (in the widest sense) in terms of the meanings that participants confer on their actions. Such approaches include Weberian sociology, symbolic interactionism, dramaturgy, phenomenology, ethnomethodology and hermeneutics. Hermeneutic textual and discourse analyses explore the ways in which a sporting social world is continually constructed and reinvented. Symbolic interactionist and ethnomethodology approaches have examined sport subcultures in terms of socialization and 'careers', defined as any time spent progressing in a sporting pursuit. Human geographical approaches have examined sports' significance as representations of places, and as rituals and spectacles (Philo 1994; Bale 2000). The figurational sociology of Elias has been one of the most important applications to sport studies (Murphy, Sheard and Waddington 2000). Such work has drawn upon Elias' concept of the long-term civilizing process (Elias 1978; Elias and Dunning 1986) as a framework which views sport as part of the refinement of manners, increasing exercize of self-control over feeling and behaviour, in a cultural shift from external to internal constraints. An Eliasian perspective also provides a framework for exploring sports cultures as people bonded in dynamic constellations, with relatively high levels of individual autonomy, but also reliant on these in networks of interdependence. The wide range of so-called, post-structuralist and critical approaches (Andrews 2000) have added critical depth to the analysis of discursive formations and the processes relating to the body, sexuality and 'identities in sports'. The so-called post-modern perspective places emphasis on the plurality of possible approaches to knowledge. Furthermore, one of the healthy aspects of sports social research has been an appreciation that there is no single optimal methodology, but rather scope to meld various approaches as appropriate in particular studies.

## Subculture and lifestyle in surfing

The narrative history of surfing (outlined and discussed in Chapter 3) provides a framework of chronologies and themes for the following consideration of subcultural, theoretical and conceptual applications to surfing, and thus an effort is made here to minimize repetition (from Chapter 3) of that basic narrative of surfing history. This section will be broadly structured in terms of, first, the appeal of the image and fashion-related style of surfing, second, socialization, identity, emotion and lifestyle, and involvement with waveriding and subcultural status and, third, the regulation of surfing etiquette in crowded conditions. The focus seeks to distinguish between the core practice (embodied waveriding), the more peripheral aspects of style and fashion, and to explore the implications of surfing's inherent 'territorial scarcity' for subcultural capital and the especial global mobility of the sport. Whilst initial sections will touch upon the macro-level of a hypothesized surfing culture, the main emphasis will be on the personal lifestyle, identity and social interactive dimensions of surfing.

## Surfing as subcultural seduction

Most of the academic analyses of surfing as a sociocultural phenomenon (e.g. Irwin 1973; Pearson 1979; Flynn 1987; Scheibel 1995; Booth 1999, 2001a, 2003; Rutsky 1999; Preston-Whyte 2002) have variously linked notions of (narrative) history to subculture and related subcultural concepts. The unfolding delineations of surfing as subculture have explored the pioneering early twentieth-century 'origins' of the sport, the appeal of the image of surfing to, or rather within, wider Western culture and society, its oppositional characteristics, incorporation, commodification and cultural impacts of the growth in participation. Furthermore, surfing meets one of Thornton's criteria of subcultural, as opposed to cultural, capital, in that its expression and internal contestations have been continually recreated and explored within a vibrant 'insider'-focused media. Indeed, in seeking to discuss surfing subculture, it would not, for instance, be appropriate to address the media within its own separate section, as the surfing media has so much bearing upon each of the themes explored in this chapter.

Irwin (1973) has discussed the initial creation of the 'scene' of surfing as a new subcultural formation, arising from two basic 'insider' and 'outsider' conditions. First, for the originators there was a need for a lull (a term resonating with the surfing experience of waiting for waves when out in the line-up) in their lives involving relative freedom from commitment to other perspectives and lifestyles, along with a shared focus on a distinctive and intense activity, involving experimentation and spontaneity. The second condition entailed the discovery or identification of the surfing scene by outsiders, to whom it represented the appeal of a cohesive and exciting lifestyle.

Irwin also noted that the subculture was formed during extended periods spent staying at remote beaches, which may be thought of as surfing's cultural spaces, serving to imbue the sport in its modern inception (for instance in terms of Fiske's semiotic analysis), with such notions as 'nature' and 'freedom'. The appeal of the surfing imaginary, along with the intense and adrenaline-arousing character of the waveriding experience, may be interpreted from the perspective of figurational sociology as pertaining to the desire within modern society for the kind of direct, exciting and elemental experience which may be channelled via sports and leisure (Elias and Dunning 1986). From the figurational perspective such sports as surfing and windsurfing serve as mimetic activities, imitating the raw passion and emotion felt in earlier societies when life held a greater degree of violence and risk (Dant 1999).

As noted in Chapter 3, practically all analyses of surfing culture highlight the important role of surfing films (both insider films such as *The Endless Summer*, and Hollywood productions such as *Gidget*) in both crystallizing ('telling surf culture to itself') and disseminating the images and subcultural connotations of surfing to wider audiences. Rutsky (1999) has analysed the enormous popularity of the surf- and beach-related films produced in Hollywood from the late 1950s through to the mid-1960s. Commentators such as Doherty (1988) and Morris (1993) have criticized films, such as *Gidget* (1959), *Beach Party* (1963) and *Bikini Beach* (1964), for a superficiality and reassuring conformity in their narrative subordination of the surfing scene to bourgeois notions of work and sexual morality. Rutsky has convincingly argued that such criticisms miss the very point of such films' appeal, and that of surfing more generally. The appeal to the audiences who flocked to see these films was the thrill of nonconformity and the attraction of a certain difference (typical qualities of subcultures), as personified in *Gidget* by the 'drop-out' 'the Great Kahuna'. Interestingly, despite the criticism that the films presented a sanitized Hollywood version of surfing subculture, the actual script of *Gidget* drew very heavily upon the actual experiences of the screenwriter's daughter in her interactions with members of the nascent surfing subculture in Southern California.

The appeal of the depicted surfers (or 'surf/beach bums') in the Hollywood beach films is derived from their association with a sense of freedom, 'dropping out' and living in the present, which 'draws heavily on the older beatnik subculture of the 1950s' (Rutsky 1999: 15). Indeed, such attributes are all classic 'subterranean values' of subcultures, which can only be understood in terms of their contrasting relation to formal work values (Young 1971 in Gelder and Thornton 1997).

The ways in which such 'subterranean values' may relate (or not) to surfers' actual lives is touched upon below in the section on lifestyles. The key point here is that surfing as a subculture may connote such values to some members of the wider society.

*Figure 4.2* Formal and subterranean values contrasted

| Formal work values | Subterranean values |
| --- | --- |
| Deferred gratification | Short-term hedonism |
| Planning future action | Spontaneity |
| Conformity to bureaucratic values | Ego-expressivity |
| Fatalism, high control over detail, little over direction (Young 1971/1997, from Gelder and Thornton, 1997; 73) | Autonomy, control of behaviour in detail and direction |
| Routine, predictability | New experience, excitement |
| Instrumental attitudes to work | Activities performed as an end-in-themselves |
| Hard productive work seen as a virtue | Disdain for work |

Source: adapted from Young 1971, in Gelder and Thornton 1997: 73

Certainly in the Birmingham CCCS period, work on subcultures was especially concerned with, and attracted to, their subversive or oppositional character in relation to advanced capitalist society. As discussed above in Chapter 3, one of the themes running through the narrative of surfing, is an antipathy towards bureaucracy and formal organization. For instance, very few surfers are members of any surfing organizations (with the exception of some surfing environmental bodies). Insofar as national surfing organizations were established, it was primarily to improve the wider societal image of surfing, to enhance legitimacy and attract sponsorship, rather than having any oppositional agenda. Indeed, rather than being oppositional Stratton (1985) has argued that the emergence of surfing subculture is firmly set in the postwar development of consumerism in America and other Western societies. In particular, Stratton has argued that surfing subculture articulates a middle class myth of holiday leisure time spent in relaxation. The 'surfie' appears to live a life of escape in the eyes of the individual trapped in a 48-hour-a-week job, and is given a certain status by his/her position as myth. Stratton further argued that, in its emphasis on individual freedom, surfing culture asserted two of the fundamentals of American capitalism, consumerism (in lifestyle) and individualism.

A further, often repeated element in writings on the narrative of surfing culture, is its subcultural quality of distinctive and expressive style (Hebdige 1979, Craig 1994), as expressed in language, clothing, non-verbal gestures, music, artistic expression in its media and so on. Regarding the development of surfing vocabulary or argot, Holmes (1991) has noted that early surfers needed to invent a way of talking, because there was no precedent to describe waveriding. Indeed, in reading accounts of some of the earliest observations of, and reflection upon, surfing (for instance J. London 1911; C. London 1922; Smith 2003), the very words they used to describe the nature of waves, waveriding and the exuberant experience are strikingly different from the words used in the contemporary surfing media and culture. It is as if such authors had a certain freedom and originality in their fumbling attempts to describe an entirely unfamiliar practice. Such observers were writing before surfers could be socialized into a surfing vocabulary, from which the shorthand of 'glassy', 'choppy', 'curl', 'peak', 'tube', 'lip', 'soup' and so on, are automatically drawn today.

Flynn observed that surfing argot and gestures were originally modelled and adapted from traditional Hawaiian surfing vocabulary. Presumably this cultural borrowing as appropriation reflected not only expedience, but also the hallowed respect for Hawaii and its culture as surfing's place of origin. Within subcultures a distinctive vocabulary is generally also used, along with other indicators, as a symbolic marker of 'insider' and 'outsider' status, and, as Flynn (1987) has argued, as a source of inter-subjective cohesion and confirmation, in what anthropologists refer to as to the process of phatic communion (Malinowski 1956; Greimas and Courtes 1982). Within youth culture part of surfing's appeal was its association with a certain 'hipness' and 'coolness'. Thornton (1997b) links the exclusiveness of 'hipness' to Bourdieu's notion of the conjoining of argot to cultural capital whereby, 'the deep-seated intention of slang vocabulary is above all the assertion of aristocratic distinction' (Bourdieu 1991: 94). The bodily ritualistic aspects of surfing subculture are discussed further in Chapter 6 in terms of Goffman's (1969) symbolic interactionist perspective.

Of greater visibility, and thus significance, to the wider society was the expression of surfing style in clothing fashion. As with language, surf-style clothing originally derived from certain functional requirements, for instance, 'baggy' knee-length shorts were developed to prevent the legs from chafing while sitting astride a surfboard (Dart 2002). Surf fashion's enormous appeal and commercial success reside in the aesthetic expression of surfing's cultural significations (such as the elemental ocean, nature, speed, power, exotic travel, sensation and so on). Some pioneering surfers in Southern California may well have developed a casual 'baggy' style of clothing, along with long hair and tanned physical appearance, and because of their prestige as skilful waveriders their 'style' may have been expected to have been imbued with a certain cultural caché. However, the crucial factor for the development of surfing fashion (as with surfing music) was the style's appropriation and elaboration by some surfing, but mostly, non-surfing, designers and artists, for its commercial packaging and marketing to the wider society.

It is interesting to note that the antipathy to mass commercialism which runs through the narrative of surfing culture parallels the narrative of inevitable incorporation and diffusion of subcultures within the wider society (Gelder 1997). Hebdige (1979) has discussed the incorporation of subcultures as a process involving commodity and ideological forms. The commodity form involves the conversion of subcultural forms (e.g. of dress and music) into mass-produced objects. Hebdige continues that, even though commercial exploitation and creativity/originality are emphatically opposed categories within most subcultures, in practice it is very difficult to maintain any absolute distinction between the two. 'Indeed, the creation and diffusion of new style is inextricably bound up with the process of production, publicity and packaging which must inevitably lead to the de-fusion of the subculture's subversive power' (Hebdige 1979: 95). Hebdige's discussion of the ideological form concerns the ways in which dominant groups label and redefine 'deviant' behaviours, dealing with the perceived threat of sub-cultures by, for instance, trivializing or transforming their signification. However, as noted with respect to Stratton's analysis, surfing was never a particularly, politically oppositional subculture. Rather than seeking to articulate contra-dictions in the advanced capitalist system, surfing culture primarily revolves around the thrilling, embodied practice of waveriding itself. Thus, rather than considering surfing's political implication, it is more useful to consider surfing culture in relation to theories of consumption.

As noted in Chapter 3, the mediascapes of globalization use images as carriers of fantasies of possible lives, seeking to influence consumption behaviour. Linking such marketing and fantasization to the individual, Baudrillard has argued 'what makes you exist is not the force of your desire . . . but the play of the world and seduction . . . the passion of illusion and appearance' (Baudrillard 1983 in Dant 1999: 119).

Contemporary analyses of consumption tend to view the consumer as cre-atively appropriating consumer objects rather than being controlled by them (Featherstone 1991). Furthermore, Falk (1994) has discussed the ways in which consumption offers the possibilities of constructing a self, as well as reflecting a current self-identity. Marketing techniques may be viewed as mobilizing the consumer by creating connections between the subject's psyche and the specific characteristics of consumer goods (Miller and Rose 1997). Thus, the com-modification of surfing culture may be viewed as connecting consumers to the possibilities of some kind of surfing identity and lifestyle associated with various values and significations connoted by surfing.

While surfing may be associated with a certain style and with 'cool' by some members of the wider society, the ways that such an appeal has been used in the commodification and commercialization of surfing subculture is regarded with some considerable ambivalence or even disdain by many surfers. Irwin (1973) has argued in his (perhaps premature!) account of the decline of surfing from the mid-1960s, that there has been suspicion of the social phenomenon of the 'pseudo-surfer' for whom surfing is an activity of secondary importance to fashion identification. Many surfers' ambivalence towards surfing as fashion is primarily about refocusing on the core of the culture, namely waveriding itself. Booth, for instance, noted that this sensibility of the suspect nature of surf fashion has led to 'labelled' surfwear being considered taboo within some 'hardcore' surfing circles in Australia (Booth 2001a: 8).

A contrasting expression of surfing's ambivalent relationship with surf fashion is, however, reflected in the processes by which some surfers are especially selective in their choice of label (Dart 2002). Holmes (1991) has noted that there is a sense of discernment concerning surfing products. 'Real' surfing products were identified with pioneering, original and specialist, surfing companies. Surfwear advertising spread from the pages of surfing magazines to the billboards of city centres, as the surf fashionwear industry underwent its colossal expansion. Their advertisements,

*Figure 4.3*    Examples of surf companies' slogans

| | |
|---|---|
| Animal | 'The world of Freedom' |
| Billabong | 'Only a surfer knows the feeling' |
| Headworx | 'Think for yourself' |
| Kuta Lines | 'Takes one to know one' |
| No Fear | 'Wimps don't surf' |
| Patagonia | 'The road less travelled' |
| Rip curl | 'The Search. Search and don't destroy' |
| Quiksilver | 'The ride can last forever' |
| Town and Country | 'Live like this' |
| Volcom Stone | 'Youth against establishment' |

Source: adapted from Williams, 2002

obviously, focus on the primal, elemental image of the surfing figure on a powerful wave. In recent years the visual aesthetic of the photographic image of surfing adverts has been increasingly complemented by company slogans (see Figure 4.3), which in the very process of seeking to expand market share, often revolve around notions of the exclusivity and authenticity of surfing.

Dart (2002) has discussed the marketing and slogans of, and preferences for, different brands of surfing clothing in relation to Bourdieu's concept of cultural capital and demographics. For instance, Dart has highlighted the ways in which Volcom Stone's oppositional and 'underground' image has a particular appeal for younger, but committed, surfers. For older surfers authenticity may be associated, along with a certain nostalgia, with surf clothing companies which go back to the 1960s. While for some younger surfers such companies are not felt to be sufficiently exclusive, as their enormous commercial expansion has tarnished their image with the taint of mass consumption. Concern with the authenticity of various surf clothing brands may also be viewed as a response not only to the increasing levels of participation in the sport, but more importantly to the global appropriation of surfing fashion by mass youth culture.

Whilst it is beyond the scope of this book, systematic analysis of the imaging of surf brands and their advertising could provide a fruitful direction for research seeking to explore the relationships between surf culture, values and commerce. As with any other form of commercial branding, emphasis and slogans have varied over time, and between companies reflecting their marketing objectives. Above all, the choice of slogan and aesthetic style of adverts have variously sought to express different cultural styles of surfing. Booth (2003: 316) has, for instance, identified six primary styles adopted by surfers:

1    the hedonism of Hawaiian beachboys
2    the highly structured and regimented sporting club lifestyle of Australian lifesavers
3    the carefree, fun lifestyles of Californians

4    the subversive spirituality of soul surfers
5    the clean-cut, health-driven, professional surfer athletes
6    the aggressive nihilism of the abusive (punk) generation.

As Booth (2001a) has emphasized surf culture is interpreted through the *Zeitgeist* of its time. In concluding this section it should be noted that surf style is probably not a major preoccupation for most surfers, who feel that the whole phenomenon of surf fashion and branding is very much secondary to the core action of wave-riding. The next section seeks to explore surfing culture in relation to the more personal concerns of socialization and identity.

## Socialization, identity, emotion and lifestyle in surfing

Following on from the preceding outline of surfing as style and subculture, this section seeks to explore lines of thinking which may assist research into the ways in which individuals become involved in, and socialized into, surfing, and some of the impacts on their lives. There are growing bodies of research that seek to examine questions of socialization, identity and emotion in sports (Donnelly 2000; Duquin 2000). Particular questions which underlie this section include: what are the ways in which individuals become socialized into surfing and surfing culture? How do individuals' perceptions of surfing and surfing culture change during the course of their deepening involvement in waveriding? What are the dynamics and nature of a sense of identity as surfer? What form does the social expression of emotion take in the process of socialization? Taking surfing involvement as a form of 'sports career', how may surfers' lifestyles be considered in the light of thinking on consumption?

   This section will initially seek to relate some of the general lines of thinking on socialization and identity to surfing; second, present and discuss some survey findings concerning the influence of involvement in surfing upon identity; and third, relate ideas of the 'sports career' to aspects of lifestyle in surfing.

   Socialization has been described as 'an active process of learning and social development that occurs as people interact with each other and become acquainted with the social world in which they live, and as they form ideas about who they are, and make decisions about their goals and behaviours' (Coakley 1998: 88). Within this process surfers may be seen as actively participating in the appropriation of meanings, interpreting the nature of waveriding and surf culture, and, in time, revising and rejecting messages received.

   There may be many different pathways by which individuals come to be involved in surfing, depending on, for example, social networks, residence and travel experience. For some young people who live near a surfbreak 'initiation' in waveriding may be a 'natural' or almost inevitable process, while for others, perhaps living some distance from the sea, initial practice of surfing may be something consciously desired and sought, requiring travel and holiday plans. Such diverse entries into surfing may be expected to have differential implications for the ways in which surfing is perceived (for instance as a subculture) prior to actually experiencing waveriding. The consensus narratives of surfing culture highlight the role of the surfing and wider media in engendering a sense of the connotations and meanings of surfing in the wider society. Such accounts and evocations of surfing and the surfing lifestyle act as narrative maps for (potential) future surfers, attracting them to both try out, or further pursue, surfing.

Irwin (1973) took the analysis of recruitment into surfing further by relating it to the (triple strata) social organization of the adolescent community in Southern California in the 1960s. Entry into surfing was seen as offering some kind of admired identity within the social competition among adolescents. Irwin's analysis may well be culturally and historically specific, but provides an interesting framework for analysis which could be undertaken in other surfing localities. Irwin's analysis linked the appeal to become involved in surfing to notions of status and prestige, which relate to Bourdieu's concept of cultural capital. The appeal could be articulated in different, but related, forms: as a desire to move towards a new identity, to develop and express some existing attributes of self-identity, or simply to gain direct experience of sensation and pleasure.

Given the breadth of surfing styles (spiritual soul surfer, clean-cut professional athlete, aggressive nihilist and so on) as, for instance, delineated by Booth (2001a), there are a wide range of surfing identities with which neophytes may feel some identification. There is scope for systematic research to explore the ways in which different individuals appropriate different idealizations of what it means to be a surfer, and the host of quite complex personal, social, cultural and situational factors which may shape such appropriations, and the changing senses of identity which may develop over the course of a surfing 'career'. The adoption of some form of surfer identity is probably best viewed as one identity among a plurality to which a given individual may subscribe. Furthermore, surfing identity is not only based on personal aspiration, but as with other subcultural identities may fluctuate in terms of level of commitment and priority, in relation to the other self-identities which an individual may conceive.

One of the most exciting new areas of research in sports studies concerns the place of emotions in identity formation, social expression and self-realization in sports and leisure (Duquin 2000). Chapter 7 is concerned with the nature and rationalizations of the emotional and sensual qualities of the waveriding experience. However, at this point it is useful to introduce some of the thinking on the socialization of emotions and emotional responses in sport.

Maguire (1991) has advocated the utility of a figurational research agenda to explore the emotional and self-expressive qualities of sports in identity formation. An example of the social expression of emotions in surfing would be surfers' celebrations (hoots, exclamations) of their own or others' rides outback. However, being excessively loud out in the line-up may be viewed, by some, as lacking a certain 'cool'. More generally, and with greater implications for the development of identity, there is the post-surfing sharing of stories, recalling exceptional waves, rides and 'wipe-outs' for example. Donnelly and Young (1988) have discussed the significance of such expression and interaction involved in the construction and confirmation of identity in subcultures. Whether or not surfing scenes form a distinct subculture, there is no doubt that there is a social bonding and friendship element to much pre-surf (finding out where and when the best waves are breaking on the day) and après-surf interaction (sharing of stories).

Taking a longer-term perspective, great surfing experiences in different places and periods of a surfer's life are often strongly etched in memory. As Duquin has noted 'memory is tied to emotion: feelings make events significant. In memory work replaying past emotions reveals the forces and everyday events that helped to shape self-identity' (2000: 480). With surfing culture's increasing self-reflexivity there is a proliferating literature which is almost shaping a canon of the great surfing events of the latter half of the twentieth century. However, probably all surfers have rich memories, evoking past, and (possibly) reinvented, emotional experiences, of their own personal surfing histories.

Jamie Williams' (2002) multi-method study of surfing and style-related identities of surf tourists visiting Newquay, UK, has yielded some intriguing quantitative findings. The schedule-structured questionnaire survey was undertaken among 200 young people mostly on surfing holidays, during the peak of the tourist season in July 2001. Many of the respondents were identified through the many 'surf lodges' that have been established in the town in recent years, to provide low-cost, dormitory style accommodation for surfing holidays. The core objective of the survey was to compare perspectives on surfing as a sport, fashion, style and lifestyle according to level of involvement in surfing, which was assessed by the proxy variable of years of surfing experience. The survey analysis was structured around four, evenly divided, categories:

Group 1  Surfing for first time
Group 2  Surfed for 2 years or less (but not for the first time)
Group 3  Surfed for 3–5 years
Group 4  Surfed for more than 6 years

The survey used a purposive sampling strategy to obtain roughly 50 respondents in each category, of which the majority were male.

With regard to pre-surfing intentions, it is notable that, one-third (34 per cent) of males and one-quarter (25 per cent) of females agreed with the statement 'I wanted to be a surfer prior to surfing', indicating that for significant minorities the image of surfing is imbued with a certain subcultural caché, before having experienced surfing itself.

Approximately half of respondents in all groups agreed with the statement 'pre- and après surf experiences are as important as surfing itself' and there was a widespread consensus that surfers are 'image-conscious' and that surfing is more a way of life than just a sport (Tables 4.2 and 4.3). Furthermore, surfing clearly has had a major influence on the way participants lead their lives (Table 4.1).

However, there were very striking differences across the groups with regard to the sense of surfing as fashion and group identity. For those who had been surfing for no more than two years, surfing was strongly associated with being stylish, 'cool' and 'carefree'. In particular there appears to be a very strong identification with

*Table 4.1* Words associated with surfing by years of involvement (%)

| | Percentage in agreement | | | |
| | Group 1<br>1st time | Group 2<br><2 years | Group 3<br>3–5 years | Group 4<br>6+ years |
| --- | --- | --- | --- | --- |
| Sport | 42 | 32 | 37 | 67 |
| Fashionable | 68 | 71 | 53 | 23 |
| Stylish | 83 | 86 | 72 | 54 |
| Individual | 46 | 49 | 63 | 94 |
| Natural | 65 | 64 | 72 | 78 |
| Culture | 54 | 44 | 53 | 65 |
| Cool | 76 | 72 | 53 | 18 |
| Carefree | 68 | 77 | 59 | 24 |
| Youth | 26 | 28 | 17 | 21 |
| Group identity | 67 | 89 | 36 | 12 |

Source: adapted from Williams, 2002: 31

*Table 4.2* Sense of surfer identity by years of involvement in surfing (%)

| | Percentage in agreement | | | |
| Statements | Group 1<br>1st time | Group 2<br><2 years | Group 3<br>3–5 years | Group 4<br>6+ years |
| --- | --- | --- | --- | --- |
| 'Surfing is more than a sport, it's a way of life' | 78 | 92 | 82 | 76 |
| 'Surfing is the most important part of my life' | 4 | 50 | 45 | 52 |
| 'Surfing has made me feel different about the way I lead my life' | 42 | 77 | 86 | 87 |
| 'Pre- and après-surf experiences are just as important as surfing itself' | 41 | 55 | 54 | 50 |
| 'Environmental consciousness is an important part of surfing' | 29 | 31 | 72 | 87 |
| 'I consider myself a surfer' | 8 | 78 | 82 | 85 |

Source: adapted from Williams, 2002

*Table 4.3* Surfing as fashion and style by years of involvement in surfing (%)

| | Percentage in agreement | | | |
| Statements | Group 1<br>1st time | Group 2<br><2 years | Group 3<br>3–5 years | Group 4<br>6+ years |
| --- | --- | --- | --- | --- |
| 'I dress like a surfer' | 41 | 81 | 52 | 40 |
| 'Surfing is about style' | 73 | 66 | 84 | 75 |
| 'Fashion is an important part of surfing' | 58 | 33 | 23 | 18 |
| 'Surfers are image conscious' | 90 | 70 | 71 | 86 |

Source: adapted from Williams, 2002

the subcultural stylistic, fashion and group identity aspects of surfing for those who have surfed for no more than about two years (Tables 4.1 and 4.3). For instance, virtually all (89 per cent) of those who had been surfing for no longer than two years, associated surfing with group identity, contrasting with a mere 12 per cent of those who had been surfing for six years or more (Table 4.1). At least for surfers from, and visiting, Newquay, with increasing years of surfing, although continuing to consider themselves as 'surfers', the sense of surfing as fashion style recedes in importance, and surfing becomes a much more personal, individualistic experience. Furthermore, for the more experienced surfers the lifestyle involves a deepening sense of environmental consciousness, and, after all, this is the home locality of the highly effective Surfers Against Sewage (SAS) pressure group, which has a national membership in excess of 10,000.

Williams' (2002) survey findings provide some striking quantitative evidence of the changes which take place in sociocultural perspectives as surfing experience increases. The surfing 'career' may gainfully be examined in relation to some of the concepts of lifestyles as consumption.

As Campbell has so eloquently expressed, 'modern individuals inhabit not just an "iron cage" of economic necessity, but a castle of romantic dreams, striving through their conduct to turn the one into the other' (1987: 227). The desire of a surfing lifestyle may be one such romantic dream. Reversing the order, it could be said that the attainment (because it is something that has to be worked at) of a surfing lifestyle (which is the pursuit of a dream of play and exhilaration) requires coming to terms with the economic realities of its pecuniary support. However, before examining such practical dynamics, some reference will be made to the aesthetic dimension of surfing lifestyles.

As with lifestyle shopping (Shields 1992) the consumption entailed in surfing is not so much that of objects, as of lifestyles. Lifestyle theorists, such as Sobel (1981) and Chaney (1996) identify some of the key characteristics of lifestyle as being a coherence and distinctiveness of pattern, congeries of sensibilities or tastes and a related aesthetic dimension. The objective of a surfing lifestyle is remarkably clear, simply to develop and maintain a way of living which enables a high level of involvement in waveriding. Indeed, those individuals enjoying some kind of hardcore surfing lifestyle are often certainly exceedingly single-minded in their pursuit of the satisfaction of their addiction.

As noted in the previous section, matters of taste, as displayed or expressed in the panoply of subcultural signifiers such as surf fashion, decrease in personal significance as years of involvement in the surfing lifestyle increase. It is not necessarily that the more experienced surfers do not wear surf apparel (after all, people have to wear something) but rather that surf fashion is just not a significant or important aspect of their lives.

The aesthetic dimension of a surfing lifestyle is better sought in terms of its obvious coherence of purpose, and the effort to sustain a continual awareness of, and relationship with, the changing state of the ocean. The centrality of the relationship to the ocean is an absolutely fundamental and recurrent theme in articulations of the surfing lifestyle. For instance, in the existential parlance of

Martin Buber, Roberts (1977) has written in an article in *Surfer* 'through this I–Thou relationship of mutuality, the surfer can find his (or her) existence in relation to the ocean. This relationship allows man (or woman) to find his (or her) identity. The aloneness in surfing helps the individual surfer develop an awareness of his(or her) existence' (Roberts 1977: 31). The reference to aloneness links with Williams' (2002) survey finding that more experienced surfers viewed surfing as individualistic, and resonates with the 'cosmic' or spiritual orientation of soul surfing.

The ideal is to be able to live, or at least spend extensive periods of time, close to surfbreaks, and to enjoy some form of labour or occupation which permits the often unscheduled time out to enable the surfer to partake of the (often fickle) waves when conditions are good. Thus, many lifestyle surfers are self-employed. A common alternative is to develop some kind of seasonal work pattern which allows travel to quality surf localities for extensive periods of time. In either case, with respect to the earlier reference to surfing's resonance with subterranean, subcultural values (Young 1971), the enjoyment of the hedonism and spontaneity of surfing is often accompanied not only by a strong 'can-do' sense of autonomy and control over behaviour in detail and direction, but also measures of deferred gratification and the careful planning of future action. On a more prosaic level when the surf is not running, lifestyle surfers 'get things done', seek to make progress in their income-generating activities, rather, for instance, than engaging in the 'hanging out at the beach', of the stereotypical image. In recent years the increased access to better surf forecasting, webcams of surf spots, television and telephone surf report services and so on, have made it much more feasible to keep in contact with surf conditions without living on the spot. This allows greater flexibility in surfing lifestyles, in terms of both residential location away from the coast and enabling better scheduling of work commitments. Some purists decry this trend towards increased reliance on 'artificial' communications technology as destroying the (wait and) search as one of the great joys of the sport' (Banks 2004). Such a perspective connects with an anti-technological and romantic counter-cultural sensibility in surfing. Although it must be added that the increasing accuracy of such technological sources of information must increase the tendency for large numbers of surfers to converge at the same locations when quality conditions arrive.

As with any sports career (in the sense of any time spent progressing in the sport) the path is rarely linear, but involves fluctuating levels of commitment, with temporary or permanent suspension of involvement, and periods of re-engagement. The demographic group which probably has the greatest opportunity for pursuit of some kind of total surfing lifestyle, is that of youth. As Thornton (1997a) has argued, after Parsons (1964), given that youth are unable to compete with adults for occupational status, they tend to seek their rewards/self-esteem/cultural capital from leisure rather than work. Furthermore, youth, at least in affluent societies, enjoys a temporary reprieve from the 'iron cage' of economic necessity, in the sense that they are not as strongly tied to the adult commitments to the accumulation of economic capital (Thornton 1997a). Thus, for many surfers high involvement in a surfing lifestyle is often derailed by the onset of various occupational and familial commitments in later life. However, surfing lifestyles are certainly not exclusive to youth. There is a growing sense in Western cultures that 'age is a myth for structuring both thought and individuals more generally' (Shurmer-Smith and Hannam 1994: 163). Traditionally the process of ageing has been intimately associated with moral questions of how people ought to behave and meet obligations at particular junctures in their lives. There is, perhaps, little indication that many hardcore surfers are prepared to grow old gracefully.

Consumption theory asserts that meeting economic needs may be addressed not only by obtaining income, but alternatively by reducing costs as in the pattern of so-called 'simple livers' and 'downshifters' (Rivers 1977; Schorr 1999). Expenditure on extensive surf travel (albeit often to low subsistence cost areas in the Tropics) must often require less spending on other spheres of consumption.

It is unclear whether the apparent frugality of many surfing lifestyles has a broader environmental ethos. Other than having an obvious interest in campaigning against marine pollution, it is uncertain whether, or maybe unlikely that, surfers are any more or less environmentally committed, than any other group of the population. Research could assess surfers' levels of sustainable behaviours (e.g. green purchasing, saving energy, recycling and so on).

Certainly in the counter-culture era some soul surfers explored forms of rural, alternative lifestyles. However, as John Severson (founding editor of *Surfer*, surf photographer and artist) has observed, 'Back to the land was our goal in the early '70s. No cost housing was the goal. It turned out to be a lot of work' (Severson 2004: 187). So-called simple living can be rather labour-demanding, crucially not necessarily affording the amounts of free time needed to enjoy the surf.[1] However, status through economic capital is probably not a high priority for most surfers. The next section seeks to examine the nature of cultural capital and prestige within surfing culture.

## Status and the regulation of scarcity in surfing

This section seeks to comment on the basis of status or subcultural capital within surfing, to explore the pervasive theme of the regulation of access to the inherent scarcity of quality waves, and consider both themes in relation to the emotive topic of localism.

As Donnelly and Young (1988) have noted, identity constructions in sports can be oriented to the two basic audiences of insider and outsider. As Williams' (2002) findings on the changing perceived meanings of surfing with experience have shown, for the beginner there is a preoccupation with the fashion and group identity aspects of surf culture, which serves to visually distinguish surfers from non-surfers, signifying subcultural membership to the outside world. In time such aspects as clothing and argot are taken for granted and, reflecting the shift of orientation to wishing to be valued as an insider in the world of surfing, the focus is increasingly on performance of surfing (Wheaton 2003).

As with other sports, insider prestige and status are overwhelmingly functions of skill in the specific sport. Dart (2002) has therefore referred to cultural capital in surfing as 'performance capital'. As discussed in Chapter 3, prestige is shaped partly by appearing in the surfing media of magazines and films. Success in contests obviously contributes to prestige in surfing, but probably only a minority of surfers are preoccupied with surfing contests, and only a very small minority actually take part in formal surfing competition. Thus, in contrast to more explicitly competitive sports, performance capital is assessed by other surfers more subjectively in terms of the combination of manoeuvres, style, capability in big waves and so on. Subcultural capital in surfing may also be related to known past achievements and places surfed, and level of commitment to surfing, as expressed in a 'hardcore' lifestyle. Thornton (1997b) has noted that some authorities claim that cultural capital's ascription as 'capital' ultimately derives from its convertibility into economic capital (or financial reward) (Garnham and Williams 1986). However, subcultural capital does not generally convert as easily into economic capital as may cultural capital. Nevertheless, Thornton points out that there are examples, for instance in rave dance subculture, of a range of occupations, such as DJ, club organizers, fashion designers and style journalists, who make a living from their subcultural capital. Similarly, within surf culture there are a (relatively small) number of surfers who derive a living from their subcultural or performance capital, notably including highly sponsored professional contest surfers, surf magazine proprietors and editors, surf journalists and photographers, the original (and thus in a sense authentic) surfboard shapers, surf fashion and equipment company owners. Subcultural activities in surfing are further elaborated in Chapter 6 in terms of their implications for bodily matters.

Given that the concept of cultural capital derives from Bourdieu (1993a) it is perhaps useful to outline his contextual notions of habitus and field in relation to surfing. Habitus refers to a system of enduring, primarily embodied, structuring structures created in response to objective conditions and acquired through socialization. As such, habitus pertains to the patterns of objectives and practices that may be developed to sustain a surfing lifestyle, which in their repeated performativity (Butler 1993) reproduce the particular ocean/surfing-oriented way of life. The field is a contextual grouping of elements within which the surfing lifestyle takes place, and includes the social and cultural institutions that establish their own hierarchies of success. Bourdieu's notion of the 'field is analysed as an arena of conflict, struggle and competitions for scarce resources and symbolic recognition related to the specific type of capital that governs success in the field' (Ritzer, Goodman and Wiedenhoft 2001: 419). At its most basic the field of surfing would include the competition to access quality waves and the media and subcultural process which shape status as cultural capital.

Within the social construction of the experience of riding a wave there is something of an ill-defined tension between the social recognition aspect of being seen to perform, and the more spiritual or individualist orientation of the lone surfer in communion with nature. Furthermore, part of the complexity of this tension is that it is not a binary, as the same person may express and enjoy both of these facets of the surfing experience, maybe giving more priority to the one or the other on different occasions and at different times in their surfing 'career'.

Being seen to perform is clearly connected with the subcultural process of the ascription of subcultural capital in surfing. Although surfers are preoccupied with finding their own waves, they are also, almost subconsciously glancing at the performance of other surfers, for example any 'new faces' in the line-up, and again may be unconsciously placing that individual in some kind of ranking in a hierarchy of those in the water at the time. This, almost unconscious and automatic, appraisal of other surfers' performances in the water is a further key element in the surfer's gaze. This aspect of the surfer's gaze involves an appraisal of skill and style, upon which there is a general consensus, but also individual variation with regard to what impresses, for instance, 'radical', explosive manoeuvres or flowing, elegant style. The suggestion is being made here that this aspect of the gaze is not merely aesthetic, but also informs an informal, social ranking with respect to performance capital, which in turn, may have functional implications in terms of respect, or even deference, in competing for peaks. In many surfing scenes excessive boasting about one's own performance, even if it is simply exuberant celebration, is regarded somewhat dismissively. Again this relates to this implicit tension between the social constructedness and oceanic communion of surfing. It may also be related to 'cool' in surfing culture.[2] Certainly among the pantheon of media-celebrated surf heroes there is something of a special place for characters like Gerry Lopez (e.g. James 1979 in George 2001: 85) and Wayne Lynch (Brisick and Pezman 1993), who, having indisputably demonstrated enormous waveriding skills, have also seemed to shun the limelight in following their own, individualistic paths. Research could be gainfully addressed to these complex matters of social and personal affirmation, modesty, 'cool' and subcultural capital in surfing performance and experience.

On a popular level the whole matter of surfing's inherent scarcity, that is questions of crowding, regulation and jockeying for position within the line-up, is so basic to contemporary surfing that it is practically taken for granted and an implicit aspect of the field of surfing. Nevertheless, because of the light that it sheds on some of the social and cultural processes operating within surfing it has been addressed in a growing proliferation of writing (Irwin 1973; Scheibel 1995; Young 2001; Dart 2002; Preston-Whyte 2002; Booth 2003; Canniford and Layne 2004; Canniford 2005; Shaw 2004). Furthermore, the negative excesses of localism and 'surf rage' (Young 2001) have long been recurrent topics in letters to surfing magazines. It is as if negativity and hostility seem particularly shocking, almost cognitively dissonant, in a pursuit which, to many, expresses counter-cultural values of harmony, nature, peace and escape, and takes place within the sacred realm of the ocean.

At the core of surfing culture resides the myth of the perfect wave (Scheibel 1995) and paradisal origins. Nostalgic recollections (reconstructions) of golden ages of surfing are framed in terms of coastal wanderings of small bands of pioneers enjoying empty line-ups. Irwin's (1973) thesis on the corruption of surf culture commences with the increasing competitiveness and invidiousness (threatening newcomers) as a response to the crowding problems in the heartlands of Southern Californian classic breaks.

In his (2002) case study of Durban in South Africa Preston-Whyte has articulated the frustration of surf crowding in terms of a geographical perspective of surfing space as a scarce resource structured by imaginary boundaries. Within these spaces locals have a sense of territorial rights defensively connected to their strong identification with their favourite surf spots. It may also be noted that the impact of crowds varies according to the straightforward characteristics of the surfbreak. For instance, reef and point breaks with their highly precise and predictable take-off points can become crowded with only 20 experienced surfers competing for waves. Alternatively, sprawling open beach breaks, with a multitude of peaks, often shifting with the movement of the tide, can accommodate much larger numbers of surfers without such a feeling of packing and jostling for position. There is also scope for systematic research to compare the response to, and management of, crowding in different cultures of the world. Some cultures appear to be more tolerant and gracious than others in these respects.

Combining the theoretical frameworks of Goffman's (1969) interaction order and Elias' figurational sociology of courtly forms, Canniford and Layne have noted that 'surfing, an apparently anarchic pursuit, under closer inspection, exhibits strict (structural) codes that are interpreted and applied in variable conditions' (2004: 1). Indeed such informal 'community regulation' is one of the guiding principles of self-management, anarchist philosophy (Woodcock 1977). Such codes revolve around the so-called 'drop-in rule', that the surfer taking off nearest to the breaking point of the wave has priority (Dart 2002; Preston-Whyte 2002; Canniford and Layne 2004). Canniford and Layne describe this process, as an 'interaction ritual', based on a consensus which informally frames and regulates competition for the scarce resource of waves. Shaw's (2004) study of the interaction of wave users in North Devon found that most surfers had been given advice about wave etiquette at some time in their careers, and that the bulk (82 per cent) of such advice was positive and helpful. This indicates that most knowledgeable surfers understood that surf etiquette is not necessarily obvious to the beginner (Shaw 2004: 28). Furthermore, it helps to present a more balanced picture than that of the surf zone as one of continuous hostility.

The consensus of the 'drop-in rule' generally serves to benefit the more skilful surfers (who can catch waves at the more critical point of take-off) and those with especial local knowledge of the breaking characteristics of a given break. However, both Scheibel (1995), through a cultural rhetorical analysis of letters to *Surfer*, and Dart (2002), through qualitative interviews with experienced surfers in Newquay, note that wave etiquette is not always observed. Both have highlighted the ways in which both those surfers who knew no better (the uncultured) and those with greater performance capital and local affiliation, often break the 'drop-in rule' against less skilful or visiting surfers in crowded conditions. Scheibel traces the origins of the surfing term to 'snake' (breaking the rules of surfing etiquette), as deriving from a sense of treachery, with 'the serpent being symbolically linked to the Garden of Eden . . . to have been "snaked" is to have been sinned against by someone who has *not resisted the temptation of acting improperly*' (Scheibel 1995: 253). Scheibel uses a Burkeian analysis of letters to *Surfer* to reflect the public argument concerning localism. Those surfers employing localism as an attempt to use various hostile methods to control access to 'their' surf spots, defended the practice in the name of cultural preservation. Scheibel discussed the ways in which such surfers used language which scapegoated, victimized, marginalized and excluded non-locals, in this case the 'hordes' of 'Vals' (surfers from the neighbouring San Fernando Valley).[3] Similarly, Dart (2002) argues that his sample of experienced surfers differentially applied surf etiquette to local surfers whom they imbued with performance capital, and those whom they termed 'weekenders' and non-locals who were perceived as having little or no performance capital and labelled, (internationally) in surfing argot, as 'kooks' and 'gremmies'. Scheibel also analyses letters that are critical of localism and which may even express the desire to dissolve the hierarchies in surfing which foster invidious behaviour. Ritz (1994) drew the graphic analogy of the popular surf spot as similar to the scene of a large kill on the Serengeti, representing the hierarchy of surfers as different animals each receiving a lesser share of the meat:

- lions – alpha predators, locals monopolizing the best waves
- hyenas – tough non-locals who can survive in packs
- jackals – just-learning surfers
- vultures – bodyboarders, picking up the final scraps.

(Ritz could also have noted how some bodyboarders in turn seek to marginalize bodysurfers.)

The tone of the argument is, in Scheibel's Burkeian terms, that 'purification and redemption will be possible only when surfers stop acting like animals' (Scheibel 1995: 263).

Shaw (2004) adopted a human geography approach to analyse the interaction of a range of wave users (shortboarders, longboarders, canoes/kayaks, bodyboarders, kitesurfers, windsurfers). Such a proliferation of surfing forms testifies to the increasingly crowded and contested nature of North Devon surf beaches. Shaw's study explored the interaction in terms of the underlying themes of identity and the landscapes of exclusion and inclusion. The study identified stereotypical views of each user group, with the shortboarders feeling a general sense of superiority over the others. Part of a shortboarder's sense of antipathy towards canoes/kayaks and longboarders is that the latter groups are able to catch waves earlier, but once riding the bulkiness of their equipment prevents them from performing manoeuvres of the same skill and finesse as those of skilled shortboarders. Hostility was found to be not just a result of competition for waves, but also arising from the sense of risk from collision, especially from the canoes/kayaks and, to a lesser extent, longboards. Indeed, in most surfing which takes place in small to medium wave size conditions, the main risk of danger is being hit by another user's waveriding vehicle. The survey found that hostility was not a common occurrence at North Devon surf breaks, but had nevertheless been experienced to some degree (verbal, gesticular or physical) at least once by 80 per cent of the male, and 45 per cent of the female, surfers.

Shaw also explored the surfers' responses to crowding, first, with respect to where they chose to locate themselves in the surf zone:

- 25 per cent chose to locate away from other users
- 15 per cent chose to locate away from other user groups
- 50 per cent chose to locate wherever the waves were best
- 10 per cent chose to locate near other users.

The study also illustrated the second, and obvious, response to crowding: seeking waves in less crowded locations. However, most wave users continued to surf at the most popular surf zones, which tended to be accessible and offering a good range of infrastructural facilities. Such patterning of the concentration of most surfers in 'honeypots', with smaller, but substantial numbers dispersing to more peripheral or even remote sites, is also replicated internationally, and reflected in patterns of surf mobility in global travels.

## Summary synthesis: the cultural practice and gaze of surfing

This summary synthesis seeks to distil some main conclusions from this chapter with respect to relating surfing to the concept of subculture, the aesthetic appropriation of values connoted by surfing by the media and commerce, changing orientations towards surfing culture with experience, surfing as an identity, the dynamics of surfing lifestyles, and subcultural (or performance) capital and the regulation of surfing's inherent scarcity.

Numerous authors have related surf culture to concepts of subculture, scene, social world and lifestyles. Clearly today surf culture transcends youth and has few attributes which are politically oppositional in the CCCS sense of subcultures. Nevertheless, surf culture's characteristics of a core embodied practice, stylistic elaboration and identity ramifications clearly provide evidence of its subcultural credentials. Chapter 2 discussed surfing as emerging (partly) from a combination of a Western, Romantic imaginary of the sea and beach, and an embodied, sensuous experience of the waves. The richness of the values, aesthetics and emotions with which this basis has imbued surfing has engendered its appropriation for creative elaboration through media (especially filmic and photographic magazines) and in commerce (clothes, music, fashion and so on). Indeed, surfing's ambivalence and antipathy towards, and yet enormous (fashion-related) commercial success as explored in terms of the narrative of surfing culture (in Chapter 3) parallels the more general narrative of the incorporation and defusion of subcultures (Hebdige 1979). For many, surfing is initially an actively sought, or creatively appropriated, identity and in the early period of many individuals' engagement with surfing the fashion-related values and perceived group identity characteristics are of considerable significance. Furthermore, the range of styles (or variations on a theme) of surfing, which are partly reinterpreted in the *Zeigeist* of the times (Booth 2001a), but always with continuing residues from earlier periods, provide diverse appropriations of surfing identities or personas according to individual taste, predispositions and desires. Surfing identity is best viewed as one of the plurality of identities, which an individual may hold, with varying levels of commitment over a 'career'. With increasing years of involvement in surfing, such image- and fashion-related aspects of surf culture become increasingly taken for granted and of less personal significance. The fashion stylistic attributes of surfing become viewed as epiphenomena to the authenticity of the experience of surfing itself.

The cultural practices of surfing, obviously, revolve around the core activity of waveriding, along with an aesthetic sense of connection with the ocean. As such, this habitus or lifestyle of surfing revolves around the structures of behaviour and consumption which facilitate and maintain the enjoyment of quality waves. Beyond youth, hardcore surfing lifestyles are materially supported by various strategies in order to come to terms with economic necessity. As with other sports, success or subcultural capital in surfing is derived from present (and past) surfing skill, which may be termed performance capital. There is a pervasive, if perhaps ill-defined, tension running through surfing, pertaining to the social recognition-seeking desire to be seen, a sense of 'coolness' which disapproves of overt self-promotion, and the sense of a private, individualist vertiginous thrill in 'a communion with nature'.

The inherent scarcity of (at least readily accessible) quality surf has become intensified by the crowding concomitant with the successive cohorts of increasing participation in the sport (as a victim of its very success, appeal and commercial and filmic promotion). In order to cope with increasing crowding an informal, but strongly understood, surfing etiquette for, if not sharing, at least apportioning waves, has developed. Whilst Irwin's notions of the corruption and increasing invidiousness of surfing in response to crowding may seem somewhat overstated, etiquette is nevertheless violated, partly on the basis of the priority taken through performance capital and 'local' status.

As with other forms of discursive formation and cultural practices, surfing culture may be construed to have its own 'gaze' (Urry 1990). Building on the attributes outlined in Chapter 2, at least three further aspects of the surfing gaze may be identified, first, a way of looking at the sea and waves for their surfing potential, second, an observation of other surfers' waveriding equipment (relating to its performance properties, challenge of usage and stereotypical imaging) and third, an appraisal of other surfers' performance on the wave, which partly informs the ascription of performance capital. It may be possible to derive further aspects of the surfing gaze, for instance with respect to clothing, but such a component is perhaps relatively trivial in comparison to the forenoted components. All three of these attributes of a surfing gaze have a simultaneously aesthetic and operational (in the sense of informing action or an orientation to behaviour) quality. Furthermore, the gaze is largely automatic and almost subconscious, although the derived information and impressions may shape conscious thinking.

# 5 Gendering the waves

## Surfing in the gender order and the gender order in surfing

Duke Kahanamoku went to Sydney. He was Hawaiian, a two time Olympic swimming champion, a waterman so strong it took the future Tarzan, Johnny Weismuller, to beat him. On 15 January, 1915 Duke left the public baths where he beat his own world record for the 100 yards freestyle, went down to the beach at Manly, carved himself a board straight from a tree, and paddled out and caught a handful of waves, finishing with a head-stand. As if by a miracle, a god like man walking on water, Australia had been converted to a surfing nation.

(Martin 2000: 80)

## Introduction

On the surface many practitioners consider there is 'no issue' with gender in surfing. Indeed, there is a distinctly liberal undertone to many of the key popular texts on surfing, women and men are included unproblematically in unequal measure due to the usually unquestioned logic that the social development of surfing was a physically and symbolically 'male' activity, that in some circumstances women also participated in (see for example Young 1994). Similarly, there is currently little critically focused academic work on surfing that addresses explicitly the theme of gender relations. The few exceptions are, however, notable, with media analyses on gender representation in surfing undertaken by Thompson (2001), Henderson (2001) and Duncan and Hasbrook (2002) and a more general historical analysis provided by Booth (2001b). With these exceptions, depictions of the surfing lifestyle tend to take the male-dominated vision of this social practice as something of a 'universal' orientation, with women's participation seen as an unproblematic inclusion into a male sphere of activity. However, we should not confuse a paucity of attention to the gendered dimension of surfing with a lack of significance of gender relations in this particular activity. In spite of very recent shifts in visibility and participation of female surfers as Booth (2001b: 4) notes, 'predictions of a more equitable gender structure in surfing are premature'.

This chapter explores surfing from the point of view of gender relations and in so doing considers a range of conceptual perspectives that help to position surfing culture within the complex web of patriarchal gender power relations that is so prevalent in nearly all institutionalized forms of sport and physical activity (Hargreaves 1994). First, it considers how we might view gender in surfing as an embodied, relational phenomenon (Hall 1996), within which gender legitimacy and hierarchy are historically constructed though the binary opposition of beliefs about femininity and masculinity. As Hall (1996: 45) puts it, the 'explication of women's oppression and subordination in and through sport is totally bound up with analysis of men and masculinity'. Second, the chapter explores how understandings of gender in surfing need to go beyond such oppositions in order to consider gender in surfing as a pluralized complex of masculinities and femininities (Connell 1995, 2000, 2001). The perspective is then broadened to consider how, in competitive surfing, these pluralities of gender become positioned into power-based hierarchy, otherwise referred to as the (world) gender order (Messner and Sabo 1990; Connell 1995; Wheaton and Tomlinson 1998; Henderson 2001) that is simultaneously locally and globally connected (Connell 1998). Finally, it is argued that these perspectives allow us to explore changing gender relations in surfing as located, rather than universal, dynamic rather than fixed, and contested rather than agreed.

## Surfing and the gender order from a relational perspective

Many aspects of masculine domination in surfing, sport and society have, until quite recently, been socioculturally *invisible*. Brod and Kaufman (1994) point out that this is so because men and masculinity often take an assumed or centred position in social discourses or narratives and thereby serve as the implicit subject around which all knowledge is constructed. They call for the need to make men and masculinity explicit, decentred in discourse and deconstructed as a unified power bloc.

In recent years this decentring has increasingly taken place at a theoretical level across a range of academic disciplines including those focused on sport. For example, Hall (1996) in her forward-looking text, *Feminism and Sporting Bodies: Essays on Theory and Practice*, contends that we need theory in the study of gender in sporting and physical activity. Moreover, she articulates the need for theory to move beyond the sort produced by the traditions of the *categorical* approach, which focuses on establishing sex differences in physical performance and embodied attribute. Similarly, there is also a need to move beyond what she refers to as *distributive* approaches, which focus on the distribution of resources, access and opportunity. While 'second wave' liberal feminism drew strongly on distributive approaches to successfully impact on sexist social policy and broadening access to cultural goods, distributive approaches generally stop short of challenging the underlying power bases of inequalities, or questioning the nature of the goods to which we all now have equal access. What is needed to examine surfing now are *relational* analyses, which 'begin with the assumption that sporting practices are historically produced, socially constructed, and culturally defined to serve the interests and needs of powerful groups in society' (Hall 1996: 12).

However, in so doing, Hall also introduces the cautionary caveat that if theory is not 'rooted in practice, it becomes prescriptive, exclusive and elitist' (1996: 31). She continues:

> Today we are in a new theoretical era, one different from the past when theoretical concepts like gender stereotyping, role conflict, socialization, and role models and mentors made sense. Now we need to focus on sport as a site for relations of domination and subordination (gender, race, class, sexuality, and other forms) and on how sport serves as a site of resistance and trans-formation.
>
> (Hall 1996: 31)

Relationships between femininity, masculinity and patriarchy centre on the thematic of power. Gender power relations, are often seen to operate in similar ways to Gramsci's (1971) theory of class hegemony, in that hegemonic structures are never absolute and are constantly shifting. Nevertheless, 'hegemonic' masculinity remains the dynamic ideological form around which these Western patriarchal relations are constructed, legitimized and defended. Moreover, relational power and legitimacy suggest that there are in evidence multiple constructions of 'masculinities', as men implicitly and explicitly are positioned and position themselves in relation to hegemonic masculinity and in opposition to multiple constructions of femininities (Connell 1995). While it needs to be qualified that women are normally most disadvantaged by the impact of hegemonic masculinity in gender relations, the ideology subordinates many men as well. Pleck's (1995: 10) view is useful here; he conceptualizes patriarchy existing as a system of two halves, both related to each other, 'in which men oppress women, and in which men oppress themselves and each other'. In moving to a relational view it is important not to imply that men and women occupy homogeneous groups. Clearly, not all women experience the same type of prejudice or subordination. For example, many white, middle class, able-bodied, heterosexual women tend to be less disadvantaged than women from working class backgrounds, women from ethnic minorities, women with a disability or women with different sexual preferences, and so on. Moreover, the positional categories used in this chapter describe the relation, not the people, thus categories may remain relatively static whereas people can and do change positions.

## Gender as embedded in the surfing body

Part of the reason for the invisibility of masculinity in sport, surfing and other physical activities is its supposed biological origin in the body. While categorical research (focusing on the differences between men and women) continues in these areas (see, for example, Seiler and Sailer 1997), it is less conclusive than popular opinion would have us believe. One example is worth considering here. The link between aggression and the hormone testosterone is now considered problematic. Men's aggressive and competitive natures were assumed to be a result of the naturally occurring higher levels the hormone in men's bodies. However, aggressive behaviour and the presence of high levels of testosterone do not correlate well in social contexts. Indeed, ironically, it may well be aggressive behaviour that actually produces more testosterone (Clare 2000). Perhaps the important contemporary conclusion on categorical work inspired by sociobiology is, as Hargreaves (1994) considers, that 'there are far greater differences within a sex than between sexes, and the fitness factor and levels of skill, agility and coordination can outweigh the sex factor anyway' (Hargreaves 1994: 282).

Hargreaves' view is supported by the empirical backdrop that in sport women's performances are improving at a more rapid rate than men's performances (Dyer 1977, 1984; Whipp and Ward 1992) a situation that suggests factors other than biological constants (whatever they may be) are at work in this shift. Perhaps nowhere is this more evident than in competitive surfing, where the development of speed and technique of female surfing champions has increased very quickly in recent years. Therefore, while contemporary social theorists quite rightly debate the relationships *between* sex and gender (Butler, 1993; Shilling 2003), or more generally between society and biology (Newton 2003; Williams 2003), the premiss that the two manifestations remain separate analytical realms continues to attract some consensual opinion (sex = biology/gender = society). Hargreaves (1994: 283) concludes that 'the complexities of the interplay between the biological and the social make it impossible to assess accurately the factors which are most important in any given situation'.

Nevertheless, gender (when separated from sex) is clearly an embodied phenomenon in the sense that gender manifests itself through bodily performance (gesture, posture, use of space and style of movement, etc.). This is perhaps best explained through allusion to Shilling's (2003) often cited observation that the body is an 'unfinished entity at birth'. How the body social is 'finished' (it never really gets finished, of course) is largely a product of complex social processes and forces that are only partially under the direct control of the gendered individual in question. One of the products of this finishing process is the gendered 'thinking body' (Burkitt 1999). He argues that, 'power relations work through the body in this way creating dispositions that lead to the performance of a specific gender and, in the process, both marks and controls bodies while also investing them with certain powers and capacities' (Burkitt 1999: 108).

Therefore, in surfing it is not so much that the body is the pre-social basis for gender power relations but that power relations become inscribed onto and embedded into the body in the projected form of gendered practices, techniques and dispositional styles. This in turn gives the gendered body quite different capacities for action that are then given differential social value. In fact, there is an identifiable hierarchy of gender in the social world and this is mirrored most strongly in sport and in surfing. As Von Der Lippe (1997: 29) describes, these relations come to form a gender orthodoxy in 'which, over time, masculine values, knowledges, and behaviours have gained power and privilege over those of women'. These orthodoxies become distilled and 'naturalized' in oppositional attributes that over time come to be seen to 'define' performances of masculinity and femininity respectively. Shields (2004) articulates some of these 'traits' in relation to surfing:

> As a social performance of stamina and fitness, of amphibian and aquatic ability, surfing ties the body to the waves as well as to the beach, to surfboard technology and to style trends of surf culture and its representation in magazines such as *Surfing*. As represented in English-language histories and the press, it is bound up with sexuality, in particular a muscular and heroic masculinity, and the competence of the individual on the surfboard.
>
> (Shields 2004: 45)

These three factors of a muscular, heroic and technically competent surfing are consistently underpinning of the dominant model of masculinity in surfing.

## Gender oppositions, alterity and the gender order

According to Connell (1998: 7) 'masculinities do not first exist and then come into contact with femininities; they are produced together, in the process that constitutes a gender order'. Although Connell (1998: 7) also acknowledges that at one level this might be counter-intuitive because 'we are so accustomed to thinking of gender as the attribute of an individual'. In this sense, masculinity, Connell (2001: 31) articulates, 'does not exist except in contrast with "femininity"'. Elsewhere, he elaborates this position stating:

> Masculinity and femininity are inherently relational concepts, which have meaning in relation to each other, as a social demarcation and a cultural opposition. This holds regardless of the changing content of the demarcation in different societies and periods of history. Masculinity as an object of knowledge is always masculinity-in-relation.
>
> (Connell 1995: 44)

In support of this viewpoint, Whithead and Barret (2001: 22) consider this understanding to be linked to the concept of 'alterity', which is best described as a process of 'Othering' – marking groups as 'different and excluded'. In Western cultures gender has been articulated through the Othering process with reference to a series of 'binary', or oppositional attributes and qualities that have over the centuries come to be associated with males and females. These binary oppositions, as they are often referred to, and the values attached to them still work to define the gender order with the ideological dominant masculine male embodying most or many of the idealized masculine traits and the emphasized feminine female embodying the idealized feminine attributes. The gender order functions to give more symbolic value to some expressions of masculinity (e.g. strength, assertiveness, courage) and femininity (e.g. grace, deference, passivity) than others. Significantly however, the dominant ideological construct that serves as the invisible core of this gender order is *hegemonic masculinity*.

## Hierarchies of positions in the gender order

Connell (1995: 77) defines hegemonic masculinity as, 'the configuration of gender practice which embodies the currently accepted answer to the problem of the legitimacy of patriarchy, which guarantees (or is taken to guarantee) the dominant position of men and the subordination of women'.

Furthermore, hegemonic masculinity, as Connell (1995: 76) considers, is 'not a fixed character type, always and everywhere the same. It is rather, the masculinity that occupies the hegemonic position in a given pattern of gender relations, a position always contestable'. This position takes the view that there are *multiple masculinities* characterized as dynamic and relational to hegemonic masculinity. Therefore, hegemonic masculinities in surfing may exhibit quite different characteristics of embodied practice, interaction patterns, and narrative forms than, for example, the types of hegemonic masculinities remarkable in a boxer, business executive, military general or even a senior member of the clergy. What unites the forms of masculinities and makes them hegemonic is their promotion of male superiority in their given sphere of human activity and, in doing so their defence and promotion of patriarchal authority. It is important to establish that the number of men who are in a position to consciously and actively promote and defend hegemonic masculinities is probably quite small. However, as a dominant ideological reference point hegemonic masculinity remains very powerful.

Identifying a range of dispositions that might constitute a hegemonic masculinity is theoretically and empirically problematic because legitimation is often based on notions of implicit superiority within a given sphere of activity and actively subordinates other ways of being as a means to justify its own position of hegemony. Therefore, the surfer who argues and seeks to demonstrate that men can and should be considered superior surfers, and that male surfing is more 'important' than female surfing would be taking a hegemonic masculine *position*.

As Booth (2001b: 6) describes, this has practical manifestations for how (male) surfers earn prestige and respect, in which they must demonstrate, 'finely-honed combinations of skill, muscular strength, endurance, cunning, aggression, toughness, and, above all, courage'. It is important to qualify, however, that this does not and should not be taken to imply that dominant positions or practices cannot be or are not assumed to be engaged in by women. As Bourdieu (2001) observes, women can occupy dominant positions and engage in dominant practices that justify the so-called masculine 'traits' (e.g. managers, politicians, military personnel and, increasingly, sportswomen to name a few). However, these have arguably done rather less to challenge the symbolic gender order that underpins social life in Western societies than many second-wave feminists may have originally thought. As Demetriou (2001) points out, the reason for this seems to be that hegemonic coalitions of men seem to accommodate changes in women's increasing participation in male associated spheres of activity without relinquishing practical or symbolic control, thereby making them *complicit*. Moreover, the hegemonic masculinities can take many forms. For example, Booth's (2003) surfing 'styles' are symbolically masculine styles because males have dominated the

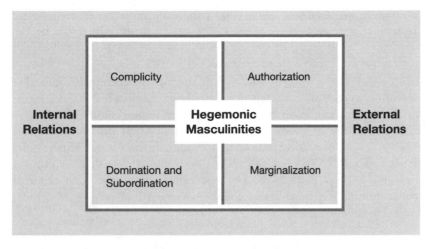

*Figure 5.1* The gender order: internal and external relations

Source: adapted from Connell, 1995

surfing subculture in the West since its revival in the early twentieth century. As we shall see some female surfers have come to adopt and adapt some of these styles without taking ownership of them.

Therefore, hegemonic masculinities must be set in their historical and contemporary context in order to see how they shape the social landscape that we live in today and the hierarchy of gender positions that emerge in relation to the dominant gendered norms. Indeed, scholarship in this area is beginning to show how hegemonic masculinities have contributed to influencing everyone's sense of social reality (see for example Connell 1995; Whithead and Barret 2001; Classen 1997), given the way in which everyone is impacted on by gender relations in some way or other. These relations are articulated in the schematic (Figure 5.1) and some explanatory articulation follows.

## Internal relations: domination, subordination and complicity

The first set of relations defines the *internal* gender order with women, homosexual men and 'effeminacy' being actively subordinated by hegemonic masculinities. The relations of domination and subordination are played out in terms of both culture and institution. A good surfing example is provided by Fiske (1989) who provides a revealing semiotic commentary on gender hierarchy in youth culture that includes surfing:

> It is worth remarking on the sexist nature of most youth subcultures, where male and female behaviour is clearly distinguished, and where males are active and dominant and females passive and subordinate. Vans, motorbikes and surfboards are conventionally driven/ridden by males and the size, skill

decoration involved in them is part of the male status order. Females are passengers, spectators, there to be won, possessed, flaunted by the male.

(Fiske 1989: 60)

Fiske successfully captures the traditional hierarchies between males and other males and between males and females. Elsewhere, Booth (2001b: 7) concurs noting that 'paradoxically the fraternal structure of surfing culture and its close association with the beach meant that women helped men define their masculinity'. It is also interesting to note that in spite of the various surfing styles identified by Booth (2003) probably all of these follow this basic underpinning gender logic. However, Fiske also goes on to identify further semiological elements of gender domination that can be found in elements of surfing subcultural discourse. He comments:

Surfers' writing mingles accounts of mastery of waves with ones of easy mastery of girls . . . They have an exclusive language for each, language that signals subcultural membership and excludes outsiders, language that performs the vital function of distinguishing *them* from *us* . . . But the key term is *hunting*, which applies equally to waves and females. Hunting is where man first denotes his mastery over nature: it is the prerequisite of cooking, which in turn, becomes the resonant metaphor for the process of culturizing nature. And consequently it is seen as a natural activity – man hunting, for food, hunting for females, hunting for waves is man behaving naturally because he acting according to his bodily needs.

(Fiske 1989: 60)

While it would be quite unrealistic and misleading to superimpose this particular reading onto the varieties of surfing styles and masculinities, it does sensitize us to how biological reductionism features strongly as an implicit defence of patriarchy employed by some surfing subcultures. It might be added that similar reductionist logics are often employed in sport with reference to the naturalization of notions of male competitiveness (see for example Dworkin and Messner 2002). Fiske's (1989: 74) semiotic analysis of surfing culture leads him to conclude that until the late 1980s at least, 'The surfie's sexuality is one of blatant male chauvinism: bushies, garudas, and so on are there for male power and pleasure'. Therefore, hegemonic masculinities can be seen to occupy the central dominant ideological and practical territory in gender relations. Clearly not all surfers (men or women) fit neatly into these dominating and subordinating categories. To make sense of these other positions there is a need to further complexify the view of gender relations.

Complicity is a subtle distinction of gender relations that is often ignored by those who would prefer to categorize men and women into a binary relation. A further position is offered by complicity as part of the *internal* gender order between men and women. Complicity refers to those men and women who might not *actively* promote hegemonic masculinity but do not attempt to challenge or change it either. Most complicit men for example appreciate and are able to display some of the stereotypical characteristics of a dominant masculinity such as assertiveness, aggressiveness, competitiveness, physical strength or power, emotional expression and so on. However, many (if not most) men cannot meet the cultural ideal of the dominant masculinity, they do not practically embody hegemonic masculinity, if they tried, they themselves might risk subordination through demonstrating their own failure. As mentioned earlier the number of men who are active in their defence of hegemonic masculinities is probably quite small. On the other hand, the number of men said to be complicit in hegemonic masculinity is likely to be very large indeed.

Connell's (1995: 77) concept of complicity is rendered more plausible given what he refers to as the *patriarchal dividend*; the sociocultural benefits that men generally gain from the subordination of women, subordinated men and marginalized groups. For the complicit male these benefits offer power and legitimacy over subordinated and marginalized others within the gender order, without having to actively defend or promote it oneself. Strategically then it would seem that most able-bodied, white, heterosexual Western men are complicit in the hegemonic masculine norm in their culture. Perhaps a little controversially it might also be argued that a number of women also come to occupy a position of complicity. Throughout second-wave feminism many women have come to occupy comfortable positions in the patriarchal order that rely on their ability to submit themselves to masculine subordination that nevertheless furthers their own social, cultural and especially economic interests. Challenging this relation would therefore undermine their own position. Pertinent examples of women occupying these positions are a select few female tennis players, who find themselves more popular, famous and wealthy due to their heterosexual good looks than for their performances, and who then pursue this avenue to social status and gain. In surfing, Fiske (1989: 74) considers that 'the women consent willingly to this male hegemony, not only in sexual activity but also in surfing'. He finds little evidence of resistance in the subculture. Rather, he contends, it 'demonstrates clearly the normalization of the surf into a comfortable reproduction of the modern marriage, where the educated woman is domestic manager in a cozy partnership' (1989: 74). However, while Fiske's description continues to hold for some relationships and positions of complicity encountered in surfing today, a generation later sees women's status as surfers and increasing resistance to subordination as a growing feature of surfing subculture.

## External relations: marginalization and authorization

Marginalization/authorization represents a second *external* set of relations (and positions) that describe the interplay of the gender order and other social structures such as class, race and ethnicity. Relationships between masculinities are made more complex and problematic by this, but by the same token the picture also becomes considerably more realistic. Within surfing we can see these external relations as a part of Thompson's (2001) analysis of surfing masculinities in South Africa; he comments:

> The history of surfing in South Africa is about the expressions of masculinity and the lure of the ocean waves. It has been a white, largely English speaking and middle class adventure/extreme sport, upholding a hegemonic white masculinity privileged in terms of class, race/ethnicity, language and social differences between women and blacks.
>
> (Thompson 2001: 91)

Marginalization therefore refers to the way hegemonic masculinities – most often white, English speaking, middle class, heterosexual and able-bodied – *use* (authorize) other forms of masculinities to construct a hegemonic gender power bloc thereby reinforcing the gender order. However, coalitions of hegemonic masculinities still remain the dominant core and seem to manage to retain institutional, cultural and symbolic power, because other men are marginalized in relation.

A classic example here is one of the white working class and black male athlete. Both of these groups of men are encouraged to foster athletic fixations with sporting prowess through their engagement with sporting institutions and businesses, that may in return provide a source of personal dignity, social mobility and, of course, revenue for the economic sports institutions (Hoberman 1997). In so doing these groups of men are encouraged to demonstrate extreme hegemonic masculine physical and narrative behaviours in the sporting arena. While some black athletes engage in acts of cultural resistance (Carrington 2002) many of these behaviours are nevertheless *authorized* because of the way they serve to reinforce actively hegemonic masculinities and the legitimacy of the white male, heterosexual vision of how the world should be (the gender order). These groups are nevertheless always slightly *marginalized* due to their social position as (at least slightly) 'Other'. This is born out by the very limited number of working class and black men who come to occupy dominant positions within the global sporting institutions.

The story of one contemporary surfer illustrates that these relations remain pertinent today. As Morton (2001: 22) describes with the case of a black South African Rasta surfer, Cass Collier, who made surfing history by becoming a 'dark horse' winner of the 1999 ISA Todos Santos big wave event, only to have one of the 'top' competitors exclaim to the media 'I've been beaten by a Rasta!'. Moreover, behind his arrival on the world surfing scene is a story of marginalization and struggle against white male supremacy, that dictates the positioning of people like Cass in relation to the dominant hegemonic norm. For example, he reported being offered bribes to deliberately loose a surfing contest, due to the reluctance of some to allow him into the elite group of (largely white) male surfers. The remainder of the chapter will begin to draw on this framework to explore the surfing and the gender order in a little more detail.

## The gender order in surfing

Despite many romanticized narrative accounts, the history of surfing, although mixed sex, is strongly textured by gender hierarchy and power relations. While the origins of surfing remain contested, it is not disputed that men and women have practised *he'e nalu* (wave-sliding) or surfing in the Polynesian Sandwich Isles since at least the fifteenth century AD, as Kampion (2003: 11) reports, surfing was 'a highly regarded and integral part of Hawaiian culture. King and queens did it. Princes and princesses did it. Kahunas and warriors did. And so did almost everyone else'.

In this culture, chiefs and warriors depended on having superior strength and stamina for ruling and surfing provided one means to achieve, maintain and demonstrate this over others. Thus, surfing can be seen as a hierarchy of cultural practice that was gendered in terms of both internal and external relations. It was internal in the sense that it positioned dominant males, warriors and princes at the top of the gender order, whose performances would define them as elites over all women and many men. 'Dropping in' on one of these social elites could have quite literally cost a surfer his/her life. It is also worth noting, that those expert women surfers of their time are now mythologized as having almost non-human qualities; the legend of Mamala is one such example. A critical feminist reading of these mythopoetics is that women 'cannot do these things' and thus there must be something divine or supernatural dictating their prowess. The gender order can also be seen to be external in the sense that while warriors and other men *were* able to show their abilities as dominant men in their culture, thus attracting some status from the proficient practice of this once exalted and spiritualized pastime, many of them did so without access to the dominant cultural goods of the time: choice of location to surf and the best boards and board makers. Moreover, ultimately, the lay surfer was marginalized in relation to the warrior and the warrior in turn had to defer to the ruling elite. Undoubtedly, some did challenge the status quo through bettering the skills or daring of their hierarchical superiors but ultimately the gender order was confirmed rather than challenged through surfing in pre-modern Polynesian culture.

A second illustration is worth articulating here. Individuals' engagement with their environment is not only 'natural' (in a practical survival sense) but socially constructed in ways which mean that actions are thereby infused with social meanings, relations and symbols. One such relationship is the way gender hierarchy was sustained through the engagement with the physical artifacts of this culture, one of the most important of which being the surfboard. The ultimate masculine status in Polynesian culture was configured around the use of heavy and long surfboards. The ability to surf with these boards and, better still, take others in tandem, served as a sign of the surfer's dominant position in the culture, both physically and socially. As Kampion (2003: 14) reminds us 'the eighteen foot long cigar-shaped olo was only ridden by very important people at exclusive surf spots'. Moreover, these boards were used by the dominant men to take others for surfing rides. Many of those who were given rides were women and 'lesser' men.

Therefore, while it is a celebrated historical 'fact' that men and women surfed, there is an important caveat that they did so with very different equipment and physical style and were differentiated in relation to the hierarchy of gender relations prevalent in the gender order at that time. Indeed, developing some of the prominent anthropological commentaries of Mauss (1954/2002) regarding the practice of *potlatch* (the ritualized ceremony for the exchange of gifts), it would be a considerable but valuable undertaking to engage in a socio-analysis of the relationships between the gender order, surfing and Polynesian society more generally.

While the near demise of surfing in the 1900s in its originating locations of Polynesian cultures saw a decline in mixed sex participation, surfing's renaissance in the modern era and its subsequent repopulation as a popular leisure activity in Western culture is undeniably a male-dominated history. The basic surfing hierarchy of relations between men and women must be seen in no small part as linked to the differential freedoms for leisure participation between men and women that was already established in societies like the United States of America, which were emerging from their industrial revolutions. In these early transitional years surfing spread between groups of men who were seeking ways of filling their newly found leisure freedom, through what Guttmann (1978) might describe as the 'ludic diffusion' of the activity. Nevertheless, it is clear that the ascriptive Polynesian modes of patriarchal domination within this activity diminished and became culturally vestigial with the spread of surfing to new shores during the early 1900s. However, one important vestige from this ancient gender order that was still visible in practices reported around the 1900s was the dominant presence of the nine foot redwood longboard. These objects, which often weighed well over 100 pounds, were only realistically usable by the largest and strongest males, at the time known as the Waikiki beachboys, the most well-known of whom was undoubtedly Duke Kahanamoku (1880–1968), often termed the 'father of modern surfing'.

In this sense, it is possible to consider the hierarchy of relations between and within the genders with dominant males justifying their position through a combination of social position, physical prowess and subcultural connections to obtain the best boards and surf the best spots with a degree of priority. In short it was (with a few notable exceptions) predominantly Western men, not women who were in the social and cultural positions to take up surfing when Kahanamoku introduced the West to the practice. However, the ideal of dominant masculinity in surfing was also to become subject to a strong, inexorable challenge by many Western males who would probably not have fitted into the Waikiki model of dominant masculinity by virtue of a lack of sheer physical stature and strength. These surfers would begin to employ technologies developed through processes of science; technology emanating from the industrialization of warfare taking place in the period between 1900 and 1950 to develop new physical artifacts that would allow them to transform the relationship between the body and the surf.

At a symbolic level, the physical production of new, lighter boards, both shaped and 'finned' provided a classically modernist reinterpretation of surfing that allowed the emergence and manifestation of a deep-seated Western masculinist ideology embedded in the core of modernist scientific enlightenment; the prediction, control and thus domination and culturization of nature, as Fiske (1989) has suggested. While this is an area that would benefit from further empirical research, a few comments on the relationship between the development of surfboard and gender are warranted here to illustrate the evolving gender order.

The newer, lighter (and later 'finned') shortboards fundamentally altered which men might ride waves and the riding styles they could adapt. These boards provided the opportunity to form different relationships with the waves that allowed surfers much more choice and control over what they did on the waves. Surfers could now begin to cutback and go against the face of the wave, create new, more dynamic turns and utilize the energy of the different parts of waves in new ways. All of these possibilities required different forms of athleticism. Embodied qualities such as quick reflexes, speed, flexibility, refined balance, dynamic (plyometric) as opposed to static strength became the new masculine standard of performance that stood in symbolic and practical opposition to the classic the 'old' 'traditional' longboard style of going with the wave (see Chapter 3 and Plates 2 and 6). In short, the Western male's preoccupation with technology gave rise to artifacts that empowered many males to lay down a challenge to the dominant masculinities in early surfing of the era. Shortboard surfing looked more dynamic and breathtaking. In reality, it was *differently* rather than *more* athletic and thereby altered the internal dynamics of the gender order by allowing a different kind of male body to rise to prominence. However, by challenging the dominance of the heavy longboard, the pioneers of shortboard surfing also paved the way for the re-democratization of surfing. While this process is still far from complete, it did begin to remove some of the physical barriers for many male and female surfers, who did not wish to build their bodies to surf with long heavy boards.

As Booth (2003) articulates, the search for social exclusiveness and distinction has led to a number of distinct surfing styles, all of which were/are male-dominated and which embody slightly different hegemonic masculine dispositions, from the Hawaiian beachboys, the Australian Lifesavers, the professional surfer athletes and, more recently, the 'abrasive' generation. While by no means generalizable, in relation to their own spheres of subcultural activity, many of the characteristics of hegemonic masculinities are shared by these styles; physical assertiveness, competitiveness, the demonstration of superior physical skill and dynamic ability all indicate a male-dominated cultural practice.

There are, of course, some notable exceptions here of female or 'Wahine' (Hawaiian for female) surf pioneers, who have become global icons in modern-day Wahine surfing subculture. The Californian, Mary Ann Hawkins, and the Australian, Isabel Letham (who was introduced to surfing by riding tandem with by Duke Kahanamoku himself) are both iconic examples of early twentieth-century female surfing pioneers. These and others such as Marge Calhoun, Linda Benson, Phyllis O'Donnell, Gail Couper and Linda Merrill should all serve as reminders that gender hegemony of the internal gender order in surfing was never total or fixed. However, the early female pioneers need to be considered in terms of the relationship to the social order of their time. Although culturally and geographically distant, Deem's (1986) work remains a powerful stimulus to ask critical questions of female leisure participation in Western cultures at this time. She points out that many of this century's female sporting pioneers came from the bourgeois or middle classes. These were women who had the combination of resources, time, knowledge, inclination and social connections to stake a serious and sustained claim to participate in an activity colonized by men. Indeed, a gender/class analysis of this dimension of the early surfing pioneers is badly needed, as we still know precious little about how gender, class, space and practice interact in relation to surfing. Equally interesting is the possible diffusing effect of social dominance through activities such as surfing in that many women also talk about being introduced to the sport as a result of intense family involvement – and usually (although not exclusively as seen in the case of Marge Calhoun and her daughters) this means fathers and brothers. However, this recolonization of an activity, while it has drifted between a number of identifiably gendered forms or transformations (see for example, Henderson 2001, Booth 2003), has nevertheless been a story of masculine engagement and colonization.

However, the gender order in surfing as we know it now is only partially the result of this traditional and subcultural development of gender relations in surfing culture. The entry of competitive surfing into the professional, commercialized sporting world also signalled a transition into a new phase of gender relations in surfing culture. This transition will be considered in the following section.

## Surfing in the (world) gender order

Connell (1998) contends that the gender order identified above is observable at a global institutional level. He continues:

> If we recognize that very large scale institutions such as the state are themselves gendered, in quite precise and specifiable ways (Connell 1990b), and if we recognize that international relations, international trade, and global markets are inherently an arena of gender formation and gender politics (Enloe 1990), then we can recognise the existence of a world gender order.
>
> (Connell 1998: 7)

In these terms, the world gender order is both a product and a reciprocal part of the globalization process, as Kimmel (2004) puts it 'Globalization was always a gendered process'. Moreover, it has real world impacts such as the feminization of poverty, due to which women now have come to occupy about 70 per cent of the 1.3 billion of the world's poorest people, and has also been linked to the rise in global terrorism, which can be interpreted as a global struggle for culturally legitimate forms of hegemonic masculinities (Kimmel 2003). Elsewhere, it is hard to fail to notice that within some of the world's leading financial institutions, the

UK stock market, for example, gender power in the boardrooms of the top 100 blue-chip companies remains remarkable through its constancy rather than change. Connell (1998) argues that globalization has provided economic and cultural power to particular groups of men on an unprecedented scale, equipping the dominant few with the resources and channels to exert their hegemony and enforce standardization over a multiplicity of localized masculinities and femininities across the developed and developing world. The primary channel for this has been the exportation of *the institution* and with it institutional power both of which are formed 'through collectivities of gender practice' (Connell 1998: 5), that is configured around a dominant ideological norm of hegemonic masculinity. While there are many forms of masculinities that have entered this institutional power bloc through colonialism and now circulate as part of this global form, the dominant form remains that configured out of, and for, the interests of the 'culture and institutions of the North Atlantic countries' (Connell 1998: 9).

It is into this world gender order that the contextualization of modern surfing, and particularly competitive surfing, must be positioned because the global gender order retains a powerful and active symbiotic relationship with the *institution* of modern competitive sport. As Hall (1996: 32) points out, 'sport, like other cultural forms and practices that become institutionalized, is profoundly affected by (and in turn affects) existing structures of power and inequality in those societies'. To this fundamental critical understanding, we must add the observation that over the past few decades surfing has made the transition from a range of diverse subcultural lifestyle practices (Booth 2003), to something that is also institutionalized, codified, commodified in ways which Guttmann (2000) has previously articulated. Henderson (2001: 323) underlines this point succinctly in commenting that, 'the professionalization of surfing places more emphasis upon competitive surfing in general, and upon the cash nexus, but it also necessitates the setting up of formal structures and institutions (contest directors, a circuit, sponsors, judging, professional associations and so on)'.

The institutionalization of surfing has led to the creation of international associations, the most significant of which is probably the International Surfing Association (ISA) that came to occupy its present position in 1976. The ISA is the world governing authority for surfing and works as an overarching coalition of surfing interests that sustain a network linking the national governing bodies (NGB) and the Association of Surfing Professionals (ASP) together. What is equally noteworthy is the way in which ISA acts as the 'legitimate' voice of surfing to the official world sporting institutions. For example, in 1982 ISA was recognized as the world governing body for surfing by the General Association of International Sport Federations (GAISF). ISA is also a member of the International World Games Federation (IWGA), the World Master Games Association (WMGA) and the Federation of University Sports (FISU). Perhaps most significantly ISA is surfing's portal to the most powerful sporting institution on the planet, the International Olympic Committee (IOC), having been granted full recognition in 1997 and becoming a part of the Olympic movement (ISA 2005).

This transition means that competitive surfing has formulated alliances with a range of global patriarchal 'structures of organized sport that reflect and reinforce established patterns of gender inequality, as well as those of class, race, and ethnicity' (Hall 1996: 32). Analyses of the connections between sport, global business and gendered political economies have long since been a preoccupation of sport sociologists (see for example Hargreaves 1986; Sage 2000; Miller 2001; Miller *et al.* 2002). One of the early commentators on these alliances, Hargreaves (1986) uses the term 'media sport' to represent what he considered to be a significant shift in power relations between individual sports, associations and sectors and the growing sport entertainment industry. This is based around the three-way coalition between sponsorship, advertising and media. While the rewards can be considerable, the costs in terms of cultural ownership are also considerable as collectively these coalitions wrestle decision-making and representative power away from individual sports, a recent example of which is provided by Villamón *et al.* (2004) who explore the institutionalization of judo. While these patriarchal alliances remain dominant and powerful, gender relations in competitive sport and physical activity more generally, are contested and change can and does take place, as Wheaton and Tomlinson (1998: 253) point out, 'since the 1970s, women have penetrated many sporting spheres. With some erosion of male spatial domination, the role sport plays in the reproduction and/or transformation of contemporary relations between, and within, the sexes is a prime concern'. In surfing, as Kampion (2003) depicts, aspects of female (and male) surfing are certainly transforming:

> By the 1980s' men's world tour prize money had topped $225,000 while the women's winnings stood at $10,000 . . . twenty years later women's surfing was side by side with tow-in surfing as the biggest phenomena [sic] to shake up the sport since the shortboard revolution of the '60's.
>
> (Kampion 2003: 141)

The question is which aspects and how? In the following sections a few of the key areas of surfing that are changing are considered in relation to the impact this may have on the gender order.

## Changing relations? Sport, surfing, resistance and transformation

In general, post-modern thinkers caution that social change is not an inevitable consequence of some singular linear process of historical development or enlightened modernization (Lyon 1994). Rather, these changes should be seen as hard-fought victories that represent precious steps towards differently organized gendered social orders in sport and society. Indeed, Booth (2001b: 6) confirms that, in spite of these advances, 'one finds increasing evidence of the male surfing fraternity closing ranks'. This point is made more pertinently by Henderson

(2001) who articulates that gender resistance and change can provoke a *backlash* by the dominant order who come to recognize that in the arena of sport, and here surfing, the struggle for equality is the struggle for social power (see also Kusz 2003). A further way of interpreting these ongoing transformations is, as Giddens (1990) points out, that all social action has both intended and unintended consequences regardless of the initial intentions.

Given the above, the first and most important task is to view gender relations in surfing as existing in a constant state of flux. While gender relations appear stable from a distance, a closer inspection usually reveals acts of social resistance, transformation and reproduction taking place at any given moment and in any given social space. This condition is aptly described by Bauman (2000) as indicative of the *fluidity* of modern social formations. The question that emerges is how to make sense of such fluidity and contradiction?

## Structural change

From a structural perspective, women's surfing has most certainly penetrated the male sporting sphere and surfing is probably practised by a wider range of classes and ethnicities than ever before. Most obvious indicators are participation figures, which are lamentably inadequate at the time of writing. Nevertheless, the figures that are available do suggest a general trend of increasing female participation. For example, the Australian Sports Commission (2005) comment that 'over 50% of current surf school participants are women and young girls' (ASC 2005). Byfield (2002) reported that 8 per cent of participants observed in his study in the southwest of the UK were female. Elsewhere, Preston-Whyte's (2002) survey in Durban, South Africa suggested that slightly less than 18 per cent of surfers there are currently women.

Competitively, relatively few female surfers have made a relatively large impact on the subculture. In common with Bauman's (2000) consideration that we live in a post-panoptical, synoptical society (in which the many watch the few) this makes some plausible sense. Media and publicity for these women command a high presence but their numbers remain few. In 2004, the World Championship Tour (WCT) had 11 male competitions with over $270,000 prize money per event, while the women's WCT had six events with prize money typically around $65,000.

A few further examples serve to highlight that some structural change has taken place and that this has been a struggle. Women's surfing organizations have for several decades been struggling to develop a successful professional circuit (Booth 2001b). As in many other sports, competitive women surfers are now a part of the historically male-dominated institution and struggle from within for greater viability and visibility (Hargreaves 1994). Some success is apparent, with women currently represented on the elected ISA executive committee with one member, the other four are male. Significantly, ISA now also publishes one set of rule guidelines for men and women surfers. Finally, ISA has established the 'women in surfing committee', whose mission is to:

Promote women's surfing on an international level. The committee's goals are to organize women's surfing competition around the world, increase the number of local women surfers (and create a favorable environment for that to happen) and lobby for more women on senior positions of the ISA.

(ISA 2005)

However, the observation that females have *penetrated* the male-dominated surfing sphere, and structural change has taken place, is considerably different than the claim of equality or wholesale changes in the gender order. In agreement with Booth (2001b) in many ways the rise of women's surfing is only just beginning. Indeed, concerns about the development of women's surfing have been taken up by a number of women who have constructed an international organization, International Women's Surfing (IWS), dedicated to furthering the cause of women in competitive and recreational surfing. The critical issues to consider here are how the gender order itself is affected by these changes and whether this constitutes a deeper and more profound challenge to the gender order or whether hegemonic masculinities are merely reorganizing their patterns of dominance in order to accommodate a broader range of masculinities and femininities?

## Commercial change

Surfing subculture is to some extent commercially underpinned by internal and external surfing sponsorship, advertisers and manufacturers. However, unlike many sports, internal, surfing-specific companies still dominate the commercial activities in surfing. While the profit motive may remain the same for both internal and external companies, external corporate sponsors do not tend have a vested interest in the real nature of surfing, so long as it yields a profit. Internal companies and sponsors on the other hand are very often surf enthusiasts and therefore tend to be more concerned about the future of surfing as changes to the sport and activity can threaten their existence (whereas corporate sponsors simply move to another sport if a sport declines in popularity). However, the commercial activities of most internal and external companies, advertisers and sponsors alike must be examined for the impact they have on transforming or reproducing gender relations in surfing. Indeed, on the very few occasions where seemingly altruistic social actions are engaged in by companies, a cursory glance often reveals that the corporation's market researchers give them reason to believe that the creation of a new desire and taste in untapped sectors of the consuming public would create fresh new markets and lead to considerable profit in the medium to long term. The example of Nike's sustained efforts to glamorize and popularize female physical activity can be considered in this way (see Lucas 2000; Shaw 1999). This is not to cynically imply, however, that corporations' interventions cannot do any good. In this example, one consequence has been the promotion of healthier lifestyles to an increasingly sedentary population in society (see for example the Institute of Youth Sport 2000).

For international competitive surfing to be commercially viable, it must represent the interests of the numerous male-dominated corporate sponsors, their coalition interests and, of course, their clients. Sponsorship of radical, new, gender-challenging sports therefore tends to be cautious at best. The global merchandizing of sponsors' products has a curious relationship in the case of surfing and gender because the target audience is simultaneously men, boys, women and girls. The issue here is that the merchandizing of surfing must take place through the manipulation of pre-existing desires, configured in, and around gendered bodies and the gender order.

One force that is providing the conditions for change in the gender order in surfing is the commodification, and sexual fetishization, of women's and men's surfing. Following Miller (2001) we should not be surprised at how sex has come to be used as a powerful marketing strategy in sport in the late twentieth and early twenty-first centuries. Constructing new markets requires the construction of desire and the translation of the sporting body into a sexualized body that might promote desire (desire for self and desire of other) is a powerful tool that draws together the body, emotions and (normally) hetero-normative reactions to socially constructed aesthetics of sexualized beauty.

Commercially, the growth of women's surfing has been most prominent in this regard. Women surfers-as-consumers have been targeted by a rapidly expanding multi-million dollar industry. A single example illustrates the growth – surf manufacturer Quiksilver's women-only brand 'Roxy' is enormously successful and in a few short years has come to be the market leader in young women's surf clothes, the following extract from the Roxy history page of the Roxy website positions its target audience and product in a gendered way:

> Roxy, Quiksilver's junior girl's line, is dedicated to active living and the extreme sports lifestyle. The line, which is designed by Dana Dartez is created with the young girl in mind. Roxy prides itself on their connection to the junior customer, progressive yet embracing all elements of life. The clothes range from basic surfwear for sport and style to vintage inspired, forward sportswear. The Roxy girl is involved in beach sports and snow sports and demands a girly fit and functional wear.
>
> (Roxy 2005)

Roxy shops now exist in Asia, USA, Europe and Australia, and the brand sponsors many competitions and is principle sponsor for a number of WCT women's competitions. The target audience for the product is therefore women and girls, but the visual fetish created by many of these products and the type of femininity being constructed through their use, is certainly in no small part normative, heterosexual and male-orientated (Craig 1994). In this regard, Roxy both typifies and drives the transformation of femininities through surfing that has taken place. On the one hand young women are now symbolically heterosexually 'safe' with enhanced secondary sexual characteristics; on the other hand they are increasingly engaging in 'risk' or extreme activities (Stranger 1999) and challenging the conventional territory-dominant masculinities. The paradoxical image and the desire it creates are both reflected and created by the competitive female surfer.

## Changing femininities in surfing – 'surf like a man' and look 'heterosexy'?

The gender order by its very nature flows through the individual body and minds of men and women who surf, something Connell (1995) refers to as body reflexive practice, where the gendered body is simultaneously a passive subject and an active agent. The implication is that, however seemingly ineffectual, individuals contribute to the gender order at personal and interpersonal levels and these actions then ripple back out into society, confirming and/or challenging the gender order. Clearly some individuals come to occupy certain social spaces that are vastly more influential than others. These mediated spaces now occupy at local and global levels in their sphere of activity and can have significant impacts on the gender order. In many ways these individuals come to symbolize change (Booth 2001b), but in the case of surfing they also most certainly embody change. Currently, some prominent individuals are the 'new' breed of professional female competitive surfers.

By way of illustration it is worth considering the representation of one of surfing's most significant contemporary surfing female exponents, Lisa Anderson, by one of surfing's most articulate cultural commentators, Drew Kampion (2003):

> Lisa Anderson was a four-in-a-row women's world surfing champion in the 1990s. For whatever reasons, she was also the catalyst that set off the women's (or girl's) surfing renaissance of the 1990s. It was the time, and she was the one. Just the looks, just the style, and everyone said she surfed like a man. There was something fresh and sexy in her, and wounded; everyone carries his or her scars somewhere. But she was successful, and that felt great. She was free, at least freer than she'd ever been, and she was surfing. That was her life – surfing and surfers and the surfing media.
>
> (Kampion 2003: 145)

In a subtle way, Kampion carefully illustrates something that surfers will already know, Lisa Anderson was different. Anderson was a pioneer as she was one of the first women to successfully begin performing the same types of radical, 'aggressive' techniques and manoeuvres normally associated with elite male surfers. Moreover, she did this on substantial waves. However, Anderson's style did not really *look* like a man's, it was a hybrid style. Commentators and other surfers united in waxing lyrical over how she combined techniques associated with male surfing and a more 'graceful' execution associated with female surfing style.

Anderson could not be positioned as subordinate on performance grounds. Indeed, she had perfected many of the male associated techniques so as to outperform many male surfers at their own game and they were forced to recognize her physical prowess on *their* own terms ('good' by their own criteria). She also outperformed the other women, the majority of whom were surfing 'differently' or 'surfing differently like women used to surf', and in so doing she was one of a few elite female surfer athletes who pioneered a shift in women's surfing performance.

Anderson had a surfer's body: a mesomorphic somatotype; low centre of gravity; high levels of flexibility; good bodyweight–strength ratio; fitness; and obviously very fast reflexes. However, Lisa Anderson was also a sexy female as well, and this term 'sexy' clearly alludes to the predominantly (although certainly not exclusively) male gaze of the normative heterosexual female body (smooth, tanned skin, blond hair, blue eyes, a feminine aesthetic and disposition). In this way she was able to offset the constant stereotyping that female surfers had hitherto sometimes faced concerning the supposed homosexual preferences of the active sportswoman (Kampion 2003; Booth 2001b). Anderson therefore, was not *challenging* the dominant men in every way, and not at all in terms of her safely sexualized identity, where she might be said to be implicitly complicit to the gender order, especially when, as a mother, she took her baby with her to competitions and won them. Rather, she was borrowing and approximating their waveriding techniques. Through this, as the quote above indicates, Anderson, as with some of her peers, came to exemplify and experience gender empowerment through surfing. Moreover, these women commanded considerable respect for their performances by male and female surfers alike. Indeed, Anderson is often cited by many of the next generation of female surfers as an inspiration for them to pursue surfing. The following comment from competitive surfer Megan Abubo is illustrative:

> Growing up, the emphasis was always on boy's sports, and we were looked at as tomboys. We didn't care. We went surfing anyway. My generation grew up with posters of Lisa Anderson and Pauline Menczer on our walls, and they were inspirational.
>
> (cited in Panniccia 2003: 54)

The issues raised by the achievements of such female pioneers as Lisa Anderson are not to be underestimated. They represent a considerable penetration into the practices that constitute a masculine orthodoxy within surfing culture itself. Moreover, her challenge to this orthodoxy in this era represents a contribution to the more general challenge to the global gender order in sport, referred to by Wheaton and Tomlinson (1998) earlier in which many women are coming to embody the practices and competencies so long denied them (see for example Wesley 2001; Mennesson 2000). However, as we shall see these challenges perhaps also demonstrate as Demetriou (2001) contends, the fluidity and flexibility of what he terms the hegemonic masculine bloc. In other words, just as many women and subordinated/marginalized men, resist being positioned as 'Other' by hegemonic masculinity in Western patriarchy, so patriarchy resists the challenges of women and subordinated men. Lisa Anderson had to negotiate her way through a life so familiar to professional sportswomen with chronic low pay, uncertain contracts, limited team support, limited media coverage and sponsorship deals that are especially noticeable in the sport of women's surfing. Henderson (2001: 329) points out that these advances of female participation need to be seen as incursions or as a 'colonization of the particularly masculine lifeworld of surfing . . . surfing is a territorial form of pleasure, dreams, and nostalgia'. As Henderson (2001: 328–329) concludes 'in her search for subcultural identity and pleasures as a surfer, the female surfer faces a difficult task of negotiating the traditional codes of femininity, difficulties not faced by men or boy surfers'.

One area where masculinist counter-resistance or even occasionally 'backlash' is seen to take place is in the void between the realities constructed through surfing practice and the realities constructed in its media representations. The reason for this is that men and male-dominated institutions still have considerable degrees of control over the participation of women and their subsequent (mis) representation via media. Moreover, as we have seen, the challenge laid down by elite women athletes to the gender order sends a ripple through the gender order that is often met with a response. However, the complexities of the position of a commercialized surfing culture in a globalized gender order is such that there is an increasingly disparate series of femininities and female positions occupied by women in surfing subculture. One articulation of this in relation to surfing is Henderson's (2001) description of 'the schizoid' treatment that she observed women receiving during her post-structuralist analysis of the interpenetration of female surfers into male surfing culture. For Henderson, there is a clear split in representation of women in the surfing media depending on whether they surf or not. Those who surf are given considerably more respect and coverage, and those who do not surf are treated as objects of desire for the largely male-dominated audience. The split is both interesting and important in terms of shifts in the gender order. Those treated as objects of desire have, in particular, their bodies 'positioned primarily as objects not only of desire, but of jokes, play grotesquery and fear' (Henderson 2001: 328). While it must be cautioned that the media she was analysing was the slightly 'unfettered', 'niche' Australian publication *Tracks*, the gendered positioning highlighted here is strongly suggestive of a dominant masculine accommodation of the female surfer, while affirming the subordinate role of the 'normal' heterosexualized female.

Surfing culture has had a traditionally male-dominated media and advertising profile both as a sport and a physical activity or leisure pursuit. Surfers are depicted as predominantly classically masculine, virile, heterosexual (normally white) men. As Henderson (2001: 326) argues when surfing entered into the sporting world, it was also thrust into the 'capitalist image culture industries', that construct surfing in the image of its main client group, the adolescent male.

While by no means in total control, the mass media have the power to position gender representations on a global stage. Through this institutional medium 'Western definitions of authoritative masculinity, criminality, desirable femininity and so on' are created (Connell 1998: 11). It is important to distinguish between the surfing media, the sporting media and the mainstream media, as all are likely to represent the interests of their journalist and core markets in subtly different ways. However, with surfing as an entry into the professional, commercialized sports business world it is perhaps the sports media that has become a unique prism for the positioning and circulation of specific forms of masculinities and femininities through sporting forms. Surfing's search for a global media presence has meant that it desperately needs representation by the media and that the media is also the single most important player in the construction of the global gender order.

A good illustration of this is provided by Duncan and Hasbrook (2002) whose comparative analysis of television portrayals of surfing and basketball is indicative of one of the global institutions that link up with sport to reconstruct the gender order in normative ways. They point out that one of society's most influential mass media, television, symbolically denies power to women by its exclusionary and denigrating tactics. More specifically in relation to surfing they conclude:

> In surfing we found that although the narratives describing male and female surfers were quite comparable and emphasized the skill of the athletes – male and female – the visuals fragmented and objectified women by presenting them in a highly sexualized way, focusing on certain body parts and depicting women in mostly passive poses . . . this juxtaposition of positive audio with negative video created a deeply ambivalent depiction of female athletes.
> (Duncan and Hasbrook 2002: 92)

Similar conclusions were reached elsewhere by Carlisle-Duncan (1990) and also by Pirinen (2002) whose study of sporting coverage of women's entry into new (previously male-only) sports was reconstructed in the Finnish media through two discernable discourses, those of trivialization/marginalization and those of equality, respectively. However, Pirinen concluded that both discourses were routinely ultimately used to justify the position, inherent values and qualities of male sport as the barometer or standard. The gender order is thus maintained as the invisible, embodied, unquestioned norm because to differing degrees both discourses 'support and reproduce the masculine values and practices of competitive sport' (Pirinen 2002: 103). The relational perspective adopted here also suggests that changes in one part of the gender order will impact on the positions and identities adopted by the others. It is appropriate that we now consider the changing masculinities in the gender order.

## Changing masculinities in surfing – surfer as athlete and the quest for the big wave

For Messner (1992) one of the effects of forced social change (such as economic collapse, war, civil unrest, institutional change, etc.) is that the traditional unquestioned logics of the order of the time (e.g. dominant masculinities) become subject to scrutiny, pressure and often result in perceptions of 'crisis'. The shifts in surfing towards a competitive sport and the pressure from female surfers to participate more, have created a certain degree of pressure on masculinities in surfing, that the fraternal surfing culture has responded to (Booth 2001b). According to the principle of alterity, when female surfers change their behaviours, actions and identities, pressure will be placed on many male surfers to make corresponding changes in order to maintain their sense of identity through difference. This becomes all the more pertinent when many female surfers are successfully adopting the skills, techniques, attitudes, principles and even lifestyles of male surfers.

Attempting to articulate a possible range of masculinities manifest in surfing is inherently difficult and perhaps an academically risky undertaking, especially given that the gender and subcultural politics involved in 'positioning' these are based on the subcultural capital that each suggestively carries in its embodiment. Nevertheless, Henderson (2001: 327) identifies a mediated heroic masculinity that contains a number of signifiers about the archetypal male surfer, 'ideally it should contain the yobbo, athlete, and rebel versions of masculinity; ease the tensions of a split subculture; and meet the fantasy needs of its large teenage male audience'. It is important to qualify that *Tracks* embodies something of the more extreme representation of the gender order in surfing.

The rise of the professional surfer athlete has been gradual but inexorable. In many ways it represents the ultimate response to the challenge of the penetration of the male sporting sphere by talented female surfers. This is even more relevant given the fact that surfing competitions were initially mixed sex. The professional surfer, such as those epitomized by Andy Irons and Kelly Slater, exemplifies and embodies not just contemporary surfing culture, but also the impact of contemporary sports culture, with its modernistic, scientific, disciplined 'Taylorized' and mechanized embodied implications (see Hoberman 1992). But clearly the professional male surfer is also iconographic in his being a living representation of the surfing aesthetic. Looking good and surfing well are synonymous, and positioned in relation to the gender order in surfing. Today's professional male surfers now occupy one of the most visible hegemonic cores around which other gendered ways of being a surfer become positioned. Henderson (2001) comments:

> Hence the pro surfer is doubly disciplined by the instrumental techniques of professional sport and by the demands of surfing as commodity form (Fitzclarence 1990: 106). Yet by virtue of his skill and his supposedly dream lifestyle, he has become the surfing ideal. Professionalism, commercialization, and hegemonic masculinity are conjoined on the utopian body of the pro.
>
> (Henderson 2001: 326)

Henderson's view is largely supported by Thompson's (2001: 99) analysis in which he considered 'the male dominated gender order can clearly be seen in the language used in *Zigzag* (a South African surfing magazine), particularly in the slippage between 'boards and broads'. Most notable was that the 'institutionalization of a masculine competitive ethos centred on men who made surfing their business' (2001: 96). Furthermore, this represented a particular set of qualities and social positions that characterized hegemonic masculinity in South African surfing beginning in the 1970s:

> It was a representation of masculinity based upon financial stability, surfing prowess and romanticization of the surfing lifestyle. In effect the young middle

class surfing businessman became a cultural icon, a configuration not isolated from the dissemination of representations of professional surfers on the world tour.

(Thompson 2001: 97)

Of course, these transitions in masculinities and in particular in the hegemonic core are in many ways ironic and riddled with tension and perhaps even lacking in desire (in the Lacanian sense). The male super pro, in order to represent this hegemonic (heroic) masculine imaginary has also become the male model who must fetishize his body and its appearance at every public opportunity in order to stimulate the desire to the consuming gaze of surf-following men and women alike. Such a process inevitably leads to an adaption and adoption of classic techniques and forms of representation that are more associated with emphasized femininity than masculinity. A similar irony was recognized by Klein's (1993) work with professional bodybuilders. In both these cases the male body becomes mirroring (reflecting that which is around it), plucked, shaved, preened and made up to look its best for its mediated contribution to a synoptical society.

There is another area where the hegemonic masculinities have pushed and redefined themselves in recent years: big waveriding (see for example Plates 8 and 9). The principle is extreme sport at its most simple: find the biggest breaking wave you can and ride it! Failure to complete riding some of these waves can mean death. It is an arena dominated by men, the hardcore male surfers, often in their forties who are driven by a quest for excitement and embodied desire to push the performance/experience envelope ever further. This defines them as hegemonically masculine. Big waveriders must be very strong, fit, technically skilled and heroically brave to pit themselves against the forces of nature. In terms of the gender order, the return to the heroic masculinities of the early days of surfing is no coincidence, it is the carving out of new territory and establishing new distance between the hegemonic masculine male surfer and the 'Other' (i.e. the females and all the other men). This heroic masculinity is enshrined in the competitive spirit of big wave competitions such as the highly culturally (if not economically) prestigious 'the Eddie', named after Eddie Aikau, a Hawaiian life-guard who died attempting to paddle to shore in heavy seas to raise the alarm for his capsized colleagues. Eddie's heroism and masculine dispositions are enshrined in the big wave surfing subculture, and are the subject of numerous dedicated texts and websites (see for example Holmes Coleman 2002). Apparently Eddie would smile (in response to being 'hailed' to surf, see Chapter 6) when the waves got to 20 feet in height in Waimea Bay, and now the competition only takes place if the waves are 20 feet high or larger. Competitors now regularly surf waves of between 20 and 40 feet. Eddie also lives on in the big waveriding vernacular through the response to indecision about whether to attempt to ride a big wave – 'Eddie would go' as they say. In so doing these men (re)configure, (re)position the gender order in surfing, with the hegemonic masculine bloc certainly broader than it was, it nevertheless seems to be re-establishing itself.

However, as Booth (2003) reminds, even here there are tensions, hierarchies and struggles that are loaded with gender positioning politics. Big waves travel much faster than small waves so catching big waves has always presented a problem. It has taken a curious collection of developments to see the rise of big wave surfing. The development of more modified (foot straps and narrower) shortboards, jetskis and tow lines now means that surfers can catch much bigger waves due to the speed attained by the pull of the jetski to assist the surfer to catch the wave. The combination of the search for new masculine territories, using technology to dominate and culturize nature and, more specifically, the waves that previously remained untameable is a coming together of the symbolic and practical expression of hegemonic masculinities that captivate many male surfers. However, there are many detractors who feel that 'real' men surf big waves without technological assistance (a much more dangerous activity). Thus, the struggle for masculine hierarchy and hegemony continues. Meanwhile, a few surfing elite women like Souza, Beachley and Gerhardt are also now surfing big waves and commanding respect (Booth 2001b), but it is just a few, for the time being . . .

## Conclusions: surfing as a site of gender resistance and accommodation, transformation and reconstruction

This chapter has considered surfing from the point of view of gender power relations. In so doing it has forwarded the view that institutionalized and competitive surfing needs to be considered an activity dominated by certain groups of men and male ideology on practical, economic and symbolic levels. This might be described as a gender order in surfing that is closely tied to the world gender order in sport and Western societies. In spite of recent challenges and transformations 'modern sport and modern society still remain predominantly andrarchic' (Dunning 1999: 238).

Nevertheless, women have certainly added ambiguity and paradox (Booth 2001b) to gender relations in surfing and challenged the boundaries of acceptable female practice. There are dangers involved in the pursuit of legitimacy in surfing by moving rapidly in the direction of men's surfing style, organizational models, competitive logics and so on. Female professionals have forced the patriarchal order in surfing not only to notice them, but also to accommodate them. However, they do remain subordinated in the gender order in surfing by emulating the men, and their co-option into the male-dominated institutions has enshrined this in bureaucratic legitimacy (through the ISA, etc.). Symbolically, the emulation precedent is evident in other sports (soccer, rugby union, cricket, etc.) that keep the symbolic comparison between men and women alive and with it the sociobiological spectre that is deployed to reduce complex social phenomena to simplistic understandings of biological difference. Co-option into a male sphere of activity has also challenged and changed *male* surfing culture as it has been forced to recognize the quality of the elite female surfer. Moreover, following Demetriou (2001) it is also important to consider that as a hegemonic bloc masculinities are capable of reorganizing and finding new ways to retain overall dominance in the gender order. He continues:

> We are used to seeing a masculine power that is a closed, coherent, and unified totality that embraces no otherness, no contradiction. This is an illusion that must be done away with because it is precisely through its hybrid and apparently contradictory content that hegemonic masculinity reproduces itself.
>
> (Demetriou 2001: 355)

Henderson's (2001) analysis provides one such example, the masculine backlash in media publications such as *Tracks'* attempts to defend the masculinized space represented by 'hardcore' surfing. Another example in this chapter has been the commercialization of women's surfing in ways that appeal to the male gaze of the heterosexual female body and a further one is the drive towards ever bigger waves, which also represents a reassertion and extension of the male surfer's heroic masculine position of dominance. The struggle over this gendered territory (both material and symbolic) will doubtless be an ongoing and, at times, a desperate one as surfers seek to lay claim to an experiential territory that has become such a valuable cultural commodity.

In conclusion, this chapter has maintained that a gender power relational view of surfing, and the overall positioning of these relations within a broader gender order, with a hierarchical dynamic, is a fruitful and insightful framework in which to understand gender in surfing. It has identified that there is a gender order in surfing and that, in turn, surfing takes places within a broader world gender order, especially through connection with the institutions of sport. Furthermore, it has been emphasized that these gender orders, and the gender identities of individual surfers within them, *are not fixed*. Gender is relatively fluid, contested, embodied, interpreted and enacted. However, Messner's (1992) play on words is useful for surfing, he reminds us that gender 'power is at play'. Hegemonic masculinity still remains the dominant force in surfing, and this is important because other ways of experiencing surfing are subordinated and marginalized in relation to it. It is important to remember that these dynamics have very real consequences for the lives and identities of men and women alike.

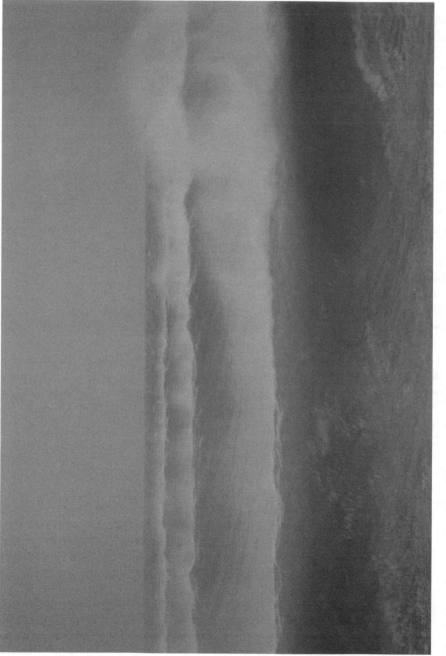

*Plate 1  Lines of corduroy* Howling offshore winds and plumes of spray as sizeable walls hold up with feathering lips. A moment of the Romantic sublime. For a surfer facing such a set of lines, there is the somewhat worrying recognition that they are about to be hammered in succession, with each wave sapping more energy and breath. Fistral, Newquay, UK. Photo: Kerstin Finke. Kerstin is a one-woman surf photography phenomenon. She takes surfing shots most days and places the best of them on her website – www.kfishsurf.com/

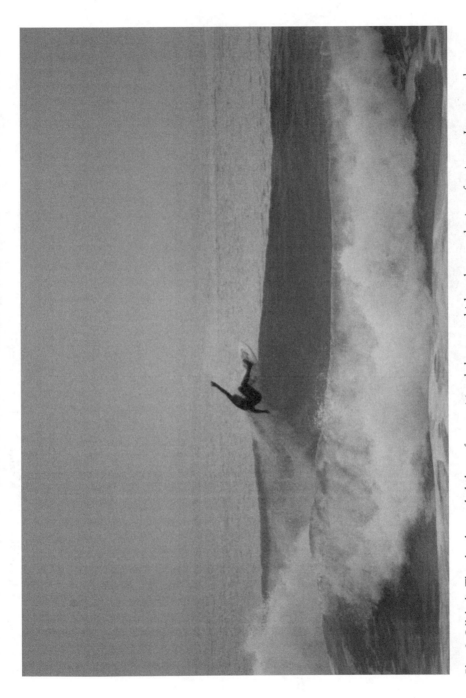

*Plate 2 Off-the-lip* This shot has a whole host of compositional elements which make up a classic surfing image. It captures the moment as the surfer is about to turn off-the-lip, silhouette of elegant posture, a single figure with merging openness of sea and sky behind. Fistral, Newquay, UK. Photo: Kerstin Finke.

*Plate 3 Getting 'air'* Capturing the spectacular moment of an 'air', the shot enhanced by the outstretched arms and the interplay of observation between the rider and the surfer paddling out, possibly just about to 'duck dive' beneath the breaking wave. 'Airs' are a good example of manoeuvres adopted by surfers in crossover from cognate pursuits, such as skateboarding. This surfer is probably about to wipe out. Justin Irons, Fistral, Newquay, UK. Photo: Kerstin Finke.

*Plate 4 The craft of surfboard making* While a few manufacturers have grown to corporate scale, all over the world most surfboard makers are fairly small scale, craft operations. 'C.J.', Newquay, UK. Photo: Kerstin Finke.

*Plate 5 Tropical perfection* Sorake (meaning in the local language 'the point with the pealing wave'), Nias, Indonesia. A pointbreak around which various narratives have been interwoven, such as paradise found, paradise lost. Set in a corner of an island with a fast-receding megalithic culture, becoming a honeypot for travelling surfers, and in recent years becoming one of the many sites for the development of indigenous Indonesian surfing. Photo: Nick Ford, 1996.

*Plate 6  Crowding at surfbreaks* It is very striking that the vast majority of surfing photographs show just one or possibly two surfers in the frame. And yet this picture captures something of the reality of most surfer's daily experience, hustling for waves, dropping in, seeking to avoid other surfers paddling out in front of the ride. Even this picture obviously does not convey the real scale of crowding at many popular, urban surfbreaks, where there may be hundreds out on good days. Fistral, Newquay, UK. Photo: Kerstin Finke.

*Plate 7 Old school/new school* The shot graphically illustrates the contrasting styles and use of the body of the more relaxed longboard surfing and the totally engaged, ever-turning, contemporary small board surfing. Guy Morgan and Simon Parish, Fistral, Newquay, UK. Photo: Kerstin Finke.

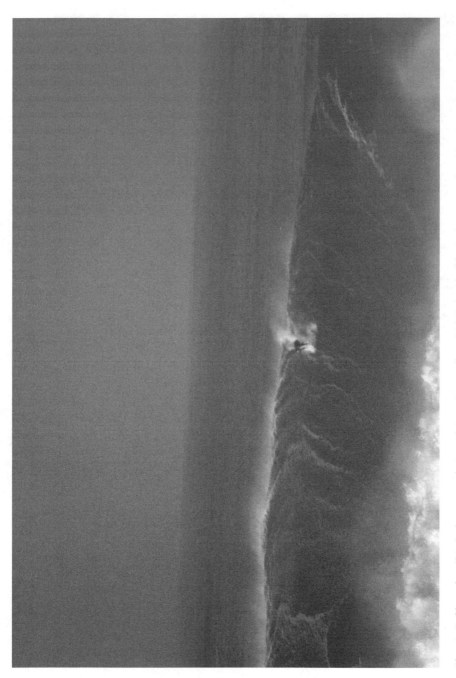

*Plate 8 Cribbar take off* A fairly routine day's surfing in Cornwall . . . NOT. South African big waverider, Chris Bertish takes off on a massive Cribbar wave, December 2004. The Cribbar (sometimes misspelt Cribber in surfing magazines) has a legendary status as probably the biggest wave in the UK. It breaks over rocks off North Pentire Head, Newquay. Photo: Kerstin Finke.

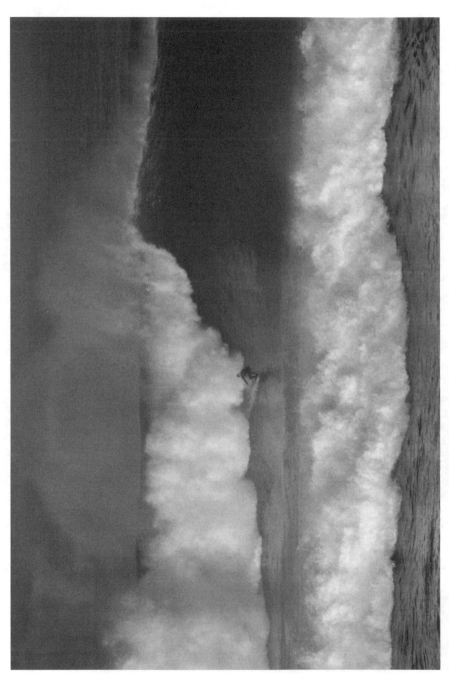

*Plate 9 Cribbar bottom turn* Chris Bertish about to make a bottom turn, on the Cribbar, (continued from Plate 8). Photo: Kerstin Finke.

# 6 Surfing and surfed bodies
## The embodiment of surfing

Surfing, the act of standing upright on a board and guiding it across the face of a breaking wave, is a form of dance in which the board rider, or surfer, 'dances' to and with a natural energy form.

(Booth 2003: 315–336)

## Introduction

The surfer's body is very much an absent presence (Leder 1990; Shilling 2003) in surfing culture, as with the quote above it is always there, but rarely made explicit. So long as they are functioning as they should, surfers' bodies normally remain absent, although on the occasions that they do go wrong they, like most performing bodies 'dys-appear' (Leder 1990), in that the 'mal-functioning' body becomes obvious through its own presence. However, in order to understand the social significance of the body in surfing there is a need to make the body visible and place it centre stage. This begins with descriptions of the qualities of the surfing body. Surfers' bodies are typically able-bodied, mesomorphic, especially those of competitive surfers (Lowdon 1980), they are lithe, almost catlike in their flexibility, and enact high levels of skill that are demonstrated through the rapid application of pre-learned moves to new 'open' skill situations. Surfers' bodies tend to work best off a low centre of gravity, with gymnast-like body dynamics that are enhanced by low levels of body fat and high levels of body strength to weight ratio, energy and stamina in the water. Surfing bodies are aquatic bodies, they must swim and dive well using oxygen efficiently when underwater. They must they feel at home in the water, in fact they must love the water. Above all, surfing bodies must be creative performing bodies that continually assemble dance-like patterns of movement across a wave. However, these bodies only depict a small fraction of the bodies that surf and are surfed. While many other body types may in reality more accurately reflect the fuller spectrum of bodies that actually surf, the qualities of the bodies articulated above form the basis of the idealized conception of the competent surfer, be they competitive, soul, or one of the many other stylized types of surfing bodies that are constantly being created since surfing was resuscitated by Western practitioners at the turn of the last century.

Given the centrality of the 'performing' body in surfing culture, it is a little surprising that, to date, very little work in research into surfing has focused more explicitly on the socialized body or embodiment. This is particularly relevent given that, as Shilling (2001: 328) points out, 'sociological studies of the body have established themselves as a significant sub-discipline and as having made a general contribution to sociological theory'.

The main purpose of this chapter is to highlight the potential of bringing the body into the study of surfing and to offer some glimpses of a range of insights that an embodied view of surfing might help to generate. However, this task is undertaken with a number of caveats, first, detailed theoretical examinations and critiques of perspectives of the body in society have been expertly conducted elsewhere (a few notable examples would include, Turner 1984; Featherstone 1991; Shilling 2003, 2005; Burkitt 1999; Williams and Bendelow 1998; Crossley 2001; Howson 2003) and these will not be replicated here. More modestly, the purpose of this analysis is to show how a few perspectives might begin to be applied to the study of surfing and the surfed body. Second, while understandings of the body, embodiment and its relationship with society and nature are by no means conceptually agreed, there are a few key points of general consensus that are worthy of mention at the outset of this chapter, as they 'frame' the underlying orientation in this chapter. The nature and degree of the relationships between the biological and the social body remain key topics for debate (see, for example, Newton 2003; Williams 2003). The overlapping and interleaving of the natural and the social body make it very difficult to assess the extent to which the biological body is in fact formed, internally and externally as a result of both single and multi-generation social processes (Burkitt 1999).

Subsequently, these relationships are best seen as dynamic and therefore the search for answers to the nature or nurture question is increasingly being seen as indicating a misguided focus. Rather, social thinkers increasingly consider the body as a simultaneously biological *and* social phenomenon (Shilling 2003). This position refocuses the questioning to consider as central, the issue of the *relationship between* the 'natural' and the 'social'. Third, the lived, material body remains elusive (Radley 1995; Shilling 2005), and is constantly at risk of disappearing behind its discursive, textual representations, which while powerful (such as the perspective offered by Michel Foucault's work 1977, 1980) often maintain rather than challenge the mind–body dualisms so evident in social science approximations of the body (Burkitt 1999). In the latter regard, this chapter does inevitably at times 'lose' the presence of the lived body as it becomes obfuscated by theoretical lenses.

Far from being some kind of genetic or social 'script' that deterministically unfolds throughout life, or indeed emerges as some formless entity that is entirely 'constructed' by society, the body is seen as having its own properties and agency, yet simultaneously being 'unfinished at birth' (Bourdieu 1984; Shilling 2003). Subsequently, the process of 'finishing' our bodies in and through practical activities such as surfing must become an important and central focus. This is especially so, as the practice of surfing is an activity that sculpts the body with often only limited intentional 'exercise'; it is a practice that materially inscribes itself into and onto the body (scars the surface) and as such becomes the 'surfed body'. It is also a relevant focus in terms of the nature of the surfing body that becomes the target of commercial processes, where the external body is finished through the consumption of lifestyle- and identity-enhancing products (Featherstone 1987).

In the following sections, three broad perspectives are drawn on that help to illuminate how the surfing body might become 'finished' (of course, the body can never be 'finished' in any absolute sense, it is more a process of refinement). Nevertheless, surfers do have a surfing 'career', bounded by time in which to maximize this refinement in relation to surfing activities. Each of these perspectives helps to raise awareness of the body's involvement (active and passive) in a number of what Goffman (1983) refers to as 'domains of activity', in which the body is productive and 'lived'. These are:

1 the practical body
2 the interacting body
3 the storied body.

It should be qualified that there is a myriad of alternative perspectives that could be drawn on and that the rationale for these lies in their structurationist leanings in the sense that all of these perspectives view a body in society that is both active and passive and body–mind integrated rather than body–mind separated. Furthermore, each of these elements is separated for analytical purposes only, and clearly surfers will experience practice, interaction and story as overlapping dimensions. In certain respects this responds to Shilling's (2005: 1) concern that the body is a 'multidimensional medium for the constitution of society'.

Each of the following sections introduces a range of conceptual 'tools', 'frameworks' or 'heuristics' from theorists whose work arguably constitutes a major input into developing these ways of viewing the body to date. In so doing, each perspective is briefly put to work to highlight some potential insights they may provide for the study of the surfing body. These three sections are followed by a rejoinder that any analysis of the surfing body and the embodiment of surfing will need to be open to an eclectic approach. However, such acts of eclecticism need to be principled and that principle might most usefully be premised around the search for ever more 'authentic' representations of the 'lived body', that is practical, emotional and simultaneously enabled and constrained by itself and its environment. The applications to surfing in this chapter necessarily revisit a number of themes including for instance, surfing lifestyles, habitus, subcultural capital, competition for waves and localism, which have been discussed in Chapters 3 and 4. However, the focus here is to build on the forenoted discussions to explore them in terms of the 'lived body'.

## Practical bodies: the logic of surfing practice

As has been suggested above, the body is 'finished' through practice. Moreover, one of the most tangible perspectives of surfing is that it is, above all, a practical activity. At the core of surfing culture is the simultaneous pursuit of practical waveriding experience and competence. Surfers immerse their bodies into particular practical engagements with the world that leave their own indelible marks on the body. In this way the body is not only the surfing body but also *the surfed body*, in the sense similar to Lewis's (2001) climbing bodies, that surfing practice *inscribes* the body with experience. These experiential inscriptions, conditionings or infoldings then provide a practical resource that the surfer draws on in future actions. Moreover, these inscriptions also form the practical basis of the construction of identity, by providing meaning and value through the surfing body.

Perhaps the most refined perspective of the practical body currently available is that developed by sociologist Pierre Bourdieu. His conceptual framework is particularly useful because it provides an explanation of the body as constituted in surfing practice and also contextualizes the value of the practical body in an embodied cultural economy of surfing practice. The perspective relies on a three-way practical relationship of field, habitus, capital, that collectively combine to provide a *logic of practice*, as Bourdieu (1990) refers to it. It should be remembered that Bourdieu was seeking to develop for his own use (initially) a perspective that bridged the gap 'between objective social conditions and the subjectivity of human agency' (Harvey and Sparks 1991: 171). Bourdieu's bodies are very much 'feeling' and aesthetic bodies, with the body formed and constantly reformed through everyday practice:

> The theory of practice as practice insists, contrary to popular positivist materialism, that the objects of knowledge are constructed, not passively recorded, and, contrary to intellectualist idealism, that the principle of this construction is the system of structured, structuring dispositions, the habitus, which is constituted in practice and is always oriented towards practical functions.
>
> (Bourdieu 1990: 52)

According to this perspective, practical logics have idiosyncrasies that can be applied to any identifiable field of human activity, but only make complete sense in relation to that field of activity that produces and gives them value. Therefore, the social logic of surfing revolves around surfing practices that, over time, inscribe or condition the body (habitus) in ways that then have a social (relating to social institutions), cultural (relating to ways of living), economic (relating to material wealth) and symbolic (relating to an association to something else that is invisible) exchange value in a cultural economy of groups of people that share a common interest in these practices (the field). In this way, surfing practices, bodies and their relative values only make 'real' sense in practical relation to one another and to surfing. The strength of this perspective is in the way the material body and its inscription through practice becomes a driver for how we orientate ourselves in our social worlds.

One of the many observations of surfing culture is that it is a way of life more than a sporting or leisure pursuit. However, moving beyond the stereotypical depictions, underpinning this way of life are the practices of surfing that only make sense when a person becomes involved in surfing. Therefore, while life*style* may usefully depict the 'gloss' that people add to their already made life choices, surfing as a way of life is constructed around the often mundane everyday logics presented by *doing the activity*. As discussed in Chapter 4, for example, the regular surfer must learn to watch the weather and find ways of checking the surf conditions, whether this is by surf forecasts on radio, TV, the internet, the coastguard or by being able to read the conditions firsthand. Most surfers must schedule these predicted surf up times around their working lives or take holiday to coincide with the best surf.

Many hardcore surfers pursue employment that gives them the flexibility to leave work at short notice, or take extended periods off work where they can travel and surf. Again, hardcore surfers may decide to move as near as possible to the surf. Added to this is another series of logics in terms of the actual surfing practice (negotiating crowded surf breaks, making the wave, 'deciding' how far to push one's technical ability on a given wave, adapting to different weather conditions, etc.). These, and a host of other practical logical 'problems' and the finite number of responses to them, inevitably shape the subcultures of surfing that are seen around the world. The following discussion articulates some of these logics in a little more detail and in so doing explores how the practical logic of surfing inscribes itself into and onto the body.

## Surfing practice and the development of habitus

Surfing as social practice is both reproductive and generative because it requires pre-existing structures (boards, waves, techniques, competitions, etc.) and yet these structures cannot be seen as 'objective' because they have to be interpreted and 'lived' before they can be appropriated and passed on by any peer or surf instructor in a number of potential ways. That said, the practical transmission of surfing knowledge, competency and legitimacy become embodied through a repeated practical engagement with the world. The result of this practical engagement is the creation of a form of 'habitus', that is a disposition resulting from a series of practical *conditionings*. In order to make better definitional sense of this term it is worth considering Bourdieu's (1990) own usage of the term in relation to social class:

> The conditionings associated with a particular class of conditions of existence produce habitus, systems of durable, transposable dispositions, structured structures predisposed to function as structuring structures, that is, as prin-ciples which generate and organise practices and representations that can be objectively adapted to their outcomes without presupposing a conscious aiming at ends or an express mastery of the operations necessary in order

to attain them. Objectively 'regulated' and 'regular' without being in any way the product of obedience to rules, they can be collectively orchestrated without being the product of the organising action of a conductor.

(Bourdieu 1990: 53)

Through their sustained practical engagement with the rules, knowledges and physical practices of the surfing field, surfers come to inscribe certain qualities into and onto their bodies that begin to define them as surfers and also begin to orientate them towards engaging with the social world in particular ways that will further define them as surfers to themselves and others. As argued above, these orientations only make sense in relation to surfing. Thus, while windsurfing may share some fundamental logics that have to do with the engagement with the water, the dynamics of that engagement are quite different (such as the relationship with the wind, the surf, the technologies and so on). To this end, the relationship between the field and surfing and what might be cautiously termed 'surfing habitus' is critical. Some illustrations are worthy of pursuing here. The surfing habitus is composed of a number of core dispositions that take a considerable amount of practice and time to acquire. A comprehensive outline of surfing practices is illustrated by Gabrielson's (1977/1995) *The Complete Surfing Guide for Coaches* that includes a compendium of practices, making it an insight into the construction of a habitus. Gabrielson begins the section on learning to surf as follows:

> Learning how to stand up on a board is not an easy thing to do. In addition, simply learning to paddle out through rough breaking waves, sit on a board outside, and then paddle into a wave takes considerable balance, strength, endurance, wave knowledge, and patience. Since these techniques take time and practice to learn, the beginner should not be expected to have success the first time out.
>
> (Gabrielson 1995: 4.1)

These qualities would seem to be fundamental to the surfing body. However, as practice inscribes itself upon the body *its* possibilities alter. Most obviously is the way in which the surfer, in practising their way from basic technique to surfer stylist, must learn to 'feel' their way into extending their surfing technique, through being self-reflexive about looking at their surfing style, gaining feedback from others, experimenting with different boards and finally seeking the experience of practice on different waves. In this final point in particular, Gabrielson implicitly anticipates habitus; he comments:

> The final way to improve style is with lots of practice in various conditions. Surf big Hawaiian waves in the winter, point breaks, quick reef breaks, beach breaks, and close beach breaks or shorebreaks. Each break type will contribute its own characteristics to your overall style.
>
> (Gabrielson 1995: 4.4)

The experiential imprint of a particular type of wave inscribes itself on the body, augmenting the habitus and extending the body's ability to feel its way in different surf conditions. It is in this way that we can come to consider the body as a *surfed* body. This differentiated conditioning of body is also typified by the 'old' and 'new' schools of surfing styles (see Plate 7) and such distinctions become increasingly evident and culturally important as surfers progress beyond the basics. Therefore, as Laberge and Sankoff (1988: 270) conclude, 'habitus, then, is both the internalization of the conditions of existence and the practice-generating principle of social agents'. Bourdieu (1990) clarifies this practical mediation in the following:

> The relation to the body is a fundamental dimension of the *habitus* that is inseparable from a relation to language and to time. It cannot be reduced to a 'body image' or even a 'body concept'. . . . This is firstly because all the schemes of perception and appreciation in which a group deposits its funda-mental structures, and the schemes of expression through which it provides them with the beginnings of objectification and therefore reinforcement, intervene between the individual and his/her body.
>
> (Bourdieu 1990: 73–74)

Through the application of those schemes in practice they become incorporated into the body; this represents an investment in the body. Furthermore, the process by which these schemes are acquired by the body is a practical mimesis which differs from imitation due to the lack of conscious effort involved in the reproduction of a gesture or action. He clarifies this by stating that, 'What is "learned by the body" is not something that one has, like knowledge that can be brandished, but something that one is' (1990: 73).

Bourdieu developed the term 'interpellation' from Althusser's (1983) ideolog-ical usage and linked it to the body through the habitus, to show how the socialized body becomes a *source* for social processes (see Shilling 2005). Loosely translated in this context it means 'called to order' or 'hailed' in embodied ways. In this way, the schemes of dispositions that constitute the surfer's habitus, are generative because, once inscribed into the body, these practical dispositions are responsive to external stimuli. Over time, a relationship between the developing surfer's habitus and the practical surfing world around them becomes stronger, more logical, until eventually the body begins to feel itself being 'hailed' by the surf. Many surfers implicitly acknowledge being hailed by the sea, especially when surf's up, or when the surf is not up but when they see images of good surf. While most surfers are mainly hailed by the presence of the real sea, even images can provide a powerful call to order as the following extract from surf writer Craig Coombs (2005) reveals in his response to looking at pictures of big waves even with no real surf outside:

> The picture on this page gets me so amped for a barrel I can't even sit still. Just looking at it makes me want to jump up and run around yelling . . .

because that is all I can do. Right now it's night time, it's cold and windy out, and even if I were up for a moonsurf the moon isn't out and the waves suck. So I wait. That's the thing about surfing . . . we wait only upon Nature, but while we wait we are helpless. Sure we can work out, watch surf vids, stare longingly into pictures of perfect, pitching lips, imagining ourselves grabbing that rail and pulling in. For the briefest moment the neurotransmitters flash through our bodies and we are there, driving through the barrel. But the daydream is never enough . . . we need that which only Mother Ocean can provide. So we wait.

(Coombs 2005)

Clearly, it is not just surfers who are hailed by the sea, but it is normally only surfers who are hailed to particular waves to perform on them specific surfing practices of the sort described above. While the embodied metaphors contained here will be considered later in the chapter, it is worth pointing out that typically there is no simulation, only the material and physical satisfaction of the practical experience, which in turn reinforces the habitus – and so it goes on.

The practical logics that sustain surfing subcultures are, therefore, embedded in the body in the form of habitus. The socially constructed habitus of many surfers will be the principle driver orientations towards the core practices of surfing waves. For example, choices of a board purchased and prepared, surf selected and a waveridden, and the style of the ride, are made on the basis of practically orientated dispositions that have already become inscribed in the body and subsequently take place without overtly direct conscious awareness of the principles that guide them. This is translated into consumer practices. As consumers, surfers buy what they can afford to obtain the best surf they can – it is important to remember that surfers are seeking surf experience. To employ Bourdieu's often used metaphor, these people are demonstrating a 'feel' for the game – but that 'feel' is anything but 'natural' in a pre-social sense. He continues:

When the properties and movements of the body are socially qualified, the most fundamental social choices are naturalised and the body with its properties and movements, is constituted as an analogical operator establishing all kinds of practical equivalences among the different divisions of the social world.

(Bourdieu 1990: 71)

The next subsection considers the value and potential for conversion of the surfing habitus, within the field of surfing.

## Accumulating and converting surfing physical capital

These experiences, and their material manifestations through the surfing habitus, are both seen and given value by other surfers (and surf judges, potential sponsors, etc.) in ways that form part of what might be considered *physical capital*.

Furthermore, while the dedicated soul surfer and surfer athlete alike exhibit similarities of habitus as a result of the generic material inscription of surfing practice on the body, there are also significant differences. Therefore, just as the practice varies so does the type of surfed body that results and some marked points of distinction are manifest, as a result of using different boards, styles of surfing, techniques of surfing, styles of talk and dress, training methods, diet, etc. The precise degree of *value* or physical capital that a surfer athlete, soul surfer or any other kind of surfer may possess will differ in relation to the various subsectors of the field of surfing they occupy and the current value of these subsectors in relation to the dominant legitimate norm of the social period in question. Therefore, Duke Kahanamoku's habitus produced a physical capital based on an expertise with heavy longboards. While legendary, this form of physical capital does not convert well in later generations where expertise in finned shortboards is the most prized form of surfing physical capital.

Therefore, what surfing (physical) capital is and its conversion value as an embodied quality (see Edwards and Imrie 2003) only makes sense in relation to the field of surfing more broadly. The surfing field is like other fields, areas of social life in which certain groups identify and structure practices, for example sport, art and education, politics and the economy. Lash (1990) considers fields to be Bourdieu's 'structures' whereas, Shilling (2003: 138) has described fields as 'dynamic organising principles'. Fields enjoy varying degrees of reliance on and autonomy from other fields. But to be defined as a field all must have some identifiable form and function and, above all, as Bourdieu (1993b) considers, that, 'in order for field to function, there have to be stakes and people prepared to play the game, endowed with the habitus that implies knowledge and recognition of the immanent laws of the field, the stakes, and so on' (Bourdieu 1993b: 72). Therefore, the field of surfing might be said to contain structures (surfing associations, etc.), rules, knowledge, practices and crucially *people*, as it is *within* and *through* people that surfing knowledge and practice are brought together, 'lived', given value and ultimately transmitted to other people largely through bodies and the practical logics that dictate our actions in relation to the social fields we occupy; Bourdieu (1990) elucidates:

> An institution, even an economy, is fully complete and viable only if it is durably objectified not only in things, that is, in logic, transcending individual agents, of a particular field, but also in bodies, in durable dispositions to recognise and comply with the demands immanent in the field.
>
> (Bourdieu 1990: 58)

There is neither the space nor warrant to pursue a more detailed application of field theory to the field of surfing here (for further applications see Lash 1990, 1993a, Brown 2005). However, it is useful to consider briefly, the habitus – capital – field relation of surfing to two of the 'six primary styles' of surfing identified by Booth (2003). The emergence of what might be determined the sub-field of *soul surfing* in the 1960s was very much a product of shifts in the broader social fields.

Postwar full employment in the United States had created unprecedented economic prosperity, the now familiar mantras of individualism, consumerism and hedonism were increasing along with a wealth of leisure goods. At the same time there was a growing disillusion with the political tensions of the Cold War and the increasingly obvious environmental destruction that people were recognizing came with capitalist late modernity. At that time (1960s to early 1970s) many novitiate surfers found an experience in surfing practices (and its logics) that helped them articulate and construct an alternative, counter-cultural lifestyle that illustrated practically their feelings of rejection for the consequences of global-ization, cultural imperialism and modernization. Many, therefore, began to load that experience with the values that expressed a rejection of the dominant social norms of the time. However, this example helps us to see that the tensions within the field of surfing, the soul surfing generation as it came to be known, with its powerfully stereotyped drug culture and anti-competitive, anti-establishment ethos led to a backlash from those in other surfing subcultures who considered surfing practices could and should be interpreted as being a more 'socially legiti-mate' activity. One of these practices, competitive surfing, gives value to a slightly different kind of body, one that is increasingly technologically invested with the disciplines of sport science, a 'clean' living body that buys into (or at least does not challenge) the Western, capitalist, meritocratic, competitive, individualist model (that competitive surfing uses for its underpinning structure), and, of course, a body that is media 'friendly', in ways that symbolize the above. Competitive surfing as a sport was thus born and, in many ways, continues to stand in *symbolic* juxtaposition to soul surfing. The field of surfing therefore, is comprised of a number of sub-fields, all of which give value to the practised, surfed body in subtly different ways and these manifest themselves through surfing styles. Moreover, these sub 'fields' have distinct practices, institutions and practitioners with subtle, but important, distinctions in their habitus that command different degrees of capital conversion. The sub-fields continue to struggle for 'prestige' as Booth (2003) describes, or embodied 'distinction' and sociocultural 'legitimacy' as Bourdieu might have put it. These struggles provide some of the tensions and disjunctures that lead to social change in surfing.

Within these contested fields the accumulation and conversion of the relevant form of physical capital is a process that takes a considerable amount of time. As detailed above, prolonged practical engagement in particular fields gives rise to states of embodiment or *habitus*. Habitus has different degrees of legitimacy and value that become commodified as *physical capital* in relation to a given field or sector of it. This physical capital is then transferred or converted into other forms of capital, which Bourdieu (1990) categorizes as generally falling into social capital (structured acknowledgement of status, e.g. awards, positions, offices, etc.); cultural capital (not structured but 'common' acknowledgement of status – the 'people's hero'; a surfer's surfer, etc.); economic capital (renumeration for valued services rendered in relation to the field); symbolic capital (visual, material con-structions that normally show a particular value in relation to the field). Bourdieu's perspective allows surfing viewers to 'see' the surfer's body a little differently, it also prompts the viewer to consider their own schemes of perception (i.e. what am I looking for that constitutes 'value' or 'quality?').

All surfers who come to invest in their surfing bodies through practice acquire physical capital (all have some, and clearly some a lot more than others!) and can begin to 'transfer' or 'convert' this capital into other forms of capital. The specific example of Kelly Slater is appropriate here as he is often seen as the ultimate competitive male surfer athlete to date, but also an intelligent athlete with certain soul surfing sensibilities. Moreover, his life story also depicts more graphically than most the development of habitus, and the accumulation and conversion of physical capital. Slater was born into a surfing family, in a surfing hot spot (Cocoa Beach, Florida, USA). A life that revolved around the water (his father was a professional lifeguard, surfer and keen fisherman) meant that Kelly began developing a habitus that quite literally immersed him in the sea and water all his life. By the age of five he was surfing, he entered and won his first competition at eight. By age ten he had accumulated enough physical capital to have earned his right to compete in the subcultural pecking order (amongst older, more experienced expert surfers) on some of the most competitive, space-scarce waves in Florida, such as Sebastian Inlet. As a result of the experience, his habitus developed and his physical capital increased still further. As a consequence, Slater again converted his capital, through being noticed and accepted as a student of one of the best surf coaches in the area, Dave Catri, a man who would know how best to develop and refine his surfing habitus. Following victory in a local competition soon afterwards, Slater again converted capital by winning a local tournament which allowed him to convert his growing physical capital into more cultural status (child superstar surfer in the making), but also economic conversion (an expenses-paid trip to surf in Hawaii). The 12-year-old boy therefore, was given the opportunity to surf bigger, and *heavier*, waves and so develop his surfing habitus through further practice, which in turn further enhanced his physical capital.

Slater continued developing and converting capital until he was the youngest world ASP tour pro winner at the age of 20. He had also converted this capital into social and economic capital by becoming a media celebrity, when he converted his physical capital as a young male surfer for a role in the TV show *Baywatch* (Slater is blessed with 'classic' good looks to match his Western aesthetically proportioned surfed body). More recently, in between winning world championships, Slater converted his physical capital into further economic/cultural capital by a series of exclusive photo-shoots (a highly valued cultural activity for surfers) in exotic locations on perfect waves. Finally, as an intelligent man with a penchant for social comment, Slater has attracted a slightly different degree of social and cultural capital for speaking out on issues as diverse as the futility of war, the excesses of capitalism and so on. Perhaps ironically (with no disrespect intended to the quality of his commentary), Slater's bodily performance provides the symbolic capital platform for the airing of his equally agile mind. As surfers will understand, the professional competitive world of surfing is a small and elite one and the vast majority of surfers do not compete. Nevertheless, in this increasingly mediatized synoptical subculture, these surfer athletes are clearly also increasingly iconic, and the potential for demonstrating *certain* qualities of the surfing habitus and physical capital is considerable.

While Slater is perhaps the most elite example of the conversion of physical capital in surfing of his generation, some of his 'acts of conversion' are regularly shared by many surfer competitors and non-competitors alike. For example, many surfers use their earnings for surfing travel, which constitutes a common form of investment in surfing. This in turn is converted into cultural capital through the development of a more 'authentic' or 'legitimate' surfing habitus by learning the 'feel' of different waves and incorporating that back into the surfing habitus. To have surfed certain places and waves is also part of the global folklore of surfing. Moreover, to surf regularly is also part of the process of surfing distinction.

There is one further example of the conversion of physical capital in surfing culture that warrants a brief illustration due to its important implications: the art, craft and science of the surfboard shaper. 'Shapers' of surfboards are usually also surfers. Shapers such as 'Art' Brewer and Greg Noll had already converted their surfing physical capital into cultural capital in terms of their surfing prowess (they are both legends of twentieth-century surfing (Kampion, 2003). Noll now converts his physical capital into the creation of handcrafted longboards out of traditional Hawaiian materials. Brewer still converts his physical capital into designing surfboards that enhance the surfing performance when riding big waves. He famously built and tested cutting-edge designs on big waves and as Kampion (2003: 51) puts it, 'credibility in the water helped build credibility on the beach'. Indeed, Brewer's boards have since been ridden by experts, champions and pioneers. Both men eventually gave up the physical act of surfing but could not and did not want to give up surfing altogether, as Noll explains:

> And you know, I'm getting up in my years and I'm not actively surfing, so I'm kind of a slug and this is my way of staying connected with the sport. I don't care, until you die, once you're involved in surfing it never gets completely out of your bloodstream.
>
> (Noll 2001: 26)

Both of these men in their different ways are drawing on their habitus of surfing and *converting* it into the production of surfboards. The surfing competence they demonstrated buys them recognition and respect for their products that are inspired by and born out of the experience inscribed onto their surfed bodies. This experience is quite literally present in the material objects they produce and as such it commands a high price that secures their financial futures through converting a physical capital that is long since exhausted in direct performance terms into an economic capital that is, nevertheless, still a resource of embodied creative potential.

Finally, all of these individuals mentioned become agents of the transmission and reconstruction of practice, habitus and valued forms of capital to the next generation of surfers. The same can be said for surf writers, coaches, teachers, surf artists and musicians who draw on their surfing habitus to inspire the performance of surfing itself. As such something of an embodied genealogy of surfers would make an enterprising application of this perspective, in order to consider, which particular forms of habitus are passed on through different practices and the manner of their transmission.

## Interacting bodies: performing surfing

On the surface, surfers may seem to be engaged in a classically individualist pursuit. The second fundamental observation of the surfing and surfed body is that it constantly and significantly *interacts* with other bodies, selves, objects and its environment. This perspective opens up a parallel yet interlinked view of the surfing and surfed body to the practical body. As such, the surfing body can be said to be an 'interacting' body. The perspective that remains full of potential for insights of this nature is that of *symbolic interactionism*, which Blumer (1962) clarifies as follows:

> The term 'symbolic interaction' refers, of course, to the peculiar and dis-tinctive character of interaction as it takes place between human beings. This peculiarity consists in the fact that human beings interpret or 'define' each others' actions. Their 'response' is not made directly to the actions of another but instead is based on the meaning which they attach to such actions. Thus, human interaction is mediated by the use of symbols, by interpretation, or by ascertaining the meaning of one another's actions. This mediation is equivalent to inserting a process of interpretation between stimulus and response in the case of human behaviour.
>
> (Blumer 1962: 180)

Although not the founder of symbolic interactionism, Erving Goffman's inter-actionist work is often celebrated because of his perspicacity of observation that frequently incorporated the interacting body into his own development of the symbolic interactionist perspective. It is also worth considering, as Collins (1979: 189) reminds us, that while Goffman used symbolic interactionism as a focus he 'transformed the explanation of these phenomena in a strongly Durkheimian direction', thus providing greater connection with broader social structures that many of his interactionist colleagues tended to ignore (Maines 2001), preferring instead to consider human behaviour as if it were taking place in a sociocultural vacuum. Furthermore, his preoccupation with the interrelationships of 'self', agency, choice, morality and existence has led Lofland (1980), amongst others, to juxtapose his work with prominent existentialist thinkers such as Jean-Paul Sartre. To this end, Lofland (1980: 46) further notes that, 'for Goffman, action is being. To engage in a particular kind of activity is to be that kind of person'. Following this it is legitimate to ask what kind of person is it that engages in surfing, how does this involve their body, and how can Goffman's constructs illuminate this?

### Managing the surfing self-identity – a surfing body idiom?

Like most interactionists, Goffman places the individual at the centre of his analysis and focuses on human agency, and the dynamic in his viewpoint is relatively straightforward and applicable in the observation of everyday life. Put simply, individuals must manage their sense of self in everyday encounters with people, objects and environments. Goffman distinguishes between social (virtual) identity and self (actual) identity (although 'actual' refers not to an absolute sense of self, but to the identity that individuals think they have and/or want to have). These identities are mutually interdependent as the identity an individual thinks he/she has will form the basis for their social performance in which their virtual social identity will be assessed. Conversely, the feedback a person receives about who they are perceived to be will have significant effects on their actual social identity. Any small disjunctures between actual and virtual identities can lead to embarrassment for the individual but are often repairable and do not affect self-identity in the long term. However, if social (virtual) identity is judged by others to be generally unsatisfactory then individuals can become stigmatized and their social identity will undergo a dramatic shift (becoming a 'spoiled' identity) that can then damage and forcibly alter their self (actual) identity.

The management of a surfing self is a complex interactional task involving, among other things, the management of one's body and its movement in and through social spaces, place and times. Furthermore, the idea that individuals 'perform' in everyday life lends a sense of the theatrical or dramaturgy to Goffman's work that is an intentional part of his perspective of the performing body–self. That surfers must perform well with their bodies is crucial if their overall identity performance is to be convincing because it is immediately visible and therefore classifiable by others. As Dyck and Archetti (2003: 10) point out, 'just as the self is embodied in performance, so is any performance an embodiment of selves'. Goffman (1971: 11) has labelled these bodily performances 'body gloss' explaining, 'by the term "externalization" or "body gloss," I refer to the process whereby an individual pointedly uses overall body gesture to make otherwise unavailable facts about his [sic] situation gleanable' (Goffman 1971: 11).

The most important 'body gloss' for a surfer is actually when waveriding. Although surfers might be motivated intrinsically by the vertigo of the activity (Chapter 8), rather like Donnelly and Young's (1988) rock climbers and rugby players they require identity confirmation by key others in the subculture as part of the construction of a surfing identity through the demonstration of the right embodied qualities while riding the wave (good balance, timing, a technical repertoire, a degree of bravado in the face of the potentially dangerous wave). The use of 'body gloss' helps surfers manage these impressions and as such can be said to be adopting a 'front', that is a presentation of the self by which an individual wishes to be perceived by others, and in so doing practically helps to develop and sustain habitus. However, it would be wrong to suggest that this 'front' is entirely conscious at all times; during waveriding, for example, there is neither the time nor the opportunity to be performing in an explicitly conscious manner. The presentation of self on the wave lays bare the surfer's self-identity.

The relative success or failure of this activity will determine an individual's sense of social identity as perceived by significant others and the individual surfer in question.

Therefore, surfers' bodies enable them to be involved in day-to-day life and the rituals of interaction that exist within a given surfing lifestyle, such as the 'search' for waves, wave-taking etiquette and the après-surf rituals of socialization. However, although individuals are seen as 'embodied', this embodiment is not autonomous because, for Goffman, interaction itself is highly structured. In *Behaviour in Public Places* (1963: 33) Goffman introduces the idea that these structured interactions operate by the use of 'shared vocabularies of body idiom'. Peoples' perceptions of bodily appearance and performance are bound up with social and cultural meanings that have been internalized through the process of 'social ritualization' that Goffman (1983: 3) describes as 'a standardization of bodily and vocal behaviour'. As Shilling (1993: 85) notes, the meanings created by, and attributed to, the interacting body, are used to classify others and for self-classification and in this sense 'we tend to perceive our bodies as if looking into a mirror which offers a reflection framed in terms of society's views and prejudices'. Within the field of sport, processes of socialization have been usefully explored by Coakley and Donnelly (1998). These processes provide opportunities and constraints on bodily actions and signals in given circumstances that give rise to the need for body management of factors including, 'bodily appearance and personal acts, dress, bearing, movement, and position, sound level, physical gestures such as waving or saluting, facial decorations and broad emotion expression' (Goffman 1963: 33).

All of these and other performances of bodily management, represent aspects of bodily behaviour which have a ritualized idiom attached to them. Consequently, social actors have an understanding of a commonly shared set of meanings that are attached to bodily behaviour. It is 'idiomatic' in the sense that these meanings are shared by both performer and observer of the behaviour. Body idiom and ritualized, normalized forms of self-expression can be seen in surfing subculture. A good synopsis of this is provided by Kampion (2003):

> Modern surfing has rich history, a unique system of rituals, distinctive language and symbolic elements, tribal hierarchies, and other unique lifestyle characteristics all of which have been broadly imitated and emulated around the world. Witness the 'shaka' hand gesture (extended pinky and thumb), praying for surf, rules of the road at surf spots, hierarchical protocols at all notable beaches, honouring of subcultural elders, related lifestyle clothing industry, and a specialized language that gives esoteric meanings to common terms such as 'green room,' 'stoke,' 'shack,' 'A-frame,' 'rip,' 'session,' and strapped.'
>
> (Kampion 2003: 59)

Most of these symbolic elements involve directly or represent aspects of *body idiom*. That body idiom has a shared set of meanings is significant for Goffman (1963:

34–35) when he states, 'Body idiom then is conventionalized discourse. We must see that in addition it is a normative one'. In terms of body idiom, an individual cannot choose to display nothing as all bodily behaviour will have its interpretation according to its normative symbolic meaning. The paradox of this is that the way to say least with one's body is to act in the way that is expected in the given situation, which is why perhaps so many novitiate surfers are so keen to 'fit in'. The body is a site of communication via a shared vocabulary and individuals use this to convey, conceal and interpret meaning in situations where two or more individuals share a presence. Rather like their linguistic metaphor, the total vocabulary of body idiom is huge indeed and, moreover, is situated within the bounds of time, space, race, culture, subculture, history, gender, etc. However, in spite of this Goffman (1963) maintains that:

> While no one in society is likely to be in a position to employ the whole expressive idiom, or even the major part of it, nevertheless everyone will possess some knowledge of the same vocabulary of body symbols. Indeed, the understanding of a common body idiom is one reason for calling an aggregate of individuals a society.
>
> (Goffman 1963: 35)

The tension here is that cross-cultural body idiom *can* differ and this leads to a problem of communication when it is encountered. In line with this perspective, the globalized subculture of surfing has many embodied interactional variations that need to be accommodated by travelling surfers as Kampion again (2003) testifies:

> At significant surf spots, the structure, rules, and strength of the local hierarchy control activity within the territory. All surfers know this. Every time we venture into a new surf spot and test a new territory, we enter into a 'force field' of hierarchy. This field might be highly organized or it could be extremely anarchic; either way, you can bet there's an organizing paradigm, and every newcomer has to 'get with it'.
>
> (Kampion 2003: 59)

Individuals in their own societies, however, tend to have the capacities to recognize and utilize the shared body idiom in ways which allow most people to meet the basic situational and contextual requirements. The notion of body management becomes a feature of interaction and is bound up with the perspective of individuals being knowledgeable actors who, wherever possible, utilize their agency. Body management, therefore, refers to the ways in which individuals manage their bodies through the sensitized application of body idiom.

## The territories of the surfing body-self: interacting with others, objects and environments

A second, body-specific construct is worth considering here. In *Relations in Public* (1971: 28–44) Goffman introduces the idea of 'territories of the self' that examines how the relationships between individuals' bodies in space are fundamental to social interaction. Goffman (1971: 42) points out that 'an egocentric territory suggests that the body is not only a preserve but also a central marker of various preserves – personal space, stall, turn, and personal effects'.

The surfing body, when seen as having a social territory, becomes a fundamental requirement of social interaction and it is therefore important not to take it for granted that interpersonal interaction will be fundamentally affected by embodied performances. Within this sensitizing concept are a number of potential sub-categories. Two worthy of identification are those of 'personal space' and 'possessional territory'.

Personal space is referred to as the 'space surrounding an individual' (1971: 29). Goffman's point here is that the fact that our bodily space may not be violated indiscriminately, and for others to enter this personal space, there is a range of contextual factors which render this an acceptable interaction or not, for example approaching a stranger and touching them is not seen as legitimate behaviour whereas bodily contact with a stranger in a lift or a busy street is to a certain degree acceptable (as long as it is either unavoidable or unintentional). On the beach and in the water in particular the surfing body requires the personal space necessary to allow itself to perform. It is possible that better surfers need and demand more space while lesser ones must make do with more confined spaces. However, it is also likely that better surfers may be more assertive (sometimes referred to as 'wave snatching') in confined spaces and crowded conditions.

Possessional territory refers to all those objects 'that can be identified with the self and arrayed around the body wherever it is' (Goffman 1971: 38). Possessions such as wetsuits, kit bags, surfboards, etc. are all possessional territory. Equally, more temporary things such as waveriding space, space in the lull, beach space and even social spaces regularly occupied by surfing groups such as pubs and cafes or beach spaces all provide significant temporary markers of self (individual or collective).

However, probably, the most fundamental example of temporary personal and possessional territory in surfing is the space that fleetingly 'belongs' to the surfer who has just committed to a wave. Here, the space around the surfing body and specifically the line they are taking on the wave become 'theirs' for the short period of the ride on that part of the wave. If, and when, others drop in on this space, there is invariably conflict ranging from mild rebuke to rather stronger forms of dissent and castigation; in short, etiquette has been broken. Moreover, in terms of an interactionist understanding, the identity of the offending surfer is called into question, and they might be said to have 'lost face'. According to etiquette, 'real' surfers do not 'drop in' on other surfers, although uncultured novitiates may and so may dominant locals who are seeking to establish their authority over 'their' waves. However, these actions are still frowned upon as discussed in greater detail in Chapter 4. In this way we can see surfing social space as policed, with wave space opening up to those who can demonstrate the skill to command a piece of this territory.

Finally, one can also view other people such as surfing family or friends as possessional territory especially in situations where one feels a sense of overriding responsibility towards or for the other. Again, the surfing fraternity can often come together in acts of collective reassurance and remembrance following the untimely death of a friend. While surfers may have a limited concern for the safety of others 'outback', this is probably not a major preoccupation. The exception to this would be those engaged in the undeniably extreme expression of the sport, of big wave surfing, who are very conscious of the safety and security of their companions.

In addition to the territoriality of the body in surfing, *artifacts* outside of the material self can act as possessions that have to be regulated and managed during social interaction; in other terms, although these are objects, surfers nevertheless *interact* with them. This is not a moot point because the ways in which surfers interact with the objects in their possession and outside their own possession (but inside their personal territory) provide significant performances of identity that will ultimately be judged by others. The best example here is, of course, the surfboard. When seen as a cultural artifact the surfboard is a critical object to interact with because it is the surfboard that facilitates very different forms of interaction with the environment (or in this case the wave). As Booth (1996b) considers:

> Throughout this century technological advances in surfboard design and materials helped transform riding style, from rigid statue-like stances, to graceful body deportment, to compact, shock-absorbing postures associated with gravity-defying aggressive maneouvers.
>
> (Booth 1996b: abstract)

Significantly, when board designers make new styles of boards they effectively evolve the potential for new interactions with the surf. A good example of this is the development of 'surfing's ultimate specialty product – the big wave gun' (Kampion 2003: 51). When these technologies were combined with the introduction of the jetski to 'tow' surfers onto giant waves that were previously moving too fast to catch, the combination of these changes facilitated interaction with waves hitherto unsurfable by a lone surfer and their 'standard' board. Therefore, the *type* of surfboard surfers choose to ride, *who* made it, and the specific *way* they choose to ride it, all contribute strongly to how they are seen by others inside and outside the subcultural group they are associated with. Therefore, as surfboards are developed, so new identities can be forged from interaction with them.

## The regionalization of body-identity performances in surfing subculture

While the territories of the self begin to facilitate the exploration of the socialized spaces and objects in those spaces with which surfing bodies must interact, it is important to consider the larger environment in which these territories and possessions are located. Indeed, to continue the illustration from above, Booth (1996b) reflects that surfboard technologies are not the only factor in the progression of surfriding styles; additionally, he considers that the beach's cultural environment must also be considered as powerful stimulant for surfer actions. He clarifies:

> Historians should not ignore the influence of beach culture on riding styles. It is no coincidence that aggressive surfing first emerged in Australia, with its highly competitive militaristic beach culture and at a time when social relations at the beach were in turmoil.
>
> (Booth 1996b: abstract)

In *Presentation of Self in Everyday Life* (1969) Goffman further develops the idea of performances and the playing out of roles in which individuals engage, in order to interact in everyday life. The behaviour is framed in relation to regions, and more specifically 'front' and 'back regions' (1969: 109–140). Front regions are situations where the individual must more consciously perform in order to maintain a desired impression of the self, and back regions represent those instances when the individual is not required to perform. Therefore, returning to Booth's (1996b) articulation above, the beach and the waves become front regions where surfers must perform. Moreover, different beaches and waves carry with them different cultures of interaction that require different embodied performances from the individuals who inhabit them. Individuals are therefore always engaged in processes of constructing and sustaining a sense of self-identity that can be enhanced by consistent performances before an audience of other surfers.

As emphasized above, the physical body and its bodily performances play a significant part in any impressions an individual wishes to give and consequently require 'face work' to present them in a way which individuals feel is representative of how they wish to be perceived socially. Therefore, the surf, specific waves, the beach and the beach bar all become 'stages' on which embodied identity performances are played out. Over time some of these performances become sedimented and culturally regulated, through invocation of moral interaction guidelines. A good example of this is provided by Kampion (2003), who describes a classic 'region' in which a particular surfing etiquette is enforced, the beach entrance:

> There's a sign – actually four wooden boards – near the stairs down to the water at Steame Lane in Santa Cruz, California. On each board is written a rule:

- First surfer on the wave has right of way.
- Paddle around wave not through it.
- Hang on to your board.
- Help other surfers.

Erected by old-school surfer Sam Reid and other devotees of a mid-twentieth-century waterman's ethic, these previously written rules evince an invisible binding force that held surf culture together in the pre- and post-World War II eras. That force has to do with respect and a shared sense of responsibility for one another and for surfing.

(Kampion 2003: 59)

The basic principles have been retained and evolved across the surfing world, in the UK for example the British Surfing Association now publishes it own surfing etiquette guidelines on the internet. In the context of surfing where the locus of the pursuit is bodywork, Goffman's interactionist perspectives provide potential for understanding the nature of embodied intention in surfing subcultures. Inter-actionism makes it clear that bodies and their presentation have a fundamental role to play in the construction of self- and social identities and the consequent successful maintenance (or not) of those identities. Finally, it should be noted that while individuals may be able to control the impressions they wish to make (within certain structural limitations) they *cannot* control the interpre-tations that others may draw from their performances. In this sense as Shilling (2003: 85) notes, individuals are 'caught in a web of communication *irrespective* of individual intentions'. While individuals are implicitly aware of this situation and while this awareness further premeditates and shapes self-presentation during interactions, the body has taken on a degree of agency that they may not be completely able to control, manipulate or that surfers may not be completely satisfied with the performance expectations of even if they can. To make better sense of this embodied agency, we need to consider a third perspective, that of the storied body.

## Storied bodies

A third fundamental observation on the surfing and surfed body is that it becomes *storied*. Following Bruner (1990), Cobley (2001: 2) reflects 'wherever there are humans there appear to be stories', and this is certainly true of surfing subculture. While there is considerable debate about whether stories have phylogenetic (sociocultural) or ontogenetic (broadly biological) origins, sociologists such as Frank (1991) seems to suggest an interrelated origin by maintaining that the stimulus for storytelling and the stories people tell about themselves are not merely cognitive, intellectual social phenomenon, but rather the outcome of the recursive *infolding* and *outfolding* of experience onto and from the material body. With this in mind the 'material' (read biologically *and* socially constructed) or lived body might be considered to have a degree of 'agency' that 'speaks' to us directly through sensation and is largely independent of our will over the body – illness and injury are probably the most obvious examples. Frank (1991) has previously argued that individuals 'story' their bodies in ways that respond to these sensations and as a result these stories are strongly indicative of the relationships that a given individual has with their body. This perspective of the storied body has taken on increasing applicability in the sociological study of the body in sport and physical activity (see, for example, Sparkes 1996, 1997, 1999; Sparkes and Silvennoinen 1999; Sparkes and Smith 2002). Sparkes and Smith's (2002) work builds on the important observation by Holstein and Gubrium (2000) that the process of 'storying' takes place within certain social limitations based around the 'storying' resources (narrative resources) that given individuals are able to construct from their situatedness in their time, culture and society. For example, a novice surfer may lack the narrative resources to describe the embodied sensations from their first experience of surfing, whereas, later in their surfing 'careers', surfers may have accumulated a wide-ranging vernacular to express their surfed body, which then allows them to articulate their experiences rather differently and in culturally 'appropriate' ways to surfing peers and others. In so doing they develop and convert their habitus and sense of surfing identity.

Therefore, the storied or 'narrative' body (Sparkes and Silvennoinen 1999) becomes an important perspective for the analysis of the surfing body because of what it can illuminate about the body–self–society relationship of individual and groups (Smith and Sparkes 2002; Sparkes and Partington 2003). This section tentatively considers the seminal perspective offered by Frank's (1991, 1995) conceptual work and its potential applications to the study of the surfing body. As such it is more exploratory in nature than the previous sections. It is also important to qualify at the outset that Frank's work and a number of its applications were initially orientated towards understanding the ill, 'dis' or mal functioning body. However, his insights are fundamental to all human activity in that they prompt a consideration of the importance of accounting for certain body problems that all individuals must face in relation to their own and others' bodies, and moreover, how this constitutes an 'agency' not often attributed to the body.

## The surfing body's problems of embodiment

Frank's (1991: 47) work begins with 'how the body is a problem *for itself*, which is an action problem rather than a system problem, proceeding from a phenomeno-logical orientation rather than a functional one'. In setting out what he refers to as a 'structuration theory of the body in society' (1991: 48) there are, Frank (1995: 29) theorizes, 'four general problems of embodiment: control, body-relatedness and other-relatedness, and desire'. Drawing on this (1991) framework these questions can be summarized as follows.

1 *Control.* The body must ask itself how predictable its performance will be
2 *Desire.* The body must constitute itself on a dimension of *desire.* Here the question is whether the body is lacking or producing.

3   *Relation to others*. Does the body relate to itself as monadic and closed in
    on itself, or as dyadic, existing in relation of mutual constitution with
    others?
4   *Self-relatedness of the body*. Does the body consciousness associate itself with
    its own being, particularly its surface, or dissociate itself from that corpo-
    reality?

(Frank 1991: 51–52)

Frank presents these relationships as a schema in which he then overlays these
problems or dimensions with four 'ideal' body types that represent typical solutions
to the four body problems that individuals arrive at (see Frank 1995: 30). As such,
they represent clusters of body–self relationships. These are: the disciplined body,
the mirroring body, the dominating body and the communicative body and will
be considered in the next section. The surfing body–self, in Frank's terms must
therefore, respond to the following series of 'action problems' and is likely in any
given example, to be a mixture of types. The relationships provide stimulating
points of departure into hitherto understudied ways of looking at the body
or the surfing body. In short, types of body–self relationships are likely to have
consequences for how surfers act and respond in their surfing 'careers'. Moreover,
there is a strong correspondence between the previous practical and interacting
outfoldings of bodies and the process of storying the body–self relationship that
can be seen to take place as the result of practice and interaction, these three
manifestations of the surfing body are thus interdependent.

The four continua of embodiment problems can be related to the surfing body,
with a view to establishing how these give rise to the 'storied body'. Each will
briefly be considered in relation to the surfing body. Predictability versus
contingency reflects the surfer's response to solving the problem of the how to
control the material body's performance. Regardless of the surfing styles identified
earlier in this chapter, the surfing body, in terms of its ideal body–self relationship,
is highly predictable in that when it takes a wave it needs to be able to respond
in an automatic, yet controlled manner to the nuances of the particular environmental conditions and return a 'quality' performance within the subcultural
benchmarks of these circumstances. However, the surfing body can, of course, also
be highly unpredictable given the conditions of surf and the surfer body's ability
to perform in them. Indeed, this is the experience of most beginners (at least) in
relation to the performing body–self in this culture. However, the practice of surfing is about the ability to instantaneously combine a series of learnt movements
and being able to perform them in an automatic and thoughtfully unmediated
fashion (see, for example, Thrift 2001, 2004). Therefore, like most sporting and
performing bodies the surfing body seems to be configured around an orientation
towards a maximum of body predictability in the sense of having the confidence
to enact a set of precise dynamic competences. However, the precise understanding of predictability is interestingly variegated by the 'open' environmental
conditions of the surf and to a lesser extent the surfing style that dictates the type
of predictability that is required. Indeed, an unpredictable body (for example a

sudden loss of balance, technique or dynamic tension) in heavy surf might be potentially dangerous. These observations suggest a number of embodied experiential implications that are further explored in Chapter 7, in relation to notions of dance, peak performance and flow.

Body-relatedness is a Cartesian dialogue that considers the nature of being associated/disassociated from one's own body, and in other words asks the question 'Do I *have* a body, or *am* I a body?' (1995: 33). Some people, Frank argues, can become disassociated from their own bodies to the point where they are unwilling to invest anything in them. In his studies of illness Frank points out that chronically ill cancer sufferers often show this disassociated tendency through their stories. Similarly, Sparkes and Smith (2002) showed how a number of rugby players with spinal cord injury experienced a disassociation with their bodies because they could no longer rely on them to construct and maintain their sporting sense of self. However, the question is an intriguing one that might also be asked of the surfing population as it suggests some significant behavioural and storied consequences. How surfers 'story' their bodies in ways that associate or disassociate with them needs to be examined. One example here might be the impact of mainstream competitive sports science discourses on the competitive surfing body which have been identified as inculcating strongly disassociated body–self relationships (see, for example, Hoberman 1992). Elsewhere, Sparkes (1996) and Sparkes and Smith (2002) have suggested that aggressive contact sports can construct strongly disassociated body–self relationships where the body becomes used as an object. Further examples of this are evident in the way in which the sporting body often carries mechanistic, objectified and militaristic metaphors, the sporting body is often represented as 'crashing' through defences, 'pulverizing the opposition' and so on (Trujillo 1995). In this sense, the performing body becomes represented as if it were a mechanistic 'it' ergo I *have* a body becomes a storyline that has strong echoes of Foucauldian discursive forms of regulation and domination.

In contrast, a brief consideration of the influence of the soul surfing generation suggests that the claims of body–mind integration that once formed a substantial counter-cultural discursive and 'narrative' resource, with which to 'story' the bodily experience and agency that emerge from the soul surfing experience, is perhaps a more generally shared phenomenon in surfing. Moreover, surfing culture is perhaps more overtly integrationist than some other sports in the ways in which the body, mind, board and sea come to be experienced and storied together when surfing.

The third, 'other-relatedness', continuum considers the question of how embodied individuals relate to other embodied individuals, the key here is the word 'embodied' because, as Frank (1995: 35) points out, 'the shared condition of being bodies becomes a basis of empathetic relations'. This points towards *dyadic* bodies which exist for each other and in strong contrast to *monadic* bodies that define themselves as existentially separate and alone in the world. These other-relatedness issues raise questions about how the different surfing body–self–other relationships may impact on the way in which surfers approach the embodied 'problem' of, for example, a crowded beach, surf or wave situation where a surfer's relationship to other bodies is exposed by the pressures created by the scarcity of bodily space and the encroaching physical proximity.

With respect to Frank's notion of other-relatedness, it is possible to identify monadic and dyadic orientations. For instance, the very desire of the cosmic surfer to be surfing alone (in the cosmos) may partially reflect a wish to dispense with the distraction of the social and the competitive aspects of surfing. Indeed, most surfers prefer to surf with just a few others around. Moreover, for many, such dyadic relatedness is evident insofar as there is an enjoyment of surfing with a few friends. The monadic/dyadic continuum seems to relate to the pervasive tension in surfing between the individualist intrinsic thrill and the more socially expressive extrinsic aspects.

The fourth and final continuum regards desire and the body. Desire is taken in the sense forwarded by the question, 'What do I *want*, and how is this desire expressed *for* my body, with my body, and *through* my body?' (1995: 37). In asking these questions, Frank applies psychologist Jacques Lacan's triadic model of desire–need–demand to make sense of how the body *produces* desire. Desire of an embodied need (e.g. basic hunger) can be fulfilled but desire when expressed as a demand cannot ever be satisfied because *the desire is the demand* (such as the desire to ride the perfect wave). As Bauman puts it (2000: 88), 'solely the desiring of desire – never its satisfaction'. The surfing body–self can therefore be explored for the desire it produces.

As considered earlier, the surfing body is generative of action, thought and feeling through *practice*. Desire is one of these manifestations and the storyings of desire are important stimuli that are likely to emerge from and infold back onto the body, thus maintaining the recursive logic. Two key terms illustrated earlier that start to open this analytical avenue are 'amped' and 'stoked'. Here, the language of body as if charged by electricity, invoked by the term 'amped' is a classically embodied metaphor that carries, better than most, the embodied response when the sea and the habitus interpellate (or the body is hailed by the sea/wave). Desire is thus created by the body in relation to the triggering of an experientially sedimented stimulus – the body literally produces desire. In comparison to this, the other important metaphor is one that describes the surfing afterglow – 'stoked'; the body's energy, captured in the simile of fire is loaded and burns on for a while, content in its afterglow – the body is again desire-producing through its satisfied, satiated state – until the next time.

Another example that relates to desire is how the surfing body might come to story the desire of the thrill of *more* waveriding or even *bigger* waveriding or *more perfect* waveriding that surpasses any cognitive need or rationale to do so. Put differently, as the surfing body–self experiences more, it might begin to demand more experiences, in the sense of an inherent experiential addictiveness that manifests itself through narrativity and embodied interactions. Given the recursive nature of the infolding of subcultural narratives about surfing these desire-filled bodies are encapsulated in what Kampion (2003) describes as the 'search', that is a culturally configured narrative, that is constantly seeking more, bigger, better waves to ride. The irony here is that there is a self-perpetuating modesty built into this narrative in that 'cool' surfers' do not talk up the wave but rather talk it down (in other words they underestimate rather than overestimate the wave sizes).

## 'Ideal' types of surfing body–self relationships

Frank (1995) then identifies four 'ideal' type body–self relationships that represent metanarratives (or stories) of the choices that 'body–selves' tend to produce and act out as a solution to the body problems that all bodies encounter (disciplined, mirroring, dominating and communicative). These types of body are presented for consideration in the same manner as Max Weber's heuristic of 'ideal types'. Frank, like Weber, concedes that these linguistic constructions represent an imposition on bodies and that in the 'really' real world people are not ideal types, rather, 'ideal types are puppets: theoretical constructions designed to describe some empirical *tendency*. Actual body–selves represent distinct mixtures of ideal types' (1995: 29). In what follows, each of these relationships is first summarized using Smith and Sparkes (2002) and then followed by a short articulation of how these types might be related to the storied surfed body:

> *The disciplined body*. Defines itself primarily in actions of self-regimentation that make itself *predictable*. Most important action problems are about control and it experiences its most serious crisis in loss of control. Desire is *lacking*. Other-relatedness is *monadic*. In terms of self-relatedness it is *disassociated* from itself.
>
> (Smith and Sparkes 2002: 150)

In these terms, the highly competitive surfing body would be most likely to gravitate towards the disciplined body–self relationship, as the type of body problem that all competitors face and seek to minimize is the contingency of their performing bodies, and begin to defer desire to the ends of their physicality (winning) rather than the process and means (participating). However, competitive surfers do tend to suggest that the disciplined body configuration needs to be somewhat revised given that most competitive surfers claim to surf for the sheer enjoyment of it, and consequently their bodies still seem to be desire-producing. Moreover, although surfing competition might be taking centre stage in media representation, experientially it constitutes a relatively small preoccupation of all but a few competitive surfers' lives. Similarly, unlike many competitive athletes, many competitive surfers do not submit themselves to regimes of 'disciplined scientific' practice, rather, they practise surfing in order to improve their surfing and as a result contemporary competitive surfers may only partially fit the disciplined body configuration.

> *The mirroring body*. Remains *predictable* as it reflects that which is around it. Its medium is *consumption* which attempts to recreate the body in the

images of other more stylish and healthier bodies. Other-relatedness remains *monadic*. It is open to an exterior world, but monadic in its appropriation of the world. Via consumption it is endlessly *producing* desires. It is associated with its own surface.

(Smith and Sparkes 2002: 150)

There are a number of ways in which the surfing body might be seen as a mirroring body. The best example would be the overt process of body judging that is manifest in surfing competition and how this has evolved from peer evaluation in everyday surfing practice. While such mirroring and careful observation is clearly present in formal competition, the mirroring body may also function on a less conscious level in many (non-competitive) surfers' development of their style.

Additionally, the perspective can be useful for exploring the storying of broader embodied experiences of the beach and surf lifestyles more generally. Of particular importance here is the way in which the mediatization and commercialization of surfing can be seen to be drawing on the body's agency and desire for itself and other bodies to construct, market and sell products to surfing audiences, particularly the male and female youth markets. Clearly, the mirroring body is vulnerable to manipulation of the *surface* of bodies, as these images become emphasized, radicalized and hyperrealized, with surf models and surf icons providing images that are often unobtainable in 'real' life, with skilled, bronzed, toned, slim and 'sexy' bodies frozen in time and naturalized through advertisements, surf photo and video shoots. Indeed, the history of surf photography and art (see Chapter 3) might be usefully examined with respect to how it constructs the performing surfing body and its relationship with the wave, beach and sea in ways that are often romanticized through particular aesthetic orientations. Surfers draw strongly on these romanticized images as a resource to stylize their own surfing performances. In these ways at least, most surfing bodies might be said to be mirroring bodies at one level or another.

> *The dominating body*. Defines itself in force. Tend to be male bodies. Characterized by a sense of lack, anxiety, and fear. Thus, this body's response to its sense of its own contingency, its disassociated self-relatedness and its dyadic other-relatedness, are all configured by lack. Although dyadic in its other-relatedness, it is *against* others rather than *for* others.
>
> (Smith and Sparkes 2002: 150–151)

While applications of this ideal type to the surfing body do not immediately stand out as a prevalent storied body–self relationship, it is a body–self–society relationship that might need to remain firmly part of the exploration of surfing culture in the future, given that competitive, professional surfing is part of an international sporting network that in many respects prizes the dominating body (for example, American football, rugby, boxing). One example of a possible dominating body–self is that of the (admittedly relatively rare) localist and elitist (often male) surfer who seeks to dominate the waves in their surf spot by dropping in on visitors and local subordinates alike. A similar example of the dominating body in surfing is the instance of 'surf rage', where some surfers are emotionally overtaken and resort to attempting to dominate the space, equipment and even bodies of other surfers, especially novitiates, who inadvertently break the surfing etiquette on the waves and in so doing destroy the surfing space previously enjoyed by the individual in question. In particular, this latter example takes on even more significance when the relationship between surfers and swimmers, bodyboarders and bodysurfers is examined in the context of the inherent scarcity of quality waves in some locations and the ever-increasing numbers of surf seekers (see Chapter 4 and Plate 6). However, while this may be a useful avenue, it needs to be qualified that these surfers may also, at others times, be observed to be fulfilling the embodied stories, practices and interactions that are more desire-producing, other-related and fully associated. As indicated, the difference of context and behaviour may well be related to the emotional context of the performance of these body types.

> *The communicative body.* Is an idealized body in process of *creating itself.* The body's contingency is no longer its problem, but its possibility. Other relatedness is *dyadic.* This desire for dyadic expression and sharing is *producing.* In terms of self-relatedness it is *associated* with itself.
>
> (Smith and Sparkes 2002: 151)

Finally, the communicative body is simultaneously an ideal type and by Frank's own admission is something of an *idealized* ideal type! Elements of surfing culture clearly appear to orientate towards the communicative body–self type. For example, the relationship between many surfers and their sharing of embodied experience is strongly suggestive of an experiential communion where individuals make their significant aspects of their social identities through the sharing of their embodied selves. This is particularly evident in the way in which surf subcultures share their 'hedonistic enjoyment' of the body, through the pleasures of immersing themselves in the sea, the coastscape and the embodied aesthetics of the sensation of surfing that is so often enjoyed in the presence of others. It would be easy, but misguided to slip into an ideal type 'idealism' with this particular concept, and perhaps overdo the search for analogous language between the communicative body type and the idealized surfer body type often expressed through the subcultural narratives. Nevertheless, communicative body types offer a potentially powerful *fully relational* alternative body-self (alternative to the atomized and individualized). In so doing it provides a potential starting point for articulating how some surfers share and collectively construct their body-self identities through immersion into the practice of surfing and the narratives that may emerge from this.

Finally, as Smith and Sparkes (2002: 167) conclude, 'coherence is not an inherent feature of the narratives told, but is artfully crafted in the telling, drawing from the available meanings, structures and linkages that comprise stories in specific cultural contexts'. The surfed storied body therefore, is likely to be a *fluid* and changing representation of self-identity that will reflect the current *state* of the body (young, old, healthy, ill, injured, getting fit, fit, novitiate, intermediate experienced, feeling 'amped', 'stoked', etc.) and the linguistic *resources* (language, vernacular, idiom, plots, sequences) that the teller has at their disposal and finally the *opportunity* to tell the story (i.e. is anyone listening? Different spaces and times for storying the body).

## Synthesis? Towards the 'surfing and the lived emotional' body

Philosopher Richard Rorty considers that many intellectual products have lost their analytical dynamism and openness, and tend to produce analyses bent on 'illustrating the applicability of their framework' (Baert 2004: 362). Instead, as Baert (2004: 362) interprets, 'Rorty pleads for a 'unmethodical criticism" which uses social analysis as an occasion for challenging and furthering accepted taxonomies and lenses rather than merely reiterating them. Therefore, however appealing it may be to 'frame' the surfing body with analyses that set out to demonstrate singular perspectives by such theorists as Foucault, Bourdieu, Goffman, Frank, Elias, or indeed any other paradigm or perspective, it is worth remembering that these cannot (and were never intended to) present the whole story, experience or the complete taxonomy of perspective of embodiment. Rather, they were (and still are) crucial ongoing intellectual interventions that suggest a review of the way embodied positions in, and engagements with, the social world are enacted. Therefore, like the bodies they attempt to explain, these perspectives are most usefully seen as unfinished projects. Concomitantly, and as indicated at the outset, it has not been the intention of this chapter to subject the various perspectives to exhaustive evaluative critique as these have already been expertly conducted elsewhere (see, for example, critiques by Shilling 1999, 2001, 2003; Burkitt 1999; Crossley 2001). Rather, in the following concluding comments some of the shared 'core' or central principles of perspectives on the body are suggested.

Howson and Inglis (2001) claim that the sociology of the body has perhaps done rather better at illuminating the 'Korper' (structural objectified body) than the 'Lieb' (living, feeling, sensing, perceiving and emotional body subject). In so doing they point to a tension in the study of the body in society that predates the modern social sciences themselves and concerns the relationship, not only between the body and nature, but also between the body and mind (see also Turner 1991; Synnott 1993). While this tension will be explored further in Chapter 7, some additional commentary is justified here. This chapter has argued for a view of the body as a fleshy, living, organic subject that carries through its social existence a fluctuating degree of agency. However, like most of the writing on the body, it rarely achieves this aim. Bodies are not 'present' in text and they never can be: all that can be done is to show bodies through data and the *nature* of the theorizing about them. All this chapter can lay claim to is a little of the latter. This standpoint is in opposition to strongly structuralist views of the body as a soulless, forceless object that merely does what its owner's (or other people's) mind tells it. Moreover, approaches that separate the experiential from the represented construct a dual focus that for many theorists creates an undesirable tension, as Shilling (2001) contends:

> Attempts to separate a 'sociology of the body' concerned with the body as objectified within society from a 'carnal' or 'corporeal' sociological concern with the body as lived subject, are seeking to institute a false dualism within the subject. The aim should instead be to construct an embodied sociology in which the discipline takes full account of the corporeal character of social life.
>
> (Shilling 2001: 341)

While expressed differently this general position seems increasingly to represent a consensus as to the way forward. Williams and Bendelow's (1998) point resonates with the above, when they conclude:

> We have sought to reconcile these former divisions through the unifying notion of the *lived*, experiential, body – an active, expressive, 'mindful' form of *embodiment* that serves not only as the existential basis of culture and self, but also of social institutions and society more generally.
>
> (Williams and Bendelow 1998: 208)

A similar conclusion is also reached by Burkitt (1999: 147) who points out, 'there is no such thing as the 'mind' considered as something separate from the body and its spatio-temporally located practices'. Perhaps nowhere are the possibilities for these developments more evident than the considerations of how the emotions might begin to play a bridging role between many of these and other perspectives. As Duquin (2000: 477) notes, 'emotion is a relatively new area of research in sociology' and even more so in our understanding of sporting and physical activities like surfing. Indeed, some principled eclecticism will be warranted in returning to consider how Elias (1991) placed emotions at the core of his understanding of social life and human endeavour (see also Elias and Dunning 1986). Conversely, as Shilling and Mellor (1996) and Shilling (1999) suggest, other perspectives consider how the emotional body might work with perspectives such as Giddens' structuration theory and Goffman's 'interaction order' in order to ask 'new' questions both *of* the theory and *with* the theory in its modified form. For example, considering the interacting body, following Shilling (1999) questions emerge about the ways in which the surfing body idiom is an emotionally expressive one and how the regionalization of the presentation of self in surfing are in fact usefully considered as arenas for quite different forms of emotional labour (see Chapter 7). Regarding the practical body, important questions emerge about how something akin to a surfing habitus might give rise to a semi-conscious series of emotional reactions that binds dispositions to the social fields that help to construct them, so enhancing the likelihood of surfers acting according to, rather than against, their dispositional drives. For example, what long since forgotten body/mind response is elicited as a big wave surfer faces a big wave and what call to action does this emotional response trigger? Finally, Frank's (1995) perspective can help us to ask questions about how certain surfing body–self–other relationships come to be storied with particular emotional 'undertones' in response to the body's emotional status and the emotional climate of the narrative resources available to the surfer, and the emotional stories they tell.

In summary, the social study of the surfing and surfed body is an intriguing area. In agreement with Shilling (2005) the body is a multidimensional phenomenon that is at once *a source, location and means for society.* The adoption of a principled eclecticism that seeks to find key points of connection between these and the practical, interacting and storytelling perspectives of the body outlined here is full of potential insight for the understanding of surfing. This discussion should not be read as an advocation to the *merger* of all these perspectives and constructs. However, there is considerable merit in utilizing these conceptual perspectives in juxtaposition in order to construct a better and more multidimensional representation of the *lived body*. Finally, in developing more rounded *bodily present* accounts, the emotions can be seen to act as the ontological 'glue' that binds, bridges and connects the practical surfing body with the social spaces that it occupies and the signifiers that would represent it. It may be useful to establish a view that balances the socially active 'living' 'doing' body in surfing, with one that is also 'done to' and on occasion more passive and represented. However, the realm of experience remains elusive as Dyck and Archetti (2003) point out:

> To understand better the ways in which athletes and dancers come to know how to use their bodies, ethnographers of sport and dance must take account of both kinaesthetic and social action that takes place within formally organized coaching and instructional regimes as well as in informally convened situations where people seek to acquire and perfect the rudiments of one or another particular form of bodily practice.
>
> (Dyck and Archetti 2003: 9)

It is this latter elusive experiential quality of the surfing body-self and the relationship between this and the social surfing body that Chapter 7 will now consider.

# 7  The experience of surfing

In surfing it is a total engagement of psychic capacities in a physical challenge
that facilitates ecstatic union with nature.

(Stranger 1999: 270)

*Surfing* research always deals in some way with the body, but one of the
challenges now is how to mend the dichotomy between mind and body that
has marginalized *surfing* for too long.

(adapted from Morris 1996: 10 with *surfing* here substituted
for the original *dance*)

## Introduction

Given the richness and vitality of the images, narratives, representations and
meanings, so powerfully associated with surfing as a cultural form, it is sometimes
easy to forget that these are all epiphenomena, and that the core of surfing has
always simply been the embodied, raw and immediate glide or slide along a wave
of energy passing through water. This chapter seeks to explore some of the
perspectives which may be addressed towards understanding the nature of the
experience of the ride along a wave. As such, although drawing upon the work of
surfer-scholars (such as Stranger 1999; Bennett and Kramer 2001) this chapter
primarily seeks to apply thinking and concepts hitherto discussed in relation to
substantive areas other than the experience of surfing.

It was emphasized in Chapter 2 that the pursuit of surfing can be viewed within
the context of the coenaesthetic (knowledge through the senses) relationship to
the sea (Corbin 1994). In Fiske's (1989) semiotic analysis of surfing, the sport and
culture is viewed as being associated with nature and wildness, in binary contrast
to society and civilization. Similarly, and with more direct reference to the body,
Lewis's (2000) analysis of adventure climbing resonates strongly with analysis of
the experience of surfing (Stranger 1999). Both Lewis and Stranger draw on the
theorizations of, first, Simmel, concerning 'modernity as rupture for embodied
experience' (Lewis 2000: 65) with 'physical exertion being superseded by an all-
pervading passivity' (Lewis 2000: 67), and, second, Elias concerning the stifling
cerebral and ocular tendencies of the civilizing process. Adventure or alternative

*Figure 7.1* Dualism of the surfing and metropolitan bodies

| Surfing body | Metropolitan body |
| --- | --- |
| Organic | Inorganic |
| Self-determined | Passive |
| Tactile | Ocular |
| Embodied contact with water | Disembodied/groundless |

Source: adapted from Lewis 2001: 59, here substituting *surfing* for *climbing*

sports such as climbing and surfing are therefore viewed as embodied attempts to redress such passive tendencies. Thus, as depicted in Figure 7.1, some elements of the surfing body may be contrasted with those of the metropolitan body, with the two 'only existing in the co-presence of the other, as part of the multiplicity of the contemporary human being' (Lewis 2000: 59).[1]

Echoing Rodaway's (1994) notion of sensuous geographies, Lewis highlights the centrality of the sense of touch in climbing, arguing that '[t]o engage with the world tactually is to situate oneself consciously in that world and to have a potentially unmediated relationship with it' (Lewis 2001: 59).[2] As will be discussed below the focal, embodied sensing in surfing is not that of touch through the hand, (as in climbing) but there is that same sense of something direct and unmediated, when actually riding the wave.

Following an initial discussion of the nature of the surfing ride, and its parallels with, and divergences from, notions of dance, this chapter is structured in relation to themes pertaining to the mind–body split and approaches to transcend it. Thus, following a section which touches briefly on some of the work on the physiology of surfing (body), the chapter turns to research on surfing motivations, peak performance, peak experience and flow (mind), narratives of flow (culture), before concluding with an exploration of the possible application of non-representational theory (mind–body integration) to surfing.

## The ride as dance?

The ('stand-up') ride on the wave is here discussed, first with reference to its distinctiveness from other forms of surfing, the relation of body to surfboard, and the kinaesthesia of balance and rhythm. Thereafter matters of performance and style lead, via Flynn's (1987) classic paper, to explorations of surfing as dance, and in relation to developments in dance studies.

There are enormous commonalities of experience across the whole range of forms of waveriding (including windsurfing, surf kayaking, surf canoeing, boogie boarding, kitesurfing, wake boarding and so on). However, practitioners who have experience of a range of waveriding vehicles generally note that the key distinctiveness of what may be termed 'stand-up' or standard surfboard riding, is the relative freedom of the body.[3] In contrast to other forms, in this kind of surfing (which is the primary focus of this book) not only does the body stand erect (as befits *Homo sapiens*' natural history), but the arms and hands are obviously not locked (or rather holding) onto any piece of equipment. The kinaesthetic movements involved in 'stand-up' surfing are extremely similar to those involved in the related practices of skateboarding and snowboarding. Indeed, many developments in surfing performance have resulted from the crossover of manoeuvres from such other pursuits. Obviously the major differences between these three highly cognate pursuits derive from their different environments (primarily urban tarmac/concrete, mountain snow and coastal waves), hence the especial concern of this text to anchor surfing within cultural relations to the coast and beach (in Chapter 2). Comparative research (between surfing, skateboarding and snowboarding) could gainfully explore the experiential and cultural ramifications of these very different environmental contexts for similar body practices.

As Flynn (1987) has noted, when riding the wave the surfboard becomes an extension of the surfer's body and mind. While care needs to be taken in extrapolating from windsurfing to 'standard' surfing, Dant's (1999) paper on material culture in the social world focusing on the windsurfboard, has usefully drawn on the work of Mead and Whitehead on human interaction with objects. Prior to any mental functioning, human beings interact bodily to master objects such as surfboards through the field of touch. In this sense the body experiences the surfboard as a 'pushiness' or a resistance to touch. Thus, the surfboard is experienced through a transference of the experience of bodily surfaces pushing against each other (Dant 1999: 120).

There would appear to be a contrasting sense of the obtrusiveness of the surfboard between paddling and riding waves. During paddling the surfer is conscious of the board as an object, however, during the ride that sense of separation between body and board seems to vanish with the board appearing more as an appendage to the moving body. While more systematic research is needed to explore such changes, it seems plausible that the shift in awareness reflects both the speed of the ride and immersion within a non-cognitive mode of consciousness.

In direct contrast to the heightened visual sense when paddling out or waiting in the line-up during surfing, during the ride there is a very little reflective awareness. As is elaborated below with reference to non-representational theory 'to be aware of an experience means it has passed' (Norretranders in Thrift 2001: 37). As with so many other practices, riding the wave is learnt through bodily knowledge, enabling an automatic set of responses to the ever-changing energy pocket and peal of the wave.

Again there is scope for systematic research on the use of the body in surfing, but as numerous observers have noted (e.g. Kampion and Brown 1998; Stranger 1999), above all surfing draws upon our kinaesthetics, that integrating sense 'that informs you of what your body is doing in space through the perception or sensation of movement in the joints, tendons and muscles' (Lewis 2000: 69). While the major expenditure of strength and energy in surfing revolves around the shoulder and back muscles mobilized in paddling the surfboard, the act of riding the wave involves the whole body.

The ride itself involves a continual process of subtly shifting pressure through the feet to shift from rail to rail on the board to both turn and accelerate from the energy in the wave – a process which has become especially accentuated in the contemporary small (and thin) board surfing of recent years. As such, the trajectory of the ride follows a series of arcing sine curves, reflecting the perpetual shifting of pressure and release. The human body pivots and aligns through the three key body weights of the skull, the thorax and the pelvis (Olsen 1998). In surfing, whilst all three are clearly involved in the continual shifting of weight and transference of pressure, the pelvic area is most focal and powerful, linking with the legs and spine. Indeed, the torquing focus of the interplay between the upper and lower parts of the body is the major source of channelling bodily energy through and with the surfboard. Further elements which body studies of surfing could also address include the (automatic?) centring (within the abdomen), lengthening of the spine and opening of the chest attendant to optimal surfing performance. This notion of centring echoes the more conscious act of centring and focusing energies in a number of the oriental martial arts.

Given its rhythmic, twisting, turning, dynamic and balancing character, it is hardly surprising that practitioners have often alluded to surfing as a dance. For instance, in his semiotic analysis of 'surfing's iconic wave dance' Flynn discusses the trajectory of the ride as 'the surfer's improvised rhythmicity and dance' (1987: 401) with the wave as the narrative field. Drawing on the work of Genette (1980), Greimas (1987), and Heidegger (1962) Flynn (1987: 402) argues that 'the surfer dances *with* the wave in a state of "anticipatory resoluteness" (past, present and future are unified)', with the synchrony of movement linked together to create a complete narrative.

The notion of surfing as dance is most strongly related to ideas of style and expressiveness in surfing. This has been discussed by Flynn in terms of 'surfing's stylistic corpus' consisting of what Bakhtin called 'body signs' (Ivanov 1973) of codified movements and evocative gestures, and later Booth (1999) referred to in terms of performance styles and 'philosophies of the wave'. Such stylistic gestures are most clearly apparent in aspects of longboard surfing deriving from the past, including, for instance such poses as 'soul arches', 'hanging ten' and 'tandem surfing'. There is almost a sense in which the more dynamic (constantly shifting rails) contemporary small board surfing makes such evocative gestures seem increasingly superfluous, if not obsolete, to the more functional concentration on remaining in the pocket of optimal wave energy. At the current juncture in the assessment and appreciation of surfing performance, although style is recognized as one of the key criteria of prowess in competition (primarily defined as the quality of flow between manoeuvres) it is possible that it has an ambiguous status, which probably relates to uncertainties regarding the concept's scope for further definition and elaboration in high performance surfing.[4] Again, there is scope for research to explore the bases and nature of different high performance surfing styles. The underlying complexities include the links of style to competence, as well as possibly personality, mood and changes over the course of the 'surfing career' and maturation. Suffice it to note at this point that an emphasis on style as 'interpretation translated into movement' (Flynn 1987: 400) or 'philosophies of the wave' (Booth 1999), seem somewhat overly cerebral, a theme which is further developed later in this chapter with respect to non-representational theory.

It may well be possible to take the analysis of the expressive and postural dimensions of waveriding further by drawing on some of the approaches, concerns and debates within the emerging and dynamic field of dance studies. Furthermore, as with surfing studies, many researchers in dance studies are dancers themselves with a concern with their own dancing bodies (Morris 1996). Both surfing and dance studies deal with an ephemeral performance, 'an event bounded in space and time, a performance [that] can be read only in its traces . . . in memory, on film . . . an endless series of distorting reflections' (Manning 1993: 12). The same pervasive tension as is found in surfing as culture (epiphenomena) and as embodied practice, structures the landscape of contemporary dance studies in terms of the cultural/interpretive and formalist (more traditional) approaches (Morris 1996). Just as the interdisciplinary trend of dance studies towards the use of social theory seeks to embed dance within culture, so surfing styles have been examined in terms of the *Zeitgeist* of the time (Booth 1999: 52). More formalist approaches are concerned with the structure of individual dances and view movement as a way of creating meaning, rather than vice versa. As noted in Chapter 4, there is something of a tension running through surfing between the individualist personal experience of the ride and the tendency to wish to be seen performing, or a surfer's pleasure in having their rides disseminated in magazines and filmic media. Such orientations are not necessarily conflicting, for instance as Lowe has noted in discussing beauty in sport, 'excellence should be viewed in athletics as a search for both greater self-realization (subjective, intrinsic) and for social recognition (objective, extrinsic)' (1977: 228). Neither is such a tension present in dance. Even though modern dance substitutes the pictorial logic of ballet with an emphasis on the affective (Dempster 1988 in Thrift 1997), performance for others to observe is almost always unproblematic within dance. In surfing just as the striking poses alluded to above as codified 'body signs' of the longboard era were staged to be seen, so today it has been argued that some (top) surfers habitually attempt particular manoeuvres for their photogenic qualities.

It seems likely that the more surfing is thought of as an artform, the greater the relevance of notions from dance studies. In seeking greater rigour and elaboration formalist approaches to dance studies have drawn on musicology and sought to explore the relationships between dance and music (Jordan 1996). Jordan has highlighted the close relationships between dance and music in terms of movement length and pitch, dynamics, legato and staccato, oppositional contrapuntal relationships, rhythmic counterpoint, theories of climax, mobility/closure, thematic analysis, and individual parameters of rhythm, harmony and melody. It is sometimes argued that for an artform to progress it needs to become literate. Just as dance studies were able to become much more movement-literate with the application of Laban Notational Movement Analysis (Desmond 1993/94 in Morris 1996), so the question is, could the analysis of surfing be enhanced by the development of a more sophisticated form of notation?

It is possible to surmise that the music of surfing as a dance would be some combination of the personal predispositions and learned/encultured repertoire of the individual surfer along with the energy and glide potentialities of any given individual wave. It is the latter aspect which ensures that despite the wealth of parallels, surfing is distinct from dance in its customary meaning of 'socially structured movement' (Morris 1996: 2). For all its possible stylistic, cultural and expressive dimensions, the movements of the surfer on a given ride are inherently and intimately improvisational, related (both as opportunities and constraints) to the flowing and changing stream of energy in the wave. This is not to say that surfing corresponds to any particular form of music – that is entirely related to personal taste. Rather, there are clear parallels with jazz and the freedom and empowerment of a physical competence to go with the flow of an ever-changing medium. Maybe rather than the 'surfer riding the wave', it could be said in a more co-constitutive way that 'the surfer is surfed', as will be further discussed below with respect to non-representational theory. Suffice it to note here that surfing as dance may be interpreted on many different levels, for instance as a narrative unfolding in a (necessarily partial) text, in more formalist terms of a series of linked moves, or as an emotional expression. In completely different terms the somatic movement of surfing can be defined in terms of the tradition of physiological analysis of surfing.

## Physiology and surfing

Although perhaps of limited relevance to this chapter's core theme of the experience of surfing, some brief reference needs to be made to the tradition of physiological research on surfing. A whole host of studies have focused on such topics as physiological requirements (e.g. Lowdon and Pateman 1980; Lowdon 1982; Meir, Lowdon and Davie 1991), surfing injuries (Lowdon, Pateman and Pitman 1983 Nathanson, Haynes and Galanis 2002), medical (Renneker 1987a) and lifestyle (Renneker 1987b) aspects of surfing. The sports medicine of surfing has been the focus of the Surfer's Medical Association (SMA) which has held numerous conferences and coordinated various research projects.[5] Research on Australian competitive surfers has shown, for instance, that they have some of the best recovery heart rates of any group of athletes (Lowdon and Pateman 1980). Such studies indicate that top surfers also have quick reflexes, dynamic balance and agility, as reflects a pursuit which involves relatively short periods of very intense activity and longer periods of inactivity.

Research on competitive surfers' somatotypes (Lowdon 1980) has indicated a general body type almost identical to Olympic swimmers. Research on surfers' musculoskeletal parameters confirmed that they have powerful shoulder flexion and extension capabilities, but with many opposing muscle groups being poorly developed (Gilliam, Ellis and Johnson 1984). The paper suggested (perhaps reflecting surf culture's 'laid-back' hedonism) that relatively few surfers follow any form of warm up or cool down stretching or counter-stretching programmes. The findings on somatotypes and muscle structure indicate ways in which the practice of surfing becomes inscribed upon the body, in a physiological, as well as embodied competence, form.

Endocrinological research has implicated endorphins as endogenous substances that have similar neurotransmitter properties to opiates (McArdle, Katch and Katch 2000). Such research has postulated that endorphins have a role in triggering a state of euphoria and exhilaration in intense exercise. Similarly, Zuckerman (1984) has suggested that such hormonal pleasure effects are part of the intrinsic rewards of engaging in high-risk and high physiological stress activities.

## Surfing motivations

A particularly useful area for the exploration of the surfing experience is the analysis of the motivations which drive and sustain the continued pursuit of surfing. Such research (Farmer 1992; Dant 1999; Stranger 1999) has generally been based on the more cultural theorizations of play (after Huizinga 1949 and Callois 1958/61), and/or the more quantitative social psychological analysis of motivations underlying sport (Kenyon 1968). The concept of play has rather more diverse meanings than that of sport, some of which pay greater attention to the psychobiological states involved (Harris and Park 1983). Bateson (1955) argued that play behaviour conveys a message not to take seriously what is occurring or about to occur. Further characteristics of play include a relative lack of commitment to the attainment of extrinsic goals (Harris 1980), intense enjoyment and 'flow' (Czikszentmihalyi 1990), and a sense of unstructured (as opposed to the tightly codified rules of sport) interaction (Turner 1972). The psychological emphasis highlights the sense that a person may vascillate into, and out of play. For instance, a professional surfer may hold a sports-related attitude in competition, carefully following rules and conscious of extrinsic reward, but slide into a play orientation when 'free-surfing'.

Callois (1958/61) drew on Huizinga's (1949) work on play as a cultural phenomenon to systematize the meanings of games and play in terms of the four basic categories of 'agon' (competition), 'alea' (chance), mimicry, and 'ilea' (vertigo or thrill) with games ranging along a continuum from the spontaneous to the disciplined and ordered. Elaborating upon Callois's categories, Kenyon (1968) identified six scales to assess attitude to physical activity as social experience, health and fitness, pursuit of vertigo, aesthetic experience, catharsis (release, recreation and relaxation) and ascetic experience (to meet a physical challenge). Applications of these scales, modified for the study of surfing motivations, have been undertaken by Farmer (1992) among 50 surfers in Torquay, Australia and Heap (2003) among 150 surfers in Croyde, North Devon, UK. Both studies found that vertigo, or the sheer thrill of the ride, was by far the primary motivation for surfing, followed by the aesthetic and cathartic dimensions. The relative lack of importance accorded to the social dimension mirrors Williams's (2002) finding that experienced surfers tended to view the surfing as a primarily individualist pursuit (Chapter 4). The emphasis on health and fitness dovetails with the anecdotal suggestion that probably relatively few surfers 'train' as such, or even undertake stretching exercises, before or after surfing.[6] As noted in earlier chapters, only a very small minority of surfers take part in competitions.

Diehm and Armatas (2004) have further explored the vertiginous motivation underlying surfing by applying Zuckerman's (1983) 'sensation seeking scale V' (SSS), and examined the aesthetic and cathartic motivations in relation to Costa and McCrae's (1992) 'openness to experience' dimension. Their study compared the motivations and personality characteristics of surfers and golfers, as high- and low-risk sports' participants. Sensation seeking is defined as 'the need for varied, novel and complex sensations and experiences, and the willingness to take physical and social risks for the sake of such experience' (Zuckerman 1979: 10). The question of risk-taking is explored below with respect to Stranger's (1999) analysis. Diehm and Armatas's analysis not only reinforces Farmer's (1992) and Heap's (2003) findings concerning the especial importance of the direct, thrilling experience of vertigo to surfing, but also highlights surfers' higher intrinsic, rather than extrinsic, motivation. Surfers' lower extrinsic (influenced from the outside) motivations may 'explain why social, health and fitness factors are found to be the least important' (Diehm and Armatas 2004: 666).

While this chapter's focus on the raw, direct experience of the surfing ride is primarily concerned with the non-cognitive and immediate, an intriguing area of enquiry is the linking of such sensual experience with the emotional and cognitive. As a practice, surfing has repeatedly been distinguished from many other sports in terms of its powerful aesthetic and cultural associations. Diehm and Armatas provide a strong indication that surfing attracts individuals with particular personality characteristics. This is evidenced by surfers' higher (than many other sports' participants, for instance comparing Shroth's 1995 findings) expression of the 'openness to experience' dimension. 'Openness to experience' (Costa and McCrae 1992) involves six aspects: an active imagination, aesthetic sensitivity, attending to inner feelings, preference for variety, intellectual curiosity and independence of judgement. Linking with the appeal and seductiveness of surfing discussed above in Chapter 3, Diehm and Armatas suggest that 'the nature of the surfing experience may thus attract individuals with stronger tendencies for fantasy, aesthetics, feelings, actions, values and ideas' (2004: 675).

The forenoted social psychological findings mirror core elements of Stranger's seminal (1999) cultural analysis of surfing. Stranger's thesis is 'that: (1) aestheticization facilitates risk-taking in the pursuit of an ecstatic, transcendent experience: and (2) the surfing aesthetic involves a postmodern incarnation of the sublime that distorts rational risk assessment' (1999: 265). The core of Stranger's analysis revolves around the nature of risk and aestheticization. Stranger notes that both the notions of 'rational recreationists' of early modernity and the 'reflective risk managers' (Giddens 1991; Beck 1992) rationalize risk-taking in terms of various efficacies such as catharsis and character building. In critique Mitchell (1988), after Simmel (1971) and Huizinga (1949), has claimed that such 'instrumentally rational language restricts our ability . . . to articulate the experience itself . . . In contrast the aesthetic reflexivity . . . (Lash 1993b) . . . enables the sensual and emotional experience to be inherently worthwhile, without having to be justified in terms of efficacious outcomes' (Stranger 1999: 269). Such a post-modern aesthetic of sensation rather than interpretation (Featherstone 1993) is clearly highly appropriate for the articulation the core experience of surfing.

Although the concept of risk is included in the titles of the Stranger and Diehm and Armatas papers, it is interesting that both analyses begin to question the centrality of risk to the experience of surfing. Diehm and Armatas note that surfing is not rated by practitioners as a high-risk, but, rather, a sensation-seeking sport. Similarly Stranger, in discussing the addictive element of seeking bigger and more powerful waves with progression in a surfer's 'career', notes that 'the increased risk is . . . simply a by-product of chasing the most intense thrills' (1999: 268). Stranger marshalls a most telling quotation from a big wave surfer of the incredible outer reef break of 'Jaws' on Maui. 'The level's always growing as what's BIG. What's big is what's going to get me that feeling . . . But . . . I'm not out there because of the challenge with fear. It's fun. I love it' (from Lyon and Lyon 1997: 180). There is probably a complex relationship between sensation, challenge and catharsis in big wave surfing (Bennett and Kramer 2001).

However, for surfers the sensation or thrill is clearly of more importance than the 'ascetic' motivation of mastering a fear and challenge experience. As Stranger puts it '[r]isk is simply a very effective catalyst for reaching those transcendent states' (1999: 274).[7] Most surfers would happily dispense with the risk of being hurt, if they could still attain the vertiginous thrill of the ride without it, possibly linking with the somewhat hedonistic and 'laid back' character of surfing culture. As Stranger notes, expressions of the thrill of surfing often take the form of intense awareness, ecstatic feelings of oneness and self-transcendence, which relate directly to the concepts of peak experience and flow, to which the following section is addressed.

## Flow, peak experience and peak performance in surfing

This section begins with a brief outline of some of the definitional and theoretical aspects of flow, peak experience and peak performance, and the application of these concepts to sports. The main body of this section then considers the application of flow, peak experience and peak performance to surfing with reference to the following themes; their relation to different facets of the surfing experience, concerns with peak performance, peak experience and surfing conditions, the narratives of flow in surfing, and implications of peak experiences for a surfer's sense of identity.

Notions of self-transcendence and ecstasy attendant to the experience of surfing (Stranger 1999) relate closely to the substantial literature on peak experience, which has emerged and proliferated following the seminal work of the humanistic psychologist Abraham Maslow (1968). Such a psychology draws on existential and phenomenological perspectives to explore human experience in both its positive and its pathological forms in a holistic way (Privette 1983). There has been considerable interest within sports studies in the related concepts of peak experience and flow (Czikszentmihalyi 1990), not only in terms of explaining the feeling of euphoria, but also because of their links, through the related notions of peak and optimal performance, to excellence in sporting practice (Privette 1983; Celsi 1992; Jackson 1995; Lipscombe 1999). While many discussions use the concepts interchangedly, Privette (1983) has sought to distinguish between them, with peak experience being viewed as a passive contemplative and intense joy, peak performance as active and superior functioning, and flow as intrinsically rewarding experience or fun. Czikszentmihalyi (1990) has stressed that flow may also have an active component in its association, for instance, with elite sporting performance. However Privette's (1983) distinguishing between different levels of peak and flow experience, for instance with respect to the considerable variations between almost mystical, self-transcendent states, and more relaxed, general senses of well-being, is a useful distinction.

Research into peak experience and flow has been concerned with identifying the range of characterizations of such experiences. For instance Maslow's 19 characterizations of the peak experience include: object unification (total harmony), total attention (complete absorption in the experience), rich perception (lost in the experience), awe and reverence (the most blissful moment, ecstasy), fusion of dichotomies (the person and the experience merge) and so on (see Lipscombe 1999). As with research in other fields, sports psychologists have been particularly involved in producing and refining accurate measuring tools to explore the peak and flow states (Jackson and Marsh 1996; Lipscombe 1999; Jackson and Eklund 2002). These measuring instruments have taken the form of both quantitative scales/inventories and qualitative thematic codings.

In applying these concepts to surfing it seems plausible to surmise that flow may relate to any aspect of surfing practice (i.e. to paddling out, catching and riding waves, waiting in the line-up for waves). On first thoughts, peak performance may be considered to apply only to the most active and absorbed aspect of actually riding the wave. However, peak performance should also be applied to the process of finding waves, especially within beach breaks with their peaks ever-shifting as the tide changes. Research is needed to explore whether the contemplative peak experience is confined to the reflective afterglow (or 'stoke' in surfing parlance) after a great wave, or may also be found during the non-cognitive experience of riding the wave itself. Peak experiences also, obviously, extend to a whole range of aesthetically oriented aspects of surfing being 'triggered', for instance, by the variety of visual (coastscape, sea, sky and water scenes) and tactile sensations surrounding, not only surfing itself, but also contacts with, and immersion in, varied cultures and places associated with travel in search of waves.

Bennett and Kramer (2001) have conducted research (using the Event Experience Scale to assess flow) into the psychology of peak performance by elite surfers. The aim of this study was to identify the psychological state attributes which relate to elite surfers' highest performance surfing, in order to assist other surfers to improve their waveriding. The seven key psychological state dimensions which Bennett and Kramer identified with such peak performance, represent a distillation from the wide range of customary peak performance/flow characterizations which are most pertinent to surfing, namely:

1 enjoyment and satisfaction
2 clarity of concentration/focus, including previously devised plans or goals pertaining to manoeuvres
3 different surfers identified alternative arousal levels: relaxed and calm *or* 'amped' physical and mental excitement, which may be related to personality type
4 performance feedback, entailing a high level of awareness of conditions, equipment and personal physical state
5 a high level of confidence and control
6 a sense of rhythm and flow, with a sense of being on 'auto-pilot', free and absorbed in the moment
7 an altered perceptual state.

Bennett and Kramer further identified a set of pre-surf factors which could enhance the possibility of peak performance. These pre-surf factors elaborated on the psychological state characterizations to note a range of strategies, which varied from individual to individual.

Czikszentmihalyi (1990) has noted that flow is often achieved in performance when there is an optimal relationship between the performer's capabilities and the demands of the encounter. In surfing terms this would entail surfers' skills being just adequate to the challenge of the size and power of the wave conditions, and clearly relates to the sense of addiction to surfing, as riders seek out progressively more challenging waves to trigger the thrill of the ride. This also explains the fact that beginners often seem to experience greater pleasure than experienced surfers in less than ideal (for instance 'sloppy') surf conditions. However, it is plausible to surmise that a basic feeling of flow may be attained in highly varied surf conditions. Within surfing culture and within individual surfers' dreams the notion of, and quest for, the perfect wave is iconic. Surfers' accounts of the most intense peak experience often revolve around surfing in such ideal conditions.

Systematic research into flow and peak experiences in surfing could gainfully explore not only the intensity of such experiences, but the settings in which they most frequently occur. Anecdotal evidence (admittedly from the UK!) suggests that peak experiences are particularly associated with overseas travel and surfing in uncrowded breaks.

While flow and peak experiences in surfing occur on a non-verbal level, the only source of their recounting is through the description of language. While surfing shares the especial emphasis on flow and peak experience with a wide range of cognate alternative/lifestyle/'whizz' sports, a particularly interesting avenue for research would be to explore the different ways in which different sports articulate these experiences (Jackson 1996). An appropriate methodology to explore the inextricable connection between a personal experience such as flow, and the social forms of meaning production through which it may be described, is that of narrative psychology (Crossley 2000; Sparkes and Partington 2003). As Smith and Sparkes (2002) have noted, coherence is not an inherent aspect of narrative, but rather something that is 'artfully crafted' in the storytelling, based on shared meanings and preoccupations of particular (sub) cultural contexts. Thus, it could be argued that the forms in which flow and peak experience are expressed and recounted by surfers would be expected to draw on themes and argot germane to surfing culture, as outlined in Chapter 3. Given the powerful mediatization of surfing culture, in terms of the quality and popularity of surfing magazines (and above all photography) and films, it is plausible to suggest that there is a reciprocal interplay (yet not determination) between accounts of the surfing experience within the media and the interactive and personal storytellings among surfers.

The predisposition towards peak experience on the part of surfers may be viewed as linking with their relatively high level of 'openness to experience' (Diehm and Armatas 2004), along with the powerful sense of a romantic aesthetic pervading the surfing imaginary (George 1999; Stranger 1999) as discussed above in Chapters 2 and 3. Romanticism's preoccupations with the senses, mystical experience, the sublime, and the lone individual estranged from civilization yet at one with nature, all feed into the rich aesthetic sensibilities which have shaped aspects of surfing culture, in particular in its 'cosmic' and soul surfing orientations.

The iconic search for perfection in surfing links with the sense of drive towards self-realization. Expressing the cosmic/soul surfing ethos Slusher (1967: 179) has noted that, 'in many ways surfing speaks to the "loner" . . . A surfing man's [sic] existence offers an opportunity to attain true being. Being, as is, might well be called the personification of perfection'.

As Stranger (1999) has emphasized with reference to Mitchell (1988), the attainment of a unifying (peak) experience is enhanced when the actions taking place (in this case the simple practice of riding waves) are given significant meanings. Stranger shows the parallels between the surfer's (almost mythic) quest for the perfect wave and Simmel's (1971) notion of the adventure, which, in order to evoke a transcendent experience, needs to connect with rich personal meanings and sense of identity. As noted in Chapter 3 narrative research has the potential to examine the process of the crafting of memories of peak experiences in surfing in relation to surfers' sense of identity and lifestyle pattern.

From the foregoing discussions of various perspectives of the direct experience of surfing there is still a certain sense of something lacking, perhaps a feeling of a lack of holism or integration in dealing with the fundamental split between mind and body. The physiological perspective seems to treat the body as machine in a reductionist scientistic sense – the sports motivations, personality orientations and peak experience perspectives clearly emphasize the mind and its constructs as being the primary nexus of agency. Narrative accounts of peak experiences and flow take the focus back to the texts and representations inherent to story-making and discourse within culture. Thus, the next section seeks to explore further the direct embodied experience of surfing, building on the earlier references to the parallels with dance (Flynn 1987; Harris 1980) and the notion of a post-modern aesthetic of sensation rather than interpretation (Featherstone 1993; Lash 1993b; Stranger 1999). In seeking to carry the discussion forward, the final section of the chapter attempts to tentatively apply some of the notions

associated with Nigel Thrift's non-representational theory (1997) to the immediate embodied experience of surfing.

## Non-representational theory and surfing

Thrift's writings on non-representational theory (1997, 2001, 2004) provide a
range of striking resonances with these efforts to explore the direct, embodied
experience of surfing. As the name implies non-representational thinking is a
(radical) departure from the overly cerebral and representation-based 'protocols
of the current social sciences and humanities' which he considers 'to be not just
mistaken, but what's worse oppressive' (2004: 81). Non-representational theory
is perhaps better viewed as an exploratory, unfolding project rather than as a
formal theory. Indeed, referring to the conventional idea of a 'body of theory that
acts out rules and conventions' Thrift notes 'it is precisely this notion of theory
that I want to junk, in favour of a notion of theory as a modest supplement to
practice, helping people to create new ways of living–thinking through which they
can explore and add to the world – rather than offering ready-made solutions'
(2004: 83). In deriving non-representational theory Thrift draws on diverse sets
of thinking, some of which (for instance, kinaesthetics, dance, peak experiences)
have been touched upon above in this chapter. It is the broad sweep of the
connections made between diverse bodies of knowledge in Thrift's writings that
is particularly illuminating. Particular lines of thinking which recur in his writings
on non-representational theory and which will here be, tentatively, related to
the embodied experience of surfing include: biological philosophy and the non-
cognitive dimension of embodiment; the present moment, expanded awareness
and ritual; critiques of the body as primarily a site for the inscription of text and
discourse; relations between bodies and things as assemblages; and the expressive
aspects of performance and Radley's notion of 'semblances' (1995). Similarly,
the work of Burkitt (1999) and Shilling (2005) also moves towards the valorizing
of the emotional, sensual and aesthetic senses of embodiment as discussed in
Chapters 6 and 8.

Thrift (2001) has drawn on biological philosophy and philosophies of biologies
(Clark 1997; Deleuze 1988) to discuss the non-cognitive dimensions of embodiment, which account for 95 per cent of embodied thought. The action of sliding
along the wave takes place on such a non-cognitive level. With practice the
learned, kinaesthetic skill of surfing becomes an automatic, almost instinctual
series of (quite complex) movements. Thrift discusses such instinctual embodied
dispositions as both 'wired in' in terms of our evolution-based natural history, and
culturally sedimented, in relation to socialization and learning. He discusses
kinaesthesia in terms of a gestalt, 'as a sixth sense based on the interactive *movement* and subsequent awareness of body parts' (2001: 41).

Thrift relates the heightened sense of 'the present moment', attendant on
kinaesthetic performance, to the sense of an expanded awareness. Such an
approach allows the peak experiences, so often reported by surfers, to be linked
more explicitly to embodiment. On a more general level, Thrift relates the

emphasis on the present moment to the perhaps mystical practices of contem-plation which, drawing on vitalist modes of thinking, allow a re-enchantment with the world. Again, this resonates powerfully with the sense of 'stoke' or afterglow of surfing, and surfing culture's more spiritual tendencies. From such perspectives surfing may be viewed as a performance technology (Hughes-Freeland 1998), the kind of ritual practice which offers 'a heightened sense of involvement' (Thrift 2001: 44). Surfers are conscious of the ritualistic aspects of 'going surfing', for instance, waxing the board, putting on wetsuits, crossing the beach, passing through the shallows and paddling out through spaces in the waves, activities in which 'the body seems to take over' and accompanied affectively by a growing sense of aliveness.[2]

In critique of representation Thrift (1997) argues that a Foucauldian approach is preoccupied with the ways in which 'the body's functions and movements are shaped by discourse . . . thus, through representation as a text the body as flesh is marginalized' (1997: 137). By contrast, a non-representational view would assert that, rather than being about signs and meanings, the body is about 'the relation between bodies and things' (Thrift 2001: 39). This involves the body's location, in this case within the ocean, passing along a line of energy, producing 'spaces through the things of nature. . . . Which in turn inhabit the body through that production' (Thrift 2001: 47). Surfers often express the sense of a feeling that the energy of the wave seems to pass through them, or even becomes incorpo-rated within them, on a somatic level. Such sentiments reflect the ways in which the direct surfing experience involves pressures and bodily physiological and emotional/affective reactions.

While the surfboard may appear to mediate the relation to the energy and water, as noted above, during the ride there is very little conscious awareness of the board, which takes on the form of a kind of hybrid extension of the body. Thrift (2004) draws on Elkaim's notion of assemblage, in which a particular embodied practice involves the interrelation of a series of elements. In the case of surfing these could include genetics, neurophysiology, tools (surfboard, wetsuit, wax), life history, personal dispositions, encultured narratives from the surfing subculture and media, and so on, all functioning together in the brief instants of non-cognitive slide along the ephemeral wave. Thrift stresses that such an assemblage is a transient *structure*, rather than a single model of causality (2004). Thus, the human being is thought of as 'a kind of machination, a hybrid of flesh, knowledge, passion and technique' (Rose 1996 in Thrift 1997: 127), with skills becoming actualized and enacted through the connecting bedrock of desire (Grosz 1994 in Thrift 1997: 128).

Notions of the practice of surfing as an assemblage, or machination, of a multiplicity of elements, link with the abovenoted, co-constituted, sense of the surfer *being surfed*, rather than *surfing*. At the heart of the embodied experience of surfing are the somatic thrill of vertigo along with the more personal expressive dimension, which associates surfing with dance. To paraphrase Isadora Duncan's comment on dance in terms of surfing 'if I could tell you what it meant, there would be no point in *surfing* it' (cited in Bateson 1977, in Thrift 1997: 139). The surfing experience has so much more to do with non-verbal 'living–thinking', embodied knowledge, or performance as 'intelligence-as-act' (Melrose 1994 in Thrift 2004: 86), than cultural interpretations.

As with the description of peak experiences, surfers face difficulties in verbally expressing the nature of the surfing experience. Indeed, some experienced surfers may express a mild and perhaps humorous aversion to the use of clichés such as 'harmony', 'lost time' and 'time standing still', being used to articulate the surfing experience (Crockett 2003). Numerous examples abound of surfers' sense of the inadequacy of verbalization to describe the surfing experience. For instance, recounting the experience of riding a 30-foot Cribbar Wave (off Newquay, UK in December 2004 [see Plates 8 and 9]) South African surfer, Chris Bertish commented 'that kind of feeling is indescribable – you can't put it into words. If you try and put it into words you just end up sounding silly' (Greenwood 2004: 5). It is possible to find articles which discuss surfing as a metaphor for life. For instance, the often-quoted musings of Timothy Leary concerning, 'evolutionary surfers. Everything is made of waves' (e.g. Pezman 1979 in George 2001). However, surfers are generally somewhat sceptical of such metaphysical thinking, indeed Pezman even titled his article 'I'm a bit leery of Timothy Leary'. A piece of dialogue in surfing novelist Kem Nunn's *Tijuana Sloughs* (2004) makes a similar point when, after the protagonist, Fahey, expresses Miki Dora's idea 'about his whole life being about outrunning the lip. . . . Magdalena . . . responds by calmly wadding up a piece of paper and bouncing it off Fahey's forehead "that's the bullshit gong" she tells Fahey' (De Cure 2004: 124). Thus, within this book the primary emphasis is on surfing as an embodied practice, rather than cultural symbol, and the tensions between the two which are articulated in the concluding chapter.

Radley's discussion of dance as being concerned with 'evolving a semblance of a world within which specific questions take their meaning . . . to articulate complexes of thought-with-meaning that words cannot name, let alone set forth. It is a way of accessing the world' (1995 in Thrift 1997: 147) appears highly apposite to the surfing experience. Surfers experientially access a specific embodied world encompassing, for instance, the feelings of the sea and energies of the waves, which have limited meaning beyond sensations and movement. As with ritual and art (Geertz 1972; Radley 1995; Thrift 1997), such activity is creating sensibilities (or semblances) rather than merely representing existing sensibilities. While participants may find it difficult to verbally express such semblances, there is, in surfing as with all such expressive and vertigo-related practices, a sense of a shared embodied knowledge, which takes on the form of a feeling of communitas (Turner 1974). Yet, being verbal, the narratives through which a subculture such as surfing seeks 'to tell itself' will always be partial and limited in contrast to the sense of an openness of being which pertains to the embodied knowledge of the direct experience.

## Conclusion

This chapter has sought to explore understanding of the direct experience of surfing in relation to a range of theoretical notions and lenses. It has been argued that these perspectives are variously placed in terms of one of the core themes of this book, namely, mind and body. For instance, physiology research has a tendency to view the body as a machine, which may be partially directed by the mind. Motivational studies of surfing highlight the primacy of the sense of, and search for, the thrill of vertigo, but, along with much work on peak experiences and flow, tend to identify the mind as the central agency. It has been argued that the project of non-representational theory (Radley 1995; Thrift 1997) provides ways of exploring the immediate or raw experience of surfing which have the potential to transcend the common mind–body dualism of the dominant, representational, scholastic traditions. It has been particularly useful to consider the surfing experience in terms of its parallels with and divergences from dance. In an academic world which is overwhelmingly preoccupied with text and representation, non-representational theory affords exciting possibilities for the study of embodied practices, from the standpoint of such disciplines as cultural geography, sport sociology and surfing studies. Such possibilities could gainfully explore the scope for experiential and performative study.

# 8 Conclusions and research directions

## Introduction

This final chapter first seeks to draw together core conclusions which emerge from the foregoing chapters into a tentative thesis concerning surfing as an embodied, cultural practice, and second, outlines a range of directions for future research into the socio-cultural and embodied dimensions of surfing.

The core theme underlying this book has been to explore surfing in terms of seeking to transcend the split between mind and body. It must be stressed that the following should be viewed as tentative and preliminary, as an attempt to sketch a framework to be challenged, elaborated and explored in further research into surfing. This chapter does not seek to repeat in detail the contents of the foregoing chapters but rather to, circumspectly, distil a range of key conclusions. For reasons of brevity these are here listed as a series of tentative propositions concerning the social, cultural and embodied dimensions of surfing.

## Core propositions

1 First and foremost surfing is an embodied practice rooted in experiential lived knowledge.
2 The embodied practice of surfing is given a rich diversity of meanings, both to surfers and the yet-to-surf, wider world, which contribute to the sense of surfing variously as a lifestyle, culture and subculture.
3 An especially important source of the wider cultural meanings ascribed to surfing is the Western imaginary of the sea, coastscape and beach. The coastscape, sea and beach comprise the place of surfing in embodied, aesthetic and cultural senses, which have powerful resonations with the surfing lifestyle. It is these especial qualities of the particular setting which distinguishes surfing from other 'alternative' or 'lifestyle' sports. In particular, this Western imaginary of the sea is infused with tropes and evocations associated with the Romantic movement in arts and philosophy.
4 The evolving perceptions of the sea and coastscape, within which the practice of surfing is embedded, have emerged in relation to the reflexive inter-play of the more cerebral and culturally strategic elements of the Western

Romantic imaginary of the sea, *and* the direct, bodily, sensual somatic practice of vigorous seabathing in turbulent waters.

5   The joy, peak experience and sheer pleasure of such an autotelic, non-instrumental activity as surfing has prompted a cultural process of reflection and storytelling, through which practitioners have sought to make sense of their obsession and passion. Through this process, and primarily over the course of the twentieth century, a fairly coherent historical narrative of surfing has emerged, by which surfing culture has sought to make itself intelligible to itself and the wider culture. Surfing's historical narrative generally involves interweaving of cultural and technological agencies.

6   Although surfing culture clearly draws on a range of sources and tendencies from the wider culture, these have been blended into a distinct surfing imaginary. Such a surfing imaginary involves a complex combination of tropes, myths and desires including, for example, an aetiological myth of tropical, paradisal origins, wanderlust in search of the perfect wave, connotations of hedonism, freedom, nature and the raw elements, a rich sense of aesthetics and so on. The strong resonances of these aesthetics has led to the appropriation of surfing as an inspiration for a range of artistic and fashion forms, in turn broadening its wider appeal.

7   In terms of practical, day-to-day visual experience the notion of a surfing imaginary may be elaborated with reference to the surfer's gaze. Such a gaze, which is shaped by a surfer's habitus involves ways of viewing the coastscape, sea and waves, other surfers' performance and equipment, social comportment and subcultural expression. The surfer's gaze thus combines operational orientations to waves and discriminative almost subconscious, ascriptions of subcultural performance capital.

8   Standard, 'stand-up' surfing may be viewed as an 'assemblage' or hybrid, bodily practice, in which, during waveriding, the surfboard as tool becomes an almost unconscious extension of the body. The technological thread within the surfing narrative highlights the ways within which progress in surfing performance has been made possible and facilitated by advances in surfboard design.

9   Despite the coherence of many aspects of the image of surfing culture, the historical narrative also revolves around a range of powerful tensions or conflicting tendencies within surfing as a culture. Core tensions include first, the complex interplay of the soul surfing and competitive orientations, which variously conceive of surfing as play or sport. Second, given surfing's spiritual and/or counter-cultural sensibilities, there is a perennial tension between the antipathy towards commercialization of surfing on the one hand, and the pragmatic desire to make a living from some aspects of the sport on the other. A core third tension revolves around the soul surfing emphasis on the personal, individualist thrill of vertigo, and the more socially expressive aspects of surfing as performance for an audience as dance or sporting competition.

10  The articulation and expression of the meta-, and sub-, narratives of surfing have been amplified and elaborated within surfing's proliferating mediatization, especially since the 1960s. While surfing as an embodied competence is

primarily set within the gestalt-like, integrative, kinaesthetic 'sixth sense', the media of surfing has been primarily visual, with the evolving and spectacular artistry of surf photography at its core. Photography has had a key role in being able to capture or 'freeze' moments of an ephemeral, non-cognitive ride, in turn facilitating surfing's reflexivity. Furthermore, above and beyond the reinforcement of a surfing narrative, the mediatization of surfing has drawn on and further imbued surfing culture with a rich and endlessly explored sense of aesthetics, perhaps unparalleled in any other sport.

11  Nevertheless despite the richness of the mediatization, photography and narrative of surfing, such aspects of the culture are essentially epiphenomena of the main embodied practice of riding waves. Indeed, most fundamental to this observation is that the relationship between surfing culture and the body is that it is desirable to consider both (although not dichotomously) the surfing and surfed body, in their active and passive senses. Moreover, while traditionally absent from writings on surfing, once identified as a focus, the body is in fact omnipresent and an extremely significant factor in any commentary on surfing culture.

12  Understanding surfing in a non-dualistic (mind and body) integrationist sense involves recognizing the ways in which the body is fundamental to the construction and maintenance of surfing culture. Three clearly emerging elements of this are that the surfing and surfed body is above all, practical, interacting and storied. These elements lead to a clear proposition that the body is *lived* and experienced directly and not through representation (i.e. constructed from thinking about), rather it is constructed through *doing* (even if that doing is thinking!). Therefore, while the surfing body can be represented in a myriad of ways, the lived body remains an important benchmark to return to and start from in any research agenda because of its integrationist standpoint. Further to this, the *lived* body is also an *emotional* body. Emotions are one of the most fundamental body–mind links that can be seen as products of the social inscriptions that are themselves the product of the surfing practices, interactions and stories. In this sense, emotions form a kind of 'ontological glue' that help to make surfers 'feel' similarly as a result of practices, interactions and stories, but also inspire them to act, to create and recreate, practices, interactions and stories.

13  The physical practice of waveriding leads to the construction of the single most important kind of subcultural capital that can be identified in surfing: embodied surfing performance capital. Because this form of subcultural capital is embodied and only acquired by the slow process of inscribing or somatizing subculturally legitimate ways of knowing and performing surfing into and onto the body, it remains the most important for conversion into other forms of capital such as the construction of subculturally legitimate identities. However, not all expressions of embodied subcultural capital are considered equally legitimate or so readily convertible.

14  While subcultural capital is consistently configured around the performing body, as above, surfing is manifestly a varied subculture with a historically

evolving range of characteristic (embodied) performative styles and adapted technologies that come together to form a differentiated, culturally distinguished (e.g. surfboard design, techniques) collection of interpretive practices, (increasingly) loosely united around the experience of waveriding. Each of these subcultural elements can be seen to be vying for social acceptability and aesthetic distinction in relation to the other surf and waveriding activities in its immediate geographical and socio-cultural locality (e.g. bodyboarding, kitesurfing, windsurfing, canoe surfing amongst others). In this sense it is possible to consider surfing subcultures as producing, possessing and 'trading' or converting forms of subcultural capital.

15  The current subcultural surfing style to attract, represent and embody the greatest subcultural capital is that of commercialized competitive professional surfing.

16  In spite of an often romanticized history of mixed sex participation in the ancient Hawaiian era, in the twentieth century there has been an identified hierarchy of gender relations in surfing that centres around the assumed centrality of the heroic male's experience of waveriding. This has more recently been consolidated by the rise of male-dominated competitive surfing and the entry of surfing into the world (and sporting) gender order. Men still clearly dominate surfing practically and symbolically in terms of organization, status, practice and visibility. However, female surfing, like other forms of female athleticism has struggled hard for visibility and recognition with some success.

17  Female surfing has quite recently adopted surfing styles that were traditionally associated with male surfers (aggressive techniques, more speed and dynamic movements) and combined them with the 'graceful emphasis' that previously demarcated female surfing style, to create a new hybrid form that commands respect from many men and women alike. These changes take place alongside the commercial commodification of women's surfing that positions women surfers' heterosexuality high on the agenda, while celebrating women's newly found empowerment through the expression of surfing physicality. The gender order is very much intact in surfing, but women have at least achieved access to the activity and, in so doing, its intrinsic and even some of its extrinsic rewards. There remains a very long way to go before surfing could be said to be non-gendered.

18  Against the stereotypical image of surfing as a hedonistic, 'easy-going' dream of unproblematic escape, the growing reality, in the face of the physical and cultural scarcity inherent to the practice, is imbued with a number of contested orders. Thus, access to waves in particular settings is structured by local/outsider ascriptions, subcultural capital, gender, and possibly also ethnic, orders. Such orders comprise power structures which contest the dream of surfing, beyond the regulation of access to the waves through surfing etiquette.

19  In terms of motivating attractions of sports or physical activity, surfing is characterized by intrinsic rewards. Of these, the thrill of vertigo is most important, but closely followed by aesthetic and cathartic appeal, which has

often been further articulated in terms of ecstatic peak and flow experiences. These findings are consistent with personality research which has suggested that surfers score particularly highly in terms of sensation-seeking and openness to experience scales, reinforcing the intrinsic motivational appeal of the practice.

20 Notions pertaining to the project of non-representational theory were found to be especially apposite in gaining some sense of the embodied experiential nature of surfing. Furthermore, the expressive and experiential dimensions of surfing parallel those in some forms of modern dance. Non-representational theory would suggest caution in deriving meanings from surfing outside of direct experiences of sensations and movement. Rather than merely representing or reflecting existing sensibilities from the wider culture, surfing is above all an embodied practice that creates (sensation-based) sensibilities or semblances.

## Directions for further research

This book has been written at a time when there is still a relatively limited amount of academic research conducted into surfing. The focus of the book has primarily been on the cultural, embodied, gendered, social and psychological aspects of surfing. It has, therefore, not had the scope to comment on the important research possibilities pertaining, for example, to the more scientific, technological, environmental and physiological dimensions of surfing. Within the social and cultural analysis of surfing there have, as yet, been a relatively small number of classic, seminal studies, most notably those of Flynn (1987), Stranger (1999) and Booth (2001a). What is clear, however, is that there is a growing groundswell (if you will excuse the pun) of research interest in surfing in many parts of the world. This book has sought to draw attention to some of the major areas of theory and literature within the context of which such future research may be gainfully developed. Surfing studies are clearly multi-, or rather trans-, disciplinary areas of research, with a fast-growing corpus of knowledge and literature.

Throughout the foregoing chapters reference has often been made to themes worthy of further study. However, given that such research suggestions have been, necessarily, scattered throughout the text, an attempt is made here in this final section to draw together and summarize some of the main directions for further research, and to make some comment on relevant methods and wider methodological debates which pertain to such work. In order to link with the reading of the text, these research directions are here broadly ordered in terms of the structure of the book. The themes and topics identified below are, of course, indicative and suggestive rather than exhaustive.

## The experience and appreciation of the sea, coastscape and beach in surfing

There is enormous scope for, both historical and contemporary, research into the cultural and experiential sensibilities towards the sea and coastscape in surfing. Textual analysis of historical sources has the potential to illuminate the unfolding of the surfing imaginary as a sociocultural construction, with its attendant set of practices and shared meanings. Specifically, such work could seek to identify the ways in which the surfing imaginary is not only related to, but also distinct from, the core Western Romantic imaginary of the sea. Given the overriding significance and primacy of the visual and photographic in representations of surfing, a whole range of visual methodologies (Rose 2001) may gainfully be employed to study the photography of the surfing media, and the ubiquitous use of surfing images within the wider (yet-to-surf) culture, in particular, in advertising.

Within the ambit of landscape studies there has been a relative neglect of coastal and beach studies. Research may gainfully be addressed to surfing localities around the world, in terms of their rich cultural constructions and powerful evocations of sense of place. The latter theme pertaining to the core elements of, and tensions within, surfing culture of its powerful territoriality, travel and wanderlust, and the implications for sense of identity, of surfers' appropriations of personal meanings of the sea and surfing places. This book has sought to emphasize that the research challenge is not so much merely to identify representations and their symbolic meanings, but rather to explore such aspects of surfing in relation to sensual experience and embodied and living knowledge, which are such powerful bases of surfers' behaviours and lifestyles. Such future research may seek to explore surfers' orientation to the sea in explicit reference to mind and body, thought and emotion and image and experiential embodiment.

## The history of surfing

Further systematic research could explore facets of the narrative history of surfing. Chapter 3 above identified, what may be thought of as, the broad meta-narrative of surfing history and culture. Within the proliferating surfing media of books and magazines there is clearly an enormous cultural enterprise taking place which is articulating surfing's heritage. It is here argued that academic analysis has a part to play in highlighting the provisional, contested and contextual nature of the surfing narrative. Indeed, the conceptual tools of narrative history may be applied to delineate the ways in which the selectivity and unfolding cultural authority of such histories reflect the patterns and structures inherent in the human cultural process of storymaking. It would be hoped that in future years a whole series of narrative histories of surfing may emerge, which may involve further reflexivity in terms of gender, ethnicity and nationality, for instance. Again, there is particular scope for textual analysis of the narratives presented within the surfing media.

Narrative analysis also has great potential to elucidate matters of identity and personal significance that underlie surfers' biographies and changing lifestyles.

Research could explore the crafted, yet apparent, coherence, of narratives in terms of their powerful implications, both for the appeal or seduction of surfing (as a personal future orientation) and in the construction of personal past through the process of memory. Research could address the ways in which different facets of surfing culture (e.g. soul surfing, commercial, professional, competitive and so on) draw on facets of surfing's narrative in different ways.

## The globalization of surfing

The mind–body interface that pervades the practice of surfing provides a particularly useful theme for analysis within various surfing localities. The historical narratives of surfing show considerable similarities across varied surfing cultures, however, research could explore the different ways in which surfing impacts upon identity, lifestyle and embodied practice in different cultural settings. Such analyses could explore the g(local)ization of the ways in which surfing culture is embedded within different sociocultural settings and places. Of particular, and as yet largely neglected, interest are the impacts and effects of surfing attendant to its growth within non-Western cultural settings, such as in Indonesia. Such work could also explore the varied cultural perspectives on surfing as mere recreation, more coherent lifestyle or as sporting phenomenon.

## The inherent scarcity and regulation of surfing

As well as further exploring the subcultural and lifestyle dynamics of surfing, there is clearly scope for further systematic research into the social regulation of access to waves. As with any cultural phenomenon which is associated with notions of 'paradise', so surfing has also been referred to (within a declensionist narrative) as a 'paradise lost'. In particular, such sentiments (expressed for instance in the 'surf noir' of Ken Nunn as 'kicking against the myth') seek to grapple with a whole host of negative expressions, such as territoriality and 'surf rage', which relate to surfing's inherent scarcity, as victim of its very success in attracting increasing numbers of participants. There is scope for research which builds on the fine work already undertaken into surf etiquette, conflict expression and management and the various orders of power (encoded for instance in subcultural capital) which pervade surfing as a social phenomenon.

## The gender order in surfing

With the growth of women's surfing, the research of gender in surfing is an area of growing interest, and considerable importance. Of particular significance here is how to explore the dynamics of the gender order in more detail to better understand how male and female surfers are shifting positions to construct and sustain their gendered identities. In any such exploration it is important to consider how changes to the position of one group are likely to be accompanied by small shifts in the others, this is particularly relevant in relation to the gendered body. While there is some understanding about the emergence of competitive and iconic female surfers who are spearheading the invasion of this 'fratriarchal' activity, as Booth (2004) refers to it, there is much less understanding of the 'everyday' female surfer and their gendered experiences. Studies of the gender order in surfing therefore need to consider surfing as a sport and surfing as a recreational/lifestyle activity in equal measure. Other avenues that require close scrutiny in future research are the gendered patterns of consumption and how female surfers' emotions are being targeted in ways which may actually reinforce their subordinated positions in the gender order. Another important question that emerges is the changing relationship between male surfers, masculinities and such themes as competition for waves in crowded conditions and the pursuit of ever-bigger, more exotic and dangerous waves.

## The surfing body

Responding to theorists such as Burkitt (1999) and Shilling (2005) the body needs to be seen as a multidimensional phenomenon, that is simultaneously the *source*, *location* and *means* for society. Therefore, explorations of how the surfing body is constructed by social forces and how the surfing body contributes to those same social forces is a key focus for future enquiry. In order to accomplish this three overlapping dimensions of socialized bodily behaviour become important avenues for future investigation: practical, interacting and storied bodies.

The analysis of how surfing culture becomes inscribed onto and into the body through practice is an important task. Developing rich and detailed accounts of the 'whats' and the 'hows' of the surfer's habitus might reveal much about this embodied, dispositional texture of this subculture. Further to this, research into surfing practice could usefully explore surfing as an embodied cultural economy where various fields and subfields of surfing struggle with each other for legitimacy and distinction (and with other water sports) and how this takes place over, as Bourdieu (1993b) puts it, the legitimate body and the legitimate uses of the body in surfing. Exploring the interacting body in surfing offers the potential for better understanding of how surfers engage in symbolic interpretive action with other surfers, their environment and objects around them such as surfboards. Ethnographic, observational work could reveal much about the body idiom, inter-action rituals, regionalization of performing space and self-management of various surfing subcultures. The storied body offers a way of focusing on the surfing body as the producer of embodied narrative of the self that can illuminate the type of relationship surfers construct with their bodies as a result of their bodies' response to a number of key problems of embodiment. How surfers story the bodily contingencies of risk, injury, performance and ageing for example are potentially illuminating angles of study. Moreover, the focus on the storied body might also reveal to a considerable degree how surfers come to acquire and apply the narrative resources that circulate in surfing culture and society more generally. All of these explorations also need to take account of the emotions and how the emotional body stimulates and is stimulated by surfing practices, interactions and stories.

Finally, all investigations into the body in surfing will need to remain mindful of the importance yet difficulty of keeping research accounts fully *embodied*. The tendency for the lived body to slip away, in our increasingly theorized and abstract explanations is ever-present. It is important therefore that research into the surfing body explores new ways of revealing the lived body (Sparkes and Smith 2002). A point that is returned to briefly below.

## Embodiment experience and expressiveness of surfing performance

A whole host of fruitful research directions emerges from the attempt to understand the core experience of surfing. Particularly useful parallels may be drawn from the cognate field of dance studies. Research could gainfully be addressed to the tension between surfing as a raw, immediate sensual and individual experience, and the more socially expressive and/or socially competitive and status-related aspects of surfing performance. The complex issues surrounding the question of style in surfing warrant systematic research. Such analysis could be facilitated by the development of more rigorous notation of the subtleties of surfing manoeuvres, along the lines of the contribution of Laban Notation to dance studies. Qualitative, in-depth analysis could also seek to explore the bases and nature of different high-performance styles of surfing. Such work could take further the excellent research undertaken into surfing and peak performance and flow (Bennett and Kramer 2001), to explore the personal, cultural and embodied bases of the contrasting styles of different elite surfers.

Given the obvious crossovers and similarities between the performance and experience of surfing with those of snowboarding and skateboarding, there is considerable scope for research that seeks to compare the experiential and embodied characteristics of the three practices. Such lines of research could explore the narrative and cultural dimensions, along with the more non-representational aspect of their embodied practice.

The substantive issues and tensions highlighted throughout the text, and summarized in the core propositions above, raise some epistemological issues that are worthy of basic commentary. It is best to begin to explore these issues by considering the production of the text itself. This text makes no claim to 'reality correspondence' in the classical neo-realist sense of the term. Nevertheless, it has employed and advocated various analytical and textual strategies that are deemed legitimate for the sociological and social geographical study of surfing. The analytical modes used have included a mixture of forms of hermeneutical textual and media analysis. Juxtaposed with these are represented ethnographic material where an embodied practical, interactional and predominantly interpretive focus is foregrounded. The textual writing strategy is overwhelmingly 'scientific realist' and is only slightly modified by the subjective voice that, on occasion, is permitted to penetrate the text via the footnotes. The analytical and textual strategies involved in producing the text do not hide but in fact reveal core underlying epistemological tensions that run through this text and scholarship in this area.

These are the inquiry into practical embodied experience and the disembodying effect of the representation of practical experience respectively.

The biographical, narrative, post-structuralist or post-modern turn in social science enquiry, as it is variously described, provides the study of a subcultural activity like surfing with some probing questions. While it might be possible to empirically identify the experiences of surfers as the key recurring element in the stories of surfers, these *remain stories*, mediated, and, by definition, limited by language. But language, as most post-structuralists point out, is inherently limiting and we are left with an embodied 'lack' in the Lacanian sense, where the desire produced through corporeality becomes impossible to convert, translate and represent in words – an embodied frustration that is always an absent presence in most probing accounts of human experience (see Belsey 2002). The response to this epistemological turn by the social sciences is, hitherto, far from coherent or unified, with some abandoning any attempt at experiential correspondence altogether and in so doing revitalizing a very old Western mind–body dualism. We must, it is conceded, learn to live with the limitations and finitude of language. However, like many researchers we will testify to the tantalizing yet elusive grasp of the 'something else' or 'more than representation' as Lorimer (2004) puts it, that 'something else', the frustration of the absent presence, will not go away and cannot be ignored. The question is how to approach this topic in ways that make epistemological sense? One such attempt is articulated by Lorimer (2004):

> During recent years, 'non-representational theory' has become as an umbrella term for diverse work that seeks better to cope with our self-evidently more-than-human, more-than-textual, multi-sensual worlds.
>
> (Lorimer 2004: 3)

The question is how do researchers 'do' non-representational work without themselves reinforcing the other side of the same dualism between mind and body mentioned above, by overzealously accepting that expression and action are somehow two separate realms? The distinction and differentiation between language (representation) and experience (non-representation) can more positively be viewed as a creative tension that produces an energy of its own and commits researchers and theorists alike to 'step outside of the box' and reconsider ways in which this more-than-experience might be solicited, captured and conveyed. Again, Lorimer (2004) offers some useful methodological orientation on this:

> To summarise lots of complex statements as simply as possible: it is multifarious, open encounters in the realm of practice that matter most. Greatest unity is found in an insistence on expanding our once comfortable understanding of 'the social' and how it can be regarded as something researchable. This often means thinking through locally formative interventions in the world. At first, the phenomena in question may seem remarkable only by their apparent insignificance. The focus falls on how life takes shape and

gains expression in shared experiences, everyday routines, fleeting encounters, embodied movements, pre-cognitive triggers, practical skills, affective intensities, enduring urges, unexceptional interactions and sensuous dispositions. Attention to these kinds of expression, it is contended, offers an escape from the established academic habit of striving to uncover meanings and values that apparently await our discovery, interpretation, judgement and ultimate representation.

(Lorimer 2004: 4)

Of course, neither the language nor direct embodied practical experience of surfing are knowable in any absolute way. However, as a focus and a direction, Lorimer's outline provides a useful signpost. Surfers are perhaps remarkable in their shared articulation of their sensory experiences, both in what they 'say' and when and how they 'say' it (surfing has a rich variety of its own 'experiential' words). In this sense, practical embodied experience remains as relative as it is elusive and intersubjective. However, surfers also consistently reiterate that the experience of surfing is the key to the cultural practice and that 'words' do not, and cannot, articulate the experience of the 'dream glide'. Researchers of surfing ignore this subcultural tension at their peril. Therefore, it is important that the contemporary study of surfing acknowledges that these debates not only exist but that they require some clear articulation between selected method and focus. As indicated above, the focus on the surfing body–mind as an interconnected duality needs to be centrally positioned, and the focus on practical sensual experience foregrounded.

Following this, approaches as diverse as hermeneutics, phenomenology, discourse and narrative analysis, ethnomethodology, symbolic interactionism and even structuration theories can all serve as important strategies for exploring experience. In forging different methodological paths, researchers must also take some risks, with both writing and representation and this is particularly the case with regard to how researchers 'show' experience. Recently qualitative enquiry in sport and physical activity has moved on to consider new ways of telling tales (Sparkes and Smith 2002). These would include confessional tales, impressionist tales, auto-ethnographic tales, poetic fictions and ethnodramas. Elsewhere, Pink (2001) shows how social anthropology has moved beyond the written text to construct a range of 'visual' anthropological techniques, which have the potential to present practical embodied experience in challenging and exciting new ways that both circumvent and augment text representation. Surfing research needs to take these methodological risks without unconsciously succumbing to the neo-positivist appeals of some greater 'reality-correspondence' that may seem to be provided by novel approaches, but it must also avoid constructivist dualisms in which the surfing body becomes reduced to what is said, and quite literally disappears thereafter. In conclusion, if the future study of surfing by sport sociologists, human geographers and others is to remain conceptually and empirically dynamic, it also requires a self-questioning attitude towards the relationship between theory, methodology and data. All three of these elements need to interact purposefully around the willingness to retain (however elusive) a focus on practical embodied experience.

This book has been written at a point in time when it is just about possible to consider most of the academic writing on the social, cultural and embodied dimensions of surfing. However, such is the growth and momentum of the study of surfing as a social and bodily phenomenon that surfing studies are fast becoming a flourishing area of transdisciplinary research in their own right. It is our hope that the perspectives that we have sought to articulate in this book may provide some basis for future forms of research that will be able to explore and capture the lived experience of surfing.

# Notes

## 2 The enchanted sea

1   As Randy Rarick has commented in a recent surfing film (*Step into Liquid* 2004), 'the lifestyle of surfing is unlike any other sport . . . How many people do you know that go and gaze at a tennis court? . . . Think of any other sport where they go and they look, and people just sit and watch waves, and it doesn't matter whether it's perfect waves like we have here in Hawaii or it's the Great Lakes!' (Brown, D. (2004) *Step into Liquid*, Artisan Films).

2   The tragic events of the December 2004 tsunami have had a particular personal resonance for many surfers. It is not so much that surfing's medium of joy has once again been shown to be the carrier of death and destruction, but that many of the very localities in which the havoc has been wrought contain some of the world's most enchanted surfspots. For instance, the islands of Nias and the Mentawai lay just off the epicentre of the earthquake. The surfing community has lost many dear Indonesian and Sri Lankan friends.

## 3 The narrative history and globalization of surfing

1   Personally, when I first saw Falzon's film *Morning of the Earth* (1974) as a teenager I related to its alternative sense of wholeness and saw it as a vision of the future. In contrast, when I watch Falzon's *Morning of the Earth* (e.g. see Kidman 2002) today, 30 years later, I am more inclined to see it as a beautiful evocation of a past. Similarly (and I expect others may agree), McCoy's film *Tubular Swells* originally represented to me the most cutting edge, high-performance surfing, while today I see the film as containing some of the most elegant and graceful surfing. The point is that when we return to evocative images of 'our' past we do not necessarily interpret them in precisely the same ways as we had originally. (NF)

2   My own, admittedly unsubstantiated, sense is that those older surfers still actively involved in surfing are probably more likely to take an interest in surfing history and culture than those who feel that they have completely left it behind in their lives. (NF)

3   Further details of these iconic figures of surfing history may be found in any one of the many excellent accounts of surfing culture (e.g. Young 1994; Finney and Houston 1996; Kampion 1997: 2003).

## 4 Surfing as subculture and lifestyle

1   It is not unimaginable that, if money were no object, many surfers' ideal would be a dream home by the beach and to scream around in Lamborghinis and Maseratis! (NF)

2   There is perhaps an anomaly to surfing's 'cool' and modest image in the ways some surfers include self-praise in magazine articles of which they are co-authors.
3   I have occasionally noticed the way in which Anglo (American, Australian and British) surfers articulate the view that 'Latino' (French, Spanish, Latin American) surfers frequently violate surf etiquette. There is uncertainty as to whether there is real evidence for this view or whether the 'Latinos' are being scapegoated as a cultural other. (NF)

## 7 The experience of surfing

1   I have been only too well aware that in order to actually write about surfing (in this book) I have had to partially restrain my surfing body, returning to my metropolitan body. I gather that Mark Stranger has had the same ironic feeling in completing his writing on surfing. (NF)
2   From the practitioner's viewpoint actually going surfing always feels like entering another world or reality. No doubt this is accentuated by the fact that surfing takes place in another realm (the sea), but there is also a sense of a bodily awareness when you know you are going to surf (a certain toning, maybe tensing and enlivening, and single-minded alertness). (NF)
3   It is certainly not being suggested by 'distinctiveness' here that 'stand-up' or standard surfboard riding is superior to other waveriding forms. Any such debate about which forms are 'better' than others is rather sterile. Individuals simply have their own preferences.
4   Even the more loosely structured 'expression sessions' today are probably less to do with providing a space for expressiveness as style, than with giving surfers greater freedom to perform explosive or experimental manoeuvres, than is the case in the usual, more formal competition format.
5   Both of the UK's Surf Science degrees have useful modules on the physiological aspects of surfing, with some students producing sound and innovative dissertations on such topics.
6   An important exception is the special case of the relatively small number of 'tow-in' monster wave surfers who, recognizing the extreme danger of their pursuit, do train to ensure that they have every possibility of surviving a 'wipe-out' at breaks such as 'Jaws' and 'Mavericks'.
7   The link between risk and peak experience has been highlighted with reference to the development of Zen Buddhism in Japan. Zen, which has an emphasis on direct experience, flourished during the Kamakura period when Japan was under threat from Mongol invasion. The Kamakura Zen teachers considered that the warrior, in wartime, had especial advantages in being able to gain access to Zen awareness, notably a sense of the transitory nature of life, total absorption in the moment and living relatively free of worldly ambitions and petty anxieties (Leggett 1978).

# Bibliography

Althusser, L. (1983). *Essays on Ideology*. London: Verso.

Anderson, B. (1983). *Imagined Communities: Reflections on the Origin and Spread of Nationalism*. London: Verso.

Anderson, R. (2004). Recorded music and practices of remembering. *Social and Cultural Geography*, 5(1), 3–20.

Andrews, D. L. (2000). Posting up: French poststructuralism and the critical analysis of contemporary sporting culture. In J. Coakley and E. Dunning (eds), *Handbook of Sports Studies*. London: Sage, pp. 106–138.

Appadurai, A. (1990). Disjuncture and difference in global cultural economy. *Theory, Culture and Society*, 7(2–3), 295–310.

Archer, M. (1990). Theory, culture and post-industrial society. *Theory, Culture and Society*, 7(2–3), 97–119.

Auden, W. H. (1951). *The Enchafed Flood, or The Romantic Iconography of the Sea*. London: Faber and Faber.

Australian Sports Commission (2005). *Membership growth – surfing*. Online at http://www.ausport.gov.au/membergrowth/surfing.asp (21 February 2005).

Baert, P. (2004). Pragmatism as philosophy of the social sciences. *European Journal of Social Theory*, 7(3).

Bale, J. (2000). Human geography and the study of sport. In J. Coakley and E. Dunning (eds), *Handbook of Sports Studies*. London: Sage, pp. 171–186.

—— and Philo, C. (1998). *Body Cultures: Essays on Sport, Space and Identity. Henning Eichberg*. London: Routledge.

Banks, M. (2004). *Is modern technology destroying the search in surfing?* Paper presented at the Proceedings of the Third Annual Conference on Contemporary Issues in Surfing, University of Plymouth, UK.

Barilotti, S. (2003). A beautiful pandemonium: How Rick Griffin, South Bay surfer cartoonist became the unlikely herald of the psychedelic revolution. *The Surfer's Journal*, 12(5), 42–59.

Bateson, G. (1955). A theory of play and fantasy. *Psychiatric Research Reports 2 of the American Psychiatric Association*, 39–51.

—— (1977). *Steps to an Ecology of Mind*. London: Picador.

Baudrillard, J. (1983). *Simulations*. New York: Semiotexte.

Bauman, Z. (2000). *Liquid Modernity*. Cambridge: Polity Press.

Bayley, S. (1991). *Taste: The Secret Meaning of Things*. London: Faber and Faber.

Beaglehole, J. C. (ed.) (1967). *The Voyage of Resolution and Adventure, 1776–1780* (Vols. 1 and 2). Cambridge: (Hakluyt Society).

Beck, U. (1992). *Risk Society: Towards a New Modernity*. London: Sage.

Belsey, C. (2002). *Poststructuralism: A Very Short Introduction*. Oxford: Oxford University Press.

Bennett, D. (2003). *Surf photography: Hoax or not?* Paper presented at the Second Annual Conference in Contemporary Issues in Surfing, University of Plymouth.

Bennett, R. and Kramer, P. (2001). The psychology of peak surfing performance. *The Surfer's Path*, 27, 92–93.

Benson, J. (2000). *Environmental Ethics: An Introduction With Readings*. London: Routledge.

Berman, M. (1983). *All that is Solid Melts into Air: The Experience of Modernity*. London: Verso.

Bilderbeck, J. (2002). John Bilderbeck: A separate reality. *The Surfer's Journal*, 11(3), 10–31.

Black, J. (1970). *The Dominion of Man*. Edinburgh: Edinburgh University Press.

Blackburn, M. (2001). *Surf's Up: Collecting the Longboard Era*. Atglen: Schiffer.

Blair, J. (ed.) (1978). *The Illustrated Discography of Surf Music 1959–1965*. Riverside: John Blair.

Blumer, H. (1962). Society as symbolic interaction. In A. Rose, M. (ed.), *Human Behaviour and Social Process: An Interactionist Approach*. Boston: Houghton Mifflin.

Boden, S. and Williams, S. J. (2002). Consumption and emotion: The romantic ethic revised. *Sociology*, 36(3), 493–512.

Bolster, W. (2002). *Warren Bolster: Masters of Surf Photography 3*. San Clemente: Journal Concepts.

Booth, D. (1995). Ambiguities in pleasure and discipline: The development of competitive surfing. *Journal of Sport History*, 22(3), 189–206.

—— (1996a). Surfing films and videos: Adolescent fun, alternative lifestyle, adventure industry. *Journal of Sport History*, 23(3), 313–327.

—— (1996b). The technological and cultural determinants of surfing. *Proceedings and Newsletter – North American Society for Sport History*, 74–75.

—— (1999). Surfing: The cultural and technological determinants. *Culture, Sport, Society*, 2(1), 36–55.

—— (2001a). *Australian Beach Cultures: The History of Sun, Sand and Surf*. London: Frank Cass.

—— (2001b). From bikinis to boardshorts: Wahines and the paradoxes of surfing culture. *Journal of Sport History*, 28(1), 3–22.

—— (2003). Expression sessions: Surfing, style and prestige. In R. E. Rinehart and S. Sydnor (eds), *To the Extreme: Alternative Sports, Inside and Out*. New York: State University of New York, pp. 315–336.

—— (2004) Surfing: From one (cultural) extreme to another. In B. Wheaton (ed.), *Understanding Lifestyle Sports: Consumption, Identity and Difference*. London: Routledge, pp. 94–110.

Bourdieu, P. (1984). *Distinction: A Social Critique of the Judgement of Taste*. London: Routledge.

—— (1990). *The Logic of Practice*. Cambridge: Polity Press.

—— (1991). Did you say popular? *Language and Symbolic Power*. Cambridge: Polity Press.

—— (1993a). Concluding remarks: For a sociogenetic understanding of intellectual works. In C. Calhoun, E. LiPuma and M. Postone (eds), *Bourdieu: Critical Perspectives*. Cambridge: Polity Press, pp. 263–275.

—— (1993b). *Sociology in Question*. London: Sage.

—— (2001). *Masculine Domination*. Stanford, CA: Stanford University Press.

Bourke, J. (1954). *The Sea as Symbol of English Poetry*. Eton: Alden and Blackwell.

Boyne, R. (1990). Culture and the world system. *Theory, Culture and Society*, 7(2–3), 57–65.

Brace, C. (1999). Cornish identity and landscape in the work of Arthur Caddick. *Cornish Studies*, 7, 130–146.

—— (2004). Landscape and identity. In I. Richardson and P. Richards (eds), *Studying Cultural Landscapes*. London: Arnold, pp. 121–140.

Brewer, A. (2001). *Art Brewer: Masters of Surf Photography 2*. San Clemente: Journal Concepts.

Brisick, J. (2003). Rushes: Viewing life's dailies with Jack McCoy. *The Surfer's Journal*, 12(3), 58–59.

—— and Pezman, S. (1993). Fringe dweller: Conversations with Wayne Lynch. *The Surfer's Journal*, 2(2), 102–123.

Brod, H. and Kaufman, M. (1994). *Theorizing Masculinities*. Thousand Oaks: Sage.

Brown, D. (2005). An economy of gendered practices? Learning to teach physical education from the perspective of Pierre Bourdieu's embodied sociology. *Sport, Education and Society*, 10(1), 3–23.

Bruner, J. (1990). *Acts of Meaning*. MA and London: Harvard University Press.

Burke, K. (1945). *A Grammar of Motives*. Berkeley: University of California Press.

Burkitt, I. (1999). *Bodies of Thought; Embodiment, Identity and Modernity*. London: Sage.

Butler, J. (1993). *Bodies That Matter: On The Discursive Limits of Sex*. London: Routledge.

Byfield, B. (2002). *Women and surfing: Gendered experiences and participatory exclusion in subcultural space*. Unpublished dissertation for BA in Geography, Exeter University, Exeter.

Callois. R. (1958/1961). *Man, Play and Games*. New York: Free Press.

Campbell, R. (1987). *The Romantic Ethic and the Spirit of Modern Consumerism*. Oxford: Basil Blackwell.

Canniford, R. (2005). Moving shadows: Suggestions for ethnography in globalized cultures. *Qualitative Market Research*, 8.

—— and Layne, N. (2004). *Riding the storm – cultural capital and surf culture*. Paper presented at the Annual Conference of the British Sociological Association, University of York.

Capra, F. (1976). *The Tao of Physics*. London: Fontana.

Carlisle-Duncan, M. (1990). Sports photographs and sexual difference: Images of women and men in the 1984 and 1988 Olympic Games. *Sociology of Sport Journal*, 7, 22–24.

Carrington, B. (2002). Sport, masculinity and black cultural resistance. In J. Sugden and A. Tomlinson (eds), *Power Games: A Critical Sociology of Sport*. London: Routledge, pp. 267–291.

Carroll, N. (ed.) (1991) *The Next Wave: A Survey of World Surfing*. London: Macdonald.

Casarino, C. (2002). *Modernity at Sea: Melville, Marx, Conrad in Crisis*. London: University of Minnesota Press.

Cawley, R. R. (1940). *Unpathed Waters: Studies in the Influence of the Voyages on Elizabethan Literature*. Princetown: Princetown University Press.

Celsi, R. L. (1992). Transcendent benefits of high-risk sports. *Advances in Consumer Research*, 19, 636–641.

Chaney, D. (1996). *Lifestyles*. London: Routledge.

Channon, B. and McLeod, H. (No date). *Surfing World Photo Annual 4*. Mona Vale: Surfing World Magazine.

Clare, A. (2000). *On Men: Masculinity in Crisis*. London: Chatto & Windus.

Clark, A. (1997). *Being There: Putting Brain, Body and World Together Again*. Cambridge: MIT Press.

Clarke, G. (1981/1997). Defending ski jumpers! A critique of theories of youth sub-cultures. In K. Gelden and S. Thornton (eds), *The Subcultures Reader*. London: Routledge, pp. 175–180.

Clarke, K. (1956). *The Nude: A study of Ideal Art*. London: Penguin.

Clash, J. M. (2004). The 100–Foot Wave? Do you have a death wish? Tow surfing lets you ride apartment-building-size waves. *Forbes*, 173(10), 198–203.

Classen, C. (1997). Engendering perception: Gender ideologies and sensory hierarchies in Western history. *Body and Society*, 3(2), 1–19.

Cloke, P. and Perkins, H. C. (1998). 'Cracking the canyon with the awesome foursome': Representations of adventure tourism in New Zealand. *Environment and Planning D*, 16(2), 185–218.

Coakley, J. (1998). *Sport in Society: Issues and Controversies*. St. Louis: Times Mirror.

—— and Donnelly, P. (eds) (1998). *Inside Sports*. London: Routledge.

—— and Dunning, E. (eds) (2000). *Handbook of Sports Studies* (1st edn). London: Sage Publications.

Cobley, P. (2001). *Narrative*. London: Routledge.

Cohen, S. (1980). *Folk Devils and Moral Panics: The Creation of the Mods and the Rockers*. Oxford: Martin Robertson.

Colburn, B. (1992). Gallery: Sandow Birk, in the heroic tradition. *The Surfer's Journal*, 1(3), 24–32.

——, Finney, B., Stallings, T., Stecyk, C. R., Stillman, D. and Wolfe, T. (2002). *Surf Culture: The Art History of Surfing*. Laguna: Laguna Art Museum.

Collins, M. (1979). *The Credential Society*. New York: Academic Press.

Congdon, K. G. and King, N. B. (2002). Teaching about surfing culture and aesthetics. *Visual Arts Research*, 28(2), 48–56.

Connell, R. W. (1995). *Masculinities*. London: Polity Press.

—— (1998). Masculinities and globalization. *Men and Masculinities*, 1(1), 3–24.

—— (2000). *The Men and the Boys*. Cambridge: Polity.

—— (2001). The social organization of masculinity. In S. Whithead, M. and F. J. Barret (eds), *The Masculinities Reader*. Cambridge: Polity Press, pp. 30–50.

Conrad, J. (1906/1992). The mirror of the sea. In J. Raban (ed.), *The Oxford Book of the Sea*. Oxford: Oxford University Press.

Coombs, C. (2005). Dropping in. *SurfShot*. Online at http://www.surfshot.com/items/magazine_item.html?context_id=247anditem_id=464 (21 February 2005).

Corbin, A. (1994). *The Lure of the Sea: The Discovery of the Seaside in the Western World 1750–1840*. Berkeley: University of California Press.

Cosgrove, D. E. (1984/1998). *Social Formations and Symbolic Landscape*. London: Croom Helm.

—— (1985). Prospect, perspective and the evolution of the landscape idea. *Transactions of the Institute of British Geographers*, 10(1), 45–62.

Costa, P. T. and McCrae, R. R. (1992). *NEO-PI-R: Revised NEO Personality Inventory*. Odessa: Psychological Assessment Resources.

Craig, J. (1994). *The Face of Fashion*. London: Routledge.

Crockett, D. (2003). *A Geographical Psychology of Surfing Consciousness*. Unpublished dissertation for BA in Geography, University of Exeter, Exeter.

Cronon, W. (1992). A place for stories: Nature, history and narrative. *Journal of American History*, 78(4), 1347–1379.

Crossett, T. and Beal, B. (1997). The use of 'subculture' and 'subworld' in ethnographic works on sport: A discussion of definitional distinctions. *Sociology of Sport*, 14(1), 73–85.

Crossley, M. (2000). *Introducing Narrative Psychology*. Buckingham: Open University Press.

Crossley, N. (2001). *The Social Body: Habit, Identity and Desire*. London: Sage.

Czikszentmihalyi, M. (1990). *Flow: The Psychology of Optimal Experience*. London: Harper and Row.

Dant, T. (1999). *Material Culture in the Social World: Values, Activities, Lifestyles*. Buckingham: Oxford University Press.

Dart, J. (2002). *Surfing, subculture and performance capital*. Unpublished dissertation for BSc in Media Studies, University of Plymouth, Plymouth.

Davis, F. (1974). *Yearning for Yesterday: A Sociology of Nostalgia*. New York: Free Press.

De Certeau, M. (1984). *The Practice of Everyday Life*. Berkeley: University of California.

De Cure, J. (2004). Dark journey. *The Surfer's Journal*, 13(5), 124–125.

Deem, R. (1986). *All Work and No Play?: A Study of Women and Leisure*. Milton Keynes: Open University Press.

Deleuze, G. (1988). *Bergsonism*. New York: Zane Books.

Demetriou, D. Z. (2001). Connell's concept of hegemonic masculinity: A critique. *Theory and Society*, 30, 337–361.

Dempster, E. (1988). Women writing the body: Let's watch a little how she dances. In S. Sheridan (ed.), *Grafts: Essays in Feminist Criticism*. London: Verso, pp. 35–54.

Desmond, J. (1993/94). Embodying difference: Issues in dance and cultural studies. *Cultural Critique*, Winter, 33–63.

Dewar, A. (1993). Would all the generic women please stand up? Challenges facing the feminist sport sociology. *Quest*, 45, 211–229.

Diehm, R. and Armatas, C. (2004). Surfing: An avenue for socially accepted risk taking, satisfying needs for sensation seeking and experience seeking. *Personality and Individual Differences*, 36, 663–677.

Divine, J. (2000). *Jeff Divine: Masters of Surf Photography 1*. San Clementes: Journal Concepts.

Doherty, T. (1988). *Teenagers and Teenpics: The Juvenilization of American Movies in the 1950s*. Boston: Unwin Hyman.

Donnelly, P. (2000). Interpretive approaches to the sociology of sport. In J. Coakley and E. Dunning (eds), *Handbook of Sports Studies*. London: Sage, pp. 77–91.

—— and Young, K. (1988). The construction and confirmation of identity in sport subcultures. *Sociology of Sport Journal*, 18, 48–65.

Drummond, M. (2002). Review of: Australian Beach Cultures: The History of Sun, Sand and Surf, by Douglas Booth. *International Review for the Sociology of Sport*, 37(2), 251–254.

Duncan, J. (1995) Landscape geography, 1993–94. *Progress in Human Geography*, 19, 414–422.

Duncan, M. C. and Hasbrook, C. A. (2002). Denial of power in televised women's sports. In S. Scraton and A. Flintoff (eds), *Gender and Sport: A reader*. London: Routledge, pp. 83–93.

Dunning, E. (1999). *Sport Matters: Sociological Studies of Sport, Violence and Civilisation*. London: Routledge.

Duquin, M. (2000). Sport and emotions. In J. Coakley and E. Dunning (eds), *Handbook of Sports Studies*. London: Sage, pp. 477–489.

Dutton, G. (1983). *Sun, Sea, Surf and Sand*. Oxford: Oxford University Press.

Dworkin, S. L. and Messner, M. (2002). Just do . . . what? Sports, bodies, gender. In S. Scraton and A. Flintoff (eds), *Gender and Sport: A Reader*. London: Routledge, pp. 17–29.

Dyck, N. and Archetti, E. P. (eds) (2003). *Sport, Dance and Embodied Identities*. Oxford: Berg.

Dyer, K. F. (1977). The trend of the male and the female performance differential in athletics, swimming and cycling, 1958–1976. *Journal of Biosocial Science*, 9, 325–339.

Dyer, K. (1984). Catching up the men. *New Scientist*, 1415(2), 25–26.

Edwards, C. and Imrie, R. (2003). Disability and bodies as bearers of value. *Sociology*, 37(2), 239–256.

Edwards, P. (1964). What is good? *Surfer Magazine*, 5, 1.

Elesh, E. (2004). Versus gallery: Eden Elesh. *The Surfer's Journal*, 13(3), 62–69.

Elias, N. (1978). *The Civilizing Process, Volume 1: The History of Manners*. Oxford: Basil Blackwell.

—— (1991). On human beings and their emotions: A process-sociological essay. In M. Featherstone, M. Hepworth and B. Turner (eds), *The Body: Social Process and Cultural Theory*. London: Sage, pp. 103–125.

—— and Dunning, E. (1986). *The Quest for Excitement: Sport and Leisure in the Civilising Process*. Oxford: Basil Blackwell.

Engell, J. (1981). *The Creative Imagination*. Cambridge: Harvard University Press.

Evans, P. (2004). Fins of fury. *Wavelength*, 136, 45.

Fahlberg , L. and Falhberg, L. (1997). Health, freedom and movement in the postmodern era. In J. M. Fernandez-Balboa (ed.), *Critical Postmodernism in Human Movement, Physical Education and Sport*. New York: State of New York University Press, pp. 65–86.

Falk, P. (1994). *The Consuming Body*. London: Sage.

Fallon, A. (1990). Culture in the mirror: Sociocultural determinants of body image. In T. Cash and T. Pruzinsky (eds), *Body Image*. London: Cultural Press, pp. 80–109.

Farmer, R. J. (1992). Surfing: Motivations, values and culture. *Journal of Sport Behaviour*, 15(3), 241–257.

Featherstone, M. (1987). Lifestyle and consumer culture. *Theory, Culture and Society*, 4(1), 55–70.

——, (1990). Global culture(s): An introduction. *Theory, Culture and Society*, 7(2–3), 1–14.

——, (1991). *Consumer Culture and Postmodernism*. London: Sage.

——, (1993). Postmodernism and the aestheticization of everyday life. In S. Lash and J. Friedman (eds), *Modernity and Identity*. Oxford: Blackwell. pp. 265–290.

Fidrus, M. (6 August 2004). Brazilian cocaine smugglers arrested. *The Jakarta Post*, pp. 1–2.

Finney, B. and Houston, J. D. (1996). *Surfing: A History of the Ancient Hawaiian Sport*. San Francisco: Pomegranate Artbook.

Fiske, J. (1989). *Reading the Popular*. London: Unwin Hyman.

Flynn, P. J. (1989). Waves of semiosis: Surfing's iconic progression. *American Journal of Semiotics*, 5(3), 397–418.

Foucault, M. (1977). *Discipline and Punish: The Birth of the Prison*. London: Allen Lane.

—— (1980). Body/Power. In C. Gordon (ed.), *Michel Foucault: Power/Knowledge. Selected Interviews and Other Writings*. Brighton: Harvester, pp. 55–62.

Frank, A. (1991). For a sociology of the body: An analytical review. In M. Featherstone, B. Hepworth and B. Turner (eds), *The Body: Social Process and Cultural Theory.* London: Sage.

—— (1995). *The Wounded Storyteller.* Chicago: University of Chicago Press.

Gabrielson, B. (1977/1995). *The Complete Surfing Guide for Coaches.* Online at www.surfcoachbook.com (13 January 2005).

Galtung, J. (1982). Sport as carrier of deep culture and structure. *Current Research on Peace and Violence,* 5, 133–143.

Garnham, N. and Williams, R. (1986). Pierre Bourdieu and the sociology of culture. In R. Collins, J. Curran, N. Garnham, P. Scannell, P. Schlesinger and C. Sparkes (eds), *Media, Culture and Society: Critical Reader.* London: Sage, pp.120–139.

Geertz, C. (1972). Deep Play: Notes on the Balinese Cockfight. *Daedalus,* 101, 1–37.

Gelder, K. (1997). Introduction: Contesting the subcultural terrain. In K. Gelder and S. Thornton (eds), *The Subcultures Reader.* London: Routledge, pp. 145–148.

—— and Thornton, S. (eds) (1997) *The Subcultures Reader.* London: Routledge.

Genette, G. (1980). *Narrative Discourse: An Essay on Method.* Ithaca, NY: Cornell University Press.

George, S. (1991). California: Land of sun, sand and surf. In N. Carroll (ed.), *The Next Wave: A Survey of World Surfing.* London: Macdonald, pp. 58–81.

—— (1999). When we were kings. *Surfer,* 40(10), 142–162.

—— (2001). *The Perfect Day: 40 Years of Surfer Magazine.* San Francisco: Chronicle.

Giddens, A. (1990). *The Consequences of Modernity.* Cambridge: Polity Press.

—— (1991). *Modernity and Self Identity: Self and Society in the Late Modern Age.* Cambridge: Polity Press.

——, Beck, U. and Lash, S. (1994). *Reflexive Modernization.* Cambridge: Polity Press.

Gilliam, I., Ellis, L. and Johnson, M. (1984). *Physiological Assessment of Surfers.* Unpublished study, Philip Insitute of Technology, Australia.

Goffman, E. (1963). *Stigma: Notes on the Management of Spoiled Identity.* New York: Prentice Hall.

—— (1969). *The Presentation of Self in Everyday Life.* London: Allen Lane.

—— (1971). *Relations in Public: Microstudies of the Public Order.* London: Allen Lane.

—— (1983). The interaction order. *The American Sociological Review,* 48, 1–17.

Grambeau, T. (2003) *Ted Grambeau: Masters of Surf Photography 4.* San Clemente: Journal Concepts.

Gramsci, A. (1971). *Selections from the Prison Notebooks.* London: Lawrence and Wishart.

Granata, C. L. (2003). *I Just Wasn't Made for These Times: Brian Wilson and the Making of Pet Sounds.* London: Unanimous.

Greenwood, A. (17 December 2004). Riding the Cribbar. Chris tames 30ft wave. *Western Morning News,* p. 5.

Greimas, A. J. (1987). *On Meaning: Selected Writings in Semiotic Theory.* Minneapolis: University of Minnesota.

—— and Courtes, J. (1982). *Semiotics and Language: An Analytical Language.* Bloomington: Indiana University Press.

Grosz, E. (1994). *Volatile Bodies: Toward a Corporeal Feminism.* St. Leonards, NSW, Australia: Allen & Unwin.

Gruneau, R. (1981). Review of: Surfing Subcultures of Australia and New Zealand. *ICSS Bulletin,* 21, 8–10.

—— (1993). The critique of sport in Modernity: Theorising power, culture, and the politics of the body. In E. G. Dunning, J. A. Maguire and R. E. Pearton (eds), *The*

*Sports Process: A Comparative and Developmental Approach.* Champaign, IL: Human Kinetics, pp. 85–110.

Gunin, J. (2004). Gallery: John Gunin, a parade of days. *The Surfer's Journal,* 13(1), 42–47.

Guttmann, A. (1978). *From the Ritual to Record. The Development of Modern Sports.* New York.

—— (2000). The development of modern sports. In J. Coakley and E. Dunning (eds), *Handbook of Sports Studies.* London: Sage, pp. 248–259.

Hadersdorfer, H. (2004). *Quantity versus quality in surfing magazines.* Paper presented at the Proceedings of the Third Annual Conference on Contemporary Issues in Surfing, University of Plymouth.

Hall, M. A. (1996). *Feminism and Sporting Bodies: Essays on Theory and Practice.* Champaign, IL: Human Kinetics.

Hannerz, U. (1990). Cosmpolitans and locals in world culture. *Theory, Culture and Society,* 7, 237–251.

Hanson, S. (1999). Isms and schisms: Healing the rift between the nature-society and space-society traditions in geography. *Annals of the Association of American Geographers,* 89, 133–143.

Hargreaves, J. (1986). *Sport, Power and Culture : A Social and Historical Analysis of Popular Sports in Britain.* Cambridge: Polity Press.

—— (1994). *Sporting Females: Critical Issues in the History and Sociology of Women's Sports.* London: Routledge.

—— (2002). Globalisation theory, global sport, and nations and nationalism. In J. Sugden and A. Tomlinson (eds), *Power Games: A Critical Sociology of Sport.* London: Routledge, pp. 25–43.

Harris, J. C. (1980). Play: A definition and implied interrelationhips with culture and sport. *Journal of Sport Psychology,* 2, 46–61.

—— and Park, R. J. (1983). *Play, Games and Sports in Cultural Contexts.* Champaign, IL: Human Kinetics.

Harvey, J. and Sparks, R. (1991) The politics of the body in the context of modernity. *Quest,* 43(2), 164–189.

Healey, J. (1991). An exploration of the relationships between memory and sport. *Sociology of Sport Journal,* 3, 213–227.

Heap, C. (2003). *Surfing Motivations and their Influence on Aesthetic, Emotional and Functional Perceptions of the Coastscape at Croyde.* Unpublished dissertation for BA in Geography, University of Exeter, Exeter.

Hebdige, D. (1979). *Subculture: The Meaning of Style.* London: Methuen.

Heidegger, M. (1962). *Being and Time.* New York: Harper and Row.

Henderson, M. (2001). A shifting line-up: Men, women, and Tracks surfing magazine. *Continuum,* 15(3), 319–332.

Hoberman, J. (1992). *Mortal Engines: The Science of Performance and the Dehumanization of Sport.* Oxford: Macmillan.

—— (1997). *Darwin's Athletes: How Sport Has Damaged Black America and Preserved the Myth of Race.* Boston: Houghton Mifflin Co.

Holmes Coleman, S. (2002). *Eddie Would Go: The Story of Edde Aikau, Hawaiian Hero.* Honolulu: MindRaising Press.

Holmes, P. (1991). Surf culture: A serious subculture. In N. Carroll (ed.), *The Next Wave: A Survey of World Surfing.* London: Macdonald, pp. 199–205.

Holstein, J. and Gubrium, J. F. (2000). *The Self We Live By.* New York: Oxford University Press.

Howson, A. (2003). *The Body in Society: An Introduction*. Cambridge: Polity Press.

—— and Inglis, D. (2001). The body in sociology: tensions inside and outside sociological thought. *The Sociological Review*, 49(3), 297–317.

Hughes-Freeland, F. (1998). *Ritual, Performance, Media*. London: Routledge.

Huizinga, J. (1949). *Homo Ludens: A Study of the Play Element in Culture*. London: Routledge.

Hulet, S. (2004). Pretty much Thomas Campbell's evident hand. *The Surfer's Journal*, 13(4), 54–71.

Institute of Youth Sport. (2000). *Towards Girl-Friendly Physical Education: The Nike/YST Girls In Sport Partnership Project*. Loughborough: IYS Loughborough.

International Surfing Association. (2004). *About ISA*. Online at http://www. isasurf.org/ (15 December 2004).

Irwin, J. (1970/1997). Notes on the status of the concept of subculture. In S. Gelder and S. Thornton (eds), *The Subcultures Reader*. London: Routledge, pp. 66–70.

—— (1973). Surfing: The natural history of an urban scence. *Urban Life and Culture*, 2, 133–146.

Ivanov, V. V. (1973). The signficance. In H. Baran (ed.), *Semiotics and Structuralism*. New York: Internal Arts and Sciences Press, pp. 310–367.

Jackson, S. (1995). Factors influencing the occurence of flow in elite athletes. *Journal of Applied Psychology*, 7, 135–163.

—— (1996). Toward a conceptual understanding of the flow experience in elite athletes. *Research Quarterly for Exercise and Sport*, 67, 76–70.

—— and Eklund, R. (2002). Assessing flow in physical activity: The Flow State Scale-2 and Dispositional Flow State Scale-2. *Journal of Sport and Exercise Psychology*, 24, 133 150.

—— and Marsh, H. (1996). Development and validation of a scale to measure optimal experience: The Flow State Scale. *Journal of Sport and Exercise Psychology*, 18, 17–35.

Jaggard, E. (2003). Review of Australian Beach Cultures: The History of Sun, Sand and Surf by Douglas Booth. *International Journal of the History of Sport*, 20(3), 179.

James, A. (1979). Gerry Lopez. *Surfer*, 20, 8.

Jameson, F. (1988). On habits of the heart. In C. H. Reynolds and R. V. Norman (eds), *Community in America: The Challenge of Habits and Heart*. Berkeley: University of California Press.

Jarratt, P. (1997). *Mr. Sunset: The Jeff Hakman Story*. Los Angeles: General Publishing Group.

Jarrett-Kerr, L. (2003). *Windsurfing: Communitas in an individual sport*. Unpublished dissertation for BA in Geography, University of Exeter, Exeter.

Jary, D. and Jary, J. (1995). *Collins Dictionary of Sociology*. Glasgow: Harper-Collins.

Jordan, S. (1996). Musical/choreographic discourse: Method music theory and meaning. In G. Morris (ed.), *Moving Words: Re-Writing Dance*. London: Routledge, pp. 15–28.

Kampion, D. (1989). *The Book of Waves: Form and Beauty on the Ocean*. Santa Barbara: Arpel Graphics.

—— (2003). *The Way of the Surfer: Living It 1935 to Tomorrow*. New York: Harry N. Abrams.

—— and Brown, B. (1997/98). *Stoked: A History of Surf Culture*. Koln: Evergreen.

Kenyon, G. S. (1968). Six scales for accessing attitude toward physical activity. *The Research Quarterly*, 39, 96–105.

Kershaw, B. (1993). *Reminiscing history: Memory, performance, empowerment*. Paper presented at the De-Traditionalization Conference, Lancaster University UK, July.

Kidman, A. (2002). Alby Falzon portfolio: The man who lives inside a flower. *The Surfer's Journal*, 11(3), 98–119.

Kimmel, M. S. (2003). Globalization and its mal(e)contents. *International Sociology*, 18, 603–620.

—— (2004). *Global masculinities: Restoration and resistance.* Online at http://gender-policy.tripod.com/journal/ (23 December 2004).

Klein, A. M. (1993). *Little Big Men: Bodybuilding Subculture and Gender Construction.* New York: State University of New York Press.

Knight, W. (1932). *The Shakespearian Tempest.* Oxford: Oxford University Press.

Kusz, K. (2003). BMX, extreme sports, and the white male backlash. In R. E. Rinhart and S. Sydnor (eds), *To the Extreme: Alternative Sports, Inside and Out.* New York: State University of New York, pp. 153–173.

Laberge, S. (1995). Toward an integration of gender into Bourdieu's concept of cultural captial. *Sociology of Sport Journal*, 12(2), 132–146.

—— and Sankoff, D. (1988). Physical activities, body habitus, and lifestyles. In J. Harvey and H. Cantelon (eds), *Not Just a Game: Essays in Canadian Sport Sociology.* Ottawa, ON: University of Ottawa Press, pp. 267–286.

Labov, W. (1972) The transformation of experience in narrative syntax. In W. Labov (ed.), *Language in the Inner City: Studies in the Black English Vernacular.* Philadelphia: University of Philadelphia Press, pp. 354–396.

Lakoff, G. and Johnson, M. (1980). *Metaphors We Live By.* Chicago: University of Chicago Press.

Lash, S. (1990). *Sociology of Postmodernism.* London: Routledge.

—— (1993a). Pierre Bourdieu: Cultural economy and social change. In C. Calhoun, E. LiPuma and M. Postone (eds), *Bourdieu: Critical Perspectives.* Cambridge: Polity Press, pp. 193–211.

Lash, S. (1993b). Reflexive modernization: The aesthetic dimension. *Theory, Culture and Society*, 10(1), 1–23.

Leder, D. (1990). *The Absent Body.* Chicago: Chicago University Press.

Leggett, T. (1978). *Zen and the Ways.* London: Routledge and Kegan Paul.

Lencek, L. and Bosker, G. (1998). *The Beach: The History of Paradise on Earth.* London: Secker and Warburg.

Leuras, L. and Leuras, L. (1997). *Surfing Indonesia: A Search for the World's Most Perfect Waves.* Hong Kong: Periplus.

Lewis, N. (2000). The climbing body, nature and the experience of modernity. *Body and Society*, 6(3–4), 58–80.

—— (2001). The climbing body, nature and the experience of modernity. In P. Macnaghten and J. Urry (eds) *Bodies of Nature.* London: Sage, pp. 58–80.

Lipovetsky, G. (1994). *The Empire of Fashion.* Princetown: Princetown Unveristy Press.

Lipscombe, N. (1999). The relevance of the peak experience to continued skydiving participation: A qualitative approach to assessing motivations. *Leisure Studies*, 18, 267–288.

Lofland, J. (1980). Early Goffman: Style, structure, substance, soul. In I. Ditton (ed.), *The view from Goffman.* London: Macmillan.

London, C. (1922). *Our Hawaii.* New York: Macmillan.

London, J. (1911). *The Cruise of the Snark.* New York: Macmillan.

Lorimer, H. (2004). The busyness of being 'more-than-representational': Some recent work in cultural geography. Online at http://web.geog.gla.ac.uk/olpapers/hlorimer003.pdf (21 February 2005).

Lowdon, B. J. (1980). The somatoypes of international surfboard riders. *Australian Journal of Sport Medicine*, 12, 34–39.

—— (1982). The fitness requirements for surfing. *Sports Coach*, 6, 35–38.

—— and Pateman, N. (1980). Physiological parameters of international surfers. *Australian Journal Sports Medicine*, 12, 30–33.

——, Pateman, N. A. and Pitman, A. J. (1983). Surfboard-riding injuries. *Medical Journal of Australia*, 2, 613–616.

Lowe, B. (1977) *The Beauty of Sport: A Cross Disciplinary Inquiry*. New Jersey: Englewood Cliffs.

Lucas, S. (2000). Nike's commercial solution: Girls, sneakers, and salvation. *International Review for the Sociology of Sport*, 35, 149–164.

Lyon, C. and Lyon, L. (1997). *Jaws Maui*. Hawaii: Peter Canon.

Lyon, D. (1994). *Postmodernity* (3rd edn). Buckingham: Open University Press.

Macnaghten, P. and Urry, J. (1998). *Contested Natures*. London: Sage.

—— (eds) (2001). *Bodies of Nature*. London: Sage.

Maguire, J. (1991). The media-sport production complex: The emergence of American sports in European culture. *European Journal of Communication*, 6, 315–336.

—— (1993). Globalization, sport development, and the media/sport production complex. *Sport Sciences Review*, 2, 29–47.

—— (1994). Sport, identity politics, and globalization: Diminishing contrasts and increasing varieties. *Sociology of Sport Journal*, 11, 398–427.

—— (2000). Sport and globalization. In J. Coakley and E. Dunning (eds), *Handbook of Sports Studies*. London: Sage, pp. 356–369.

Maines, D. R. (2001). *The Faultline of Consciousness: A View of Interactionism in Sociology*. New York: Aldine de Gruyter.

Malinowski, B. (1956). The problem of meaning in primitive languages. In O. Ogden and I. Richards (eds), *The Meaning of Meaning*. London: International Library of Psychology, pp. 296–336.

Manning, S. (1993). *Ecstasy and the Demon: Feminism and Nationalism in the Dances of Mary Wigman*. Berkeley: University of California Press.

Maquet, J. (1986). *The Aesthetic Experience: An Anthropologist Looks at the Visual Arts*. London: Yale University Press.

Martin, A. (2000). Beach. In S. Coates and A. Stetter (eds), *Impossible Worlds*. Boston: Birkhauser, pp. 79–81.

Maslow, A. H. (1964). *Religions, Values and Peak Experiences*. Columbus: Ohio State University.

Maslow, A. H. (1968). *Towards a Psychology of Being*. New York: Van Nostrand Reinholt.

Mauss, M. (1935/1973). Techniques of the body. *Economy and Society*, 2, 70–88.

—— (1954/2002). *The Gift: Forms and Functions of Exchange in Primitive Societies*. London: Routledge Classics.

McArdle, W. D., Katch, K. I. and Katch, V. L. (2000). *Essentials of Exercise Physiology*. Baltimore: Lippincott Williams and Williams.

McKee, R. (1998). *Story: Substance, Structure, Style and the Principles of Screenwriting*. London: Methuen.

Meir, R. A., Lowdon, B. J. and Davie, A. J. (1991). Heart rates and estimated energy expenditure during recreational surfing. *The Australian Journal of Science and Medicine in Sport*, 23, 70–74.

Melrose, S. (1994). *A Semiotics of the Dramatic Text*. London: Macmillan.

Mennesson, C. (2000). 'Hard' women and 'soft' women: The social construction of identities among female boxers. *International Review for the Sociology of Sport*, 35(1), 21–33.

Mercer, C. (2003). *Joining the Dots: Cultural Sector Research in the South West of England.* Exeter: Culture South West.

Meredith, K. (2003). *Reading the Beach Preservation–Development Dichotomy: A Critical Analysis of Management, Conservation and Beach Users' Perceptions with Special Reference to Fistral Bay Surf Centre Centre Newquay.* Unpublished dissertation for BSc in Geography, University of Exeter, Exeter.

Merleau-Ponty, M. (1964). *Signs.* London: RKP.

—— (1965). *The Strucuture of Behaviour.* London: Methuen.

—— (1968). *The Visible and the Invisible.* Evanston, IL: Northwestern University Press.

—— (1969). *Humanism and Terror.* Boston, Beacon Press.

—— (1971). *Sense and Non-sense.* Evanston, IL: Northwestrn University Press.

—— (1973). *Adventures of the Dialectic.* Evanston, IL: Northwestern University Press.

—— (1988). *In Praise of Philosophy and Themes from the Lectures at the College de France.* Evanston, IL: Northwestern University Press.

Messner, M. (1992). *Power at Play: Sports and the Problem of Masculinity.* Boston: Beacon Press.

—— and Sabo, D. (eds) (1990). *Sport, Men and the Gender Order.* Champaign, IL: Human Kinetics Press.

Michaels, S. (1981). "Sharing Time": Children's narrative styles and differential access to literacy. *Language and Society*, 10, 423–424.

Midol, N. and Broyer, G. (1995) Towards an anthropological analysis of new sport cultures: The case of whizz sports in France. *Sociology of Sport Journal*, 12, 204–212.

Miller, J. H. (1995). Narrative. In F. Lentricchio and T. McLaughlin (eds), *Critical Terms of Literary Study.* London: Chicago Literary Press, pp. 66–79.

Miller, T. (2001). *Sportsex.* Philadelphia, PA: Temple University Press.

——, Lawrence, G., McKay, J. and Rowe, D. (2002). *Globalisation and Sport.* London: Sage.

Miller, P. and Rose, N. (1997) Mobilizing the consumer: Assembling the subject of consumption. *Theory, Culture and Society*, 14(1), 1–36.

Mitchell, R. (1988). Sociological implications of flow experience. In M. Czikszentmihalyi and I. S. Czikszentmihalyi (eds), *Optimal Experience: Psychological Studies of Flow Experiences.* Cambridge: Cambridge University Press, pp. 36–59.

Mitchell, W. J. T. (1994). *Landscape and Power.* Oxford: Blackwells.

Morgan, R. (1999). A novel user-based rating for tourist beaches. *Tourist Management*, 20(4), 393–410.

Morin, K. M. (2003). Landscape and environment: Representation and interpreting the world. In S. L. Holloway, S. P. Rice and G. Valentine (eds), *Key Concepts in Geography.* London: Sage, pp. 319–334.

Morris, G. (1993). Beyond the beach: Social and formal aspects of AIP's Beach Party movies. *Journal of Popular Film and Television*, 21, 5.

—— (ed.) (1996). *Moving Words: Re-Writing Dance.* London: Routledge.

Morton, S. (2001). Let he who is thirsty drink clear water. *The Surfer's Journal*, 10(4), 10–23.

Murphy, P., Sheard, K. and Waddington, I. (2000). Figurational sociology and its application to sport. In J. Coakley and E. Dunning (eds), *Handbook of Sports Studies.* London: Sage, pp. 92–105.

Nash, C. (1999). Landscape. In P. Cloke, P. Crang and M. Goodwin (eds), *Introducing Human Geographies*. London: Hodder Arnold, pp. 217–225.

Nathanson, A., Haynes, P. and Galanis, D. (2002). Surfing injuries. *American Journal of Emergency Medicine*, 20(3), 155–160.

Newton, T. (2003). Truly embodied sociology; marrying the social and the biological? *The Editorial Board of the Sociological Review*, 20–42.

Noble, S. (2004). *The need for windsurfing technology in surfboard construction*. Paper presented at the Proceedings of the Third Annual Conference on Contemporary Issues in Surfing, University of Plymouth.

Noll, G. (2001). Noll's wood. *The Surfer's Journal*, 10, 24–35.

Norretranders, T. (1998). *The User Illusion: Cutting Consciousness Down to Size*. Boston: Harvard Business School Press.

Nunn, K. (1998). *Tapping the Source*. Harpenden: No Exit Press.

—— (1998). *Dogs of Winter*. Harpenden: No Exit Press.

—— (2004). *Tijuana Sloughs*. Los Angeles: Scribner.

Olsen, A. (1998). *Bodystories: A Guide to Experiential Anatomy*. New York: Station Hill.

O'Riordan, T. (1981). *Environmentalism*. London: Pion.

Osborn, M. (1977). The evolution of the archetypal sea in rhetoric and poetics. *Quarterly Journal of Speech*, 63, 347–363.

Owen, T. and Dickson, D. (1999). *High Art: A History of the Psychedelic Poster*. London: Sanctuary.

Pacteau, F. (1994). *The Symptom of Beauty*. Cambridge, Mass.: Harvard University Press.

Panniccia, P. (2005). Progressions. *The Surfer's Journal*, 12(2), 36–61.

Parmenter, D. (1989). Iconoclast now! *Surfer*, 30, 2.

Parsons, T. (1964). *Essays on Sociological Theory*. New York: The Free Press.

Pearson, K. (1979). *Surfing Subcultures of Australia and New Zealand*. St. Lucia, Queensland: University of Queensland Press.

Perkins, H. C. and Thoms, D. C. (2001). Gazing or performing: Reflections on Urry's tourist gaze of contemporary experience in the Antipodes. *International Sociology*, 16, 185–204.

Pezman, S. (1979). I'm a bit leery of Timothy Leary. *Surfer*, 20, 8.

Philo, C. (1994). In the same ballpark? Looking in on the new sports geography. In J. Bale (ed.), *Community, Landscape and Identity: Horizons in a Geography of Sport*. Keele: Department of Geography, Keele University, pp. 1–11.

Pink, S. (2001). *Doing Visual Ethnography: Images, Media and Representation in Research*. London: Sage.

Pirinen, R. (2002). Catching up with the men? Finnish newspaper coverage of women's entry into traditionally male sport. In S. Scraton and A. Flintoff (eds), *Gender and Sport: A Reader*. London: Routledge, pp. 94–104.

Pleck, J. (1995). Men's power with women, other men, and society: A men's movement analysis. In K. Kimmel and M. Messner (eds), *Men's Lives*. New York: Allyn & Bacon Press, pp. 5–12.

Preston-Whyte, R. (2002). Constructions of surfing space at Durban, South Africa. *Tourism Geographies*, 4(3), 307–328.

Privette, G. (1983). Peak experience, peak performance, and flow: A comparative analysis of positive human experience. *Journal of Personality and Social Psychology*, 45, 1361–1368.

Raban, J. (1992). *The Oxford Book of the Sea*. Oxford: Oxford University Press.

Radley, A. (1995). The elusory body in social constructionist theory. *Body and Society*, 1(2), 3–24.

Rees, C. (2003). *The Sea Never Stops Moving: Surfers, Sewage and the Social Constructions of the Sea*. Unpublished dissertation for BA in Geography, University of Exeter, Exeter.

Reissman, C. K. (1993). *Narrative Analysis*. London: Sage.

Renneker, M. (1987a). Surfing: The medical aspects of surfing. *Physician Sportsmedicine*, 15(12), 97–104.

—— (1987b). Surfing: The sport and the life-style. *Physician Sportsmedicine*, 15(10), 157–162.

—— (No date). *Surfing*. Online at http://www.sportsci.org/encyc/drafts/Surfing.doc (21 February 2005).

Richardson, J. (1994). *Selected Poems of Baudelaire*. Harmondsworth: Penguin.

Rinehart, R. (1998). Inside of the outside: Pecking orders within alternative sport at ESPN's 1995 "The extreme Games". *Journal of Sport and Social Issues*, 22(4), 398–414.

Rinehart, R. E. (2000). Emerging arriving sport: Alternatives to formal sports. In J. Coakley and E. Dunning (eds), *Handbook of Sports Studies*. London: Sage, pp. 504–519.

—— and Sydnor, S. (2003). *To the Extreme: Alternative Sports, Inside and Out*. New York: State University of New York.

Ritz, E. (1994). Charlie (Darwin) don't surf (letter to the editor). *Surfer*, 22, 24.

Ritzer, G., Goodman, D. and Wiedenhoft, W. (2001). Theories of consumption. In G. Ritzer and B. Smart (eds), *Handbook of Social Theory*. London: Sage, pp. 410–442.

Rivers, P. (1977). *Living Better on Less*. London: Turnstone.

Roberts, J. W. (1977). The essence of surfing. *Surfer*, 18, 29–33.

Roberts, M. (1998). The end(s) of pictorial representation: Merleau-Ponty and Lyotard. In H. J. Silverman (ed.), *Cultural Semiosis: Tracing the Signifier*. London: Routledge, pp. 129–139.

Roberts, T. J. (1975). Sport and the sense of beauty. *Journal of Philosophy of Sport*, 2(9), 1–11.

Robertson, R. (1992). *Globalization: Social Theory and Global Culture*. London: Sage.

Rodaway, P. (1994). *Sensuous Geographies: Body, Sense and Place*. London: Routledge.

Rojek, C. (1985). *Capitalism and Leisure Theory*. London: Tavistock.

—— and Urry, J. (1997). *Touring Cultures: Transformations in Travel and Theory*. London: Routledge.

Rolston III, M. (1994a). *Considering Natural Value*. New York: Columbia University Press.

—— (1994b). Environmental ethics: Values in the duties to the natural world. In L. Gruen and D. Jamieson (eds), *Reflecting on Nature in Environmental Philosophy*. Oxford: Oxford University Press.

Rorty, R. (1980). *Philosophy and the Mirror of Nature*. Oxford: Blackwell.

Rose, G. (2001). *Visual Methodologies*. London: Sage.

Rose, N. (1996). Identity, genealogy, history. In S. Hall and P. du Gay (eds), *Questions of Cultural Identity*. London: Sage, pp. 128–150.

Roszak, T. (1972). *Where the Wasteland Ends: Politics and Transcendence in Post Industrial Society*. London: Faber and Faber.

Roxy. (2005). *Roxy The History*. Online at http://www.roxy.com/ (25 January 2005).

Rundell, J. (2001). Modernity, enlightenment, revolution and romanticism: Creating social theory. In G. Ritzer and B. Smart (eds), *Handbook of Social Theory*. London: Sage, pp. 13–29.

Rutsky, R. L. (1999). Surfing the Other: Ideology on the beach. *Film Quarterly*, 52(4), 12–23.

Sage, G. (2000). Political economy and sport. In J. Coakley and E. Dunning (eds), *Handbook of Sports Studies*. London: Sage, pp. 260–276.

Sage, S. J. (1998). Eliminating the distance. From Barthes' *Ecriture-lecture* to *Ecriture-Vue*. In H. J. Silverman (ed.), *Cultural Semiosis: Tracing the Signifier*. London: Routledge, pp. 105–128.

Scheibel, D. (1995). "Making waves" with Burke: Surf Nazi culture and the rhetoric of localism. *Western Journal of Communication*, 59, 253–269.

Schorr, J. (1999). *The Overspent America*. New York: Harper Collins.

Scott, A. (ed.). (2003). *The Cultural Industries Reader*. London: Routledge.

Seiler, S. and Sailer, S. (1997, May–June). The gender gap: Elite women are running further behind. *Sportscience News*.

Severson, J. (2004). *Surf Fever: John Severson Surfer Photography*. San Clemente: Journal Concepts.

Shaw, D. (2004). *An Investigation of the Surf Zone and the Interaction of Coastal Sports*. Unpublished dissertation for BA in Geography, University of Exeter, Exeter.

Shaw, R. (1999). *Reclaiming America: Nike, Clean Air, and the New National Activism*. California: The University of California Press.

Shibutani, T. (1955). Reference groups as perspectives. *American Journal of Sociology*, 111, 562–569.

Shields, R. (1991). *Places on the Margin: Alternative Geographies of Modernity*. London: Routledge.

—— (2004). Surfing: Global space or dwelling in the waves? In M. M. Sheller and J. Urry (eds), *Tourism Mobilities: Places to Stay, Places in Play*. London: Routledge, pp. 44–51.

—— (1992). *Lifestyle Shopping: The Subject of Consumption*. London: Routledge.

Shilling, C. (1992). Reconceptualising structure and agency in the sociology of education: Structuration theory and schooling. *British Journal of Sociology of Education*, 13(1), 69–87.

—— (1999). Towards an embodied understanding of the structure/agency relationship. *British Journal of Sociology*, 50(4), 543–562.

—— (2001). Embodiment, experience and theory: In defence of the sociological tradition. *The Editorial Board of the Sociological Review*, 327–344.

—— (2003). *The Body and Social Theory* (2nd edn). London: Sage.

—— (2005). *The Body in Culture, Technology and Society*. London: Sage.

—— and Mellor, P. (1996) Embodiment, structuration theory and modernity: Mind/body dualism and the repression of sensuality. *Body and Society*, 2(3), 1–15.

Short, K. (2002). Gallery: Kevin Short, Trestles Suite. *The Surfer's Journal*, 11(3), 32–39.

Shroth, M. L. (1995). Comparison of sensation seeking among different groups of athletes and non-athletes. *Personality and Individual Differences*, (18), 219–222.

Shurmer-Smith, P. and Hannam, K. (1994). *Worlds of Desire, Realms of Power: A Cultural Geography*. London: Edward Arnold.

Simmel, G. (1971). *George Simmel on Individuality and Social Forms*. Chicago: University of Chicago Press.

Slusher, H. S. (1967). *Men, Sport and Existence*. Philadelphia: Lea and Febiger.

Smith, B. and Sparkes, A. C. (2002). Men, sport, spinal cord injury and the construction of coherence: Narrative practice in action. *Qualitative Research*, 2(2), 143–171.

Smith, T. D. (2002). Open ocean surfing for increased range and endurance. *Oceans*, 3, 1629–1634.

Snyder, E. (1991). Sociology of nostalgia: Sport halls of fame and museums in America. *Sociology of Sport Journal*, 7(3), 228–238.

Sobel, M. E. (1981). *Lifestyle and Social Structure: Concepts, Definitions and Analyses*. New York: Academic Press.

Sparkes, A. (1996). The fatal flaw: A narrative of the fragile body self. *Qualitative Enquiry*, 2(4), 263–494.

—— (1997). An elite body, illness, and the fragmentation of self: a collaborative exploration. *Auto/Biography*, 1(3), 27–38.

—— (1999). Exploring body narratives. *Sport, Education and Society*, 4(1), 17–30.

—— and Silvennoinen, M. (eds) (1999). *Talking Bodies: Men's Narratives of the Body and Sport*. SoPhi: University of Jyvaskyla.

—— and Smith, B. (2002). Sport, spinal cord injury, embodied masculinities and the dilemmas of narrative identity. *Men and Masculinities*, 4(3), 258–285.

—— and Partington, S. (2003). Narrative practice and its potential contribution to sport psychology: The example of flow. *The Sport Psychologist*, 17, 292–317.

Steinberg, P. E. (1999a). The maritime mystique: Sustainable development, capital mobility and nostalgia in the world ocean. *Environment and Planning D*, 17, 403–426.

—— (1999b). Navigating the multiple horizons: Towards a geography of ocean space. *The Professional Geographer*, 51, 366–375.

—— (2001). *The Social Construction of the Ocean*. Cambridge: Cambridge University Press.

Stranger, M. (1999). The aesthetics of risk: A study of surfing. *International Review for the Sociology of Sport*, 34(4), 265–276.

Stratton, J. (1985/1997). On the importance of subcultural origins. In K. Gelder and S. Thornton (eds), *The Subcultures Reader*. London: Routledge, pp. 181–190.

Synnott, A. (1993). *The Body Social: Symbolism Self and Society*. London: Routledge.

Thompson, G. (2001). Making waves, making men: The emergence of a professional surfing masculinity in South Africa during the late 1970s. In R. Morrell (ed.), *Changing Men in Southern Africa*. London: Zed Books, pp. 91–104.

Thornton, S. (1995). *Club Cultures: Music, Media and Subcultural Capital*. Cambridge: Polity.

—— (1997a). The social logic of subcultural capital. In K. Gelder and S. Thornton (eds), *The Subcultures Reader*. London: Routledge, pp. 200–209.

—— (1997b). General Introduction. In K. Gelder and S. Thornton (eds), *The Subcultures Reader*. London: Routledge, pp. 1–7.

Thrift, N. (1997). The still point: Resistance, expressive embodiment and dance. In S. Pile and M. Keith (eds), *Geographies of Resistance*. London: Routledge, pp. 124–151.

—— (2001). Still life in nearly present time: The object of nature. In P. Macnaghten and J. Urry (eds), *Bodies of Nature*. London: Sage, pp. 34–57.

—— (2004). Summoning life. In P. Cloke, P. Crang and M. Goodwin (eds), *Envisioning Human Geographies*. London: Arnold, pp. 81–103.

Trujillo, N. (1995). Machines, missiles, and men: Images of the male body on ABC's Monday Night Football. *Sociology of Sport Journal*, 12, 403–423.

Tuan, Y. F. (1974) *Topophilia: A Study of Environmental Perception, Attitudes and Values*. New Jersey: Prentice Hall.

Turner, B. S. (1984). *The Body and Society*. Oxford: Blackwell Ltd.

—— (1987). A note on notstaglia. *Theory, Culture and Society*, 4, 147–156.

—— (1991). Recent developments in the theory of the body. In M. Featherstone, M. Hepworth and B. Turner (eds), *The Body: Social Process and Cultural Theory*. London: Sage, pp. 1–35.

Turner, V. (1972/1978). Passages, margins and poverty: Religious symbols of communities. *Worship*, 46(7–8), 390–412/482–494.

Turner, V. (1974). Liminal or liminoid, in play, flow and ritual: An essay in comparative symbology. *Rice University Studies*, 60, 53–92.

Urry, J. (1990). *The Tourist Gaze*. London: Sage.

—— (2000). *Sociology Beyond Societies: Mobilities for the Twenty-First Century*. London: Routledge.

Van Gennep, A. (1909/1960). *The Rites of Passage*. London: Routledge and Kegan Paul.

Villamón, M., Brown, D., Espartero, J. and Gutiérrez, C. (2004). Modernization and the disembedding of Judo from 1946 to the 2000 Sydney Olympics. *International Review for the Sociology of Sport*, 39(2), 139–156.

Von Der Lippe, G. (1997). Gender discrimination in Norwegian academia: A hidden male game or an inspiration for postmodern feminist praxis. In J.-M. Fernandez-Balboa (ed.), *Critical Postmodernism in Human Movement, Physical Education and Sport*. New York: State University of New York Press, pp. 27–38.

Wallerstein, I. (1987). World-Systems Analysis. In A. Giddens and J. Turner (eds), *Social Theory Today*. Stanford: Stanford University Press.

Warshaw, M. (1997). *Above the Roar: 50 Surfer Interviews*. Santa Cruz: Waterhouse.

Wesley, J. K. (2001). Negotiating gender: Bodybuilding and the natural/unnatural continuum. *Sociology of Sport Journal*, 18(2), 162–180.

Wheaton, B. (2003). Windsurfing: A subculture of commitment. In R. Rinehart and S. Sydnor (eds), *To the Extreme: Alternative Sports, Inside and Out*. New York: State University of New York, pp. 75–101.

—— (ed.). (2004). *Understanding Lifestyle Sports: Consumption, Identity and Difference*. London: Routledge.

—— (2004). 'Just Do It': Consumption, commitment, and identity in the windsurfing subculture. *Sociology of Sport Journal*, 17(3), 254–27.

Wheaton, B. and Tomlinson, A. (1998). The changing gender order in sport? The case of windsurfing subcultures. *Journal of Sport and Social Issues*, 22(3), 254–274.

Whipp, B. J. and Ward, S. A. (1992). Will women soon outrun men? *Nature*, 355, 25.

White, L. (1967). The historical roots of our ecological crisis. *Science*, 155, 1203–1207.

Whitehead, S. M. and Barret, F. J. (eds) (2001). *The Masculinities Reader*. Cambridge: Polity Press.

Williams, J. (2002). *A study of the influence of surfing and surf culture on the identity of its participants, inside the case study of surf tourism in Newquay*. Unpublished dissertation for BA in Geography, University of Exeter, Exeter.

Williams, S. J. (2003). Marrying the social and the biological? A rejoinder to Newton. *The Editorial Board of The Sociological Review*, 550–561.

Williams, S. J. and Bendelow, G. (1998). *The Lived Body: Sociological Themes, Embodied Issues*. London: Routledge.

Wilson, P. (1991). Hossegor. In N. Carroll (ed.), *The Next Wave: A Survey of World Surfing*. London: Macdonald, pp. 172–173.

Wise, N. (1994). *The Beach Boys: In Their Own Words*. London: Omnibus.

Woodcock, G. (1977). *The Anarchist Reader*. London: Penguin.

Young, J. (1971/1997). The Subterranean world of play. In K. Gelder and S. Thornton (eds), *The Subcultures Reader*. London: Routledge, pp. 71–80.

Young, K. G. (1987). *Taleworlds and Story Realms: The Phenomenology of Narrative*. Boston: Martinus Nijhoff.

Young, N. (1994). *A History of Surfing*. Angourie, NSW, Australia: Palm Beach.

—— (ed.) (2001). *Surf Rage: A Surfer's Guide to Turning Negatives into Positives*. Angourie, NSW, Australia: Nymboida.

Zuckerman, M. (1979). *Sensation Seeking: Beyond the Optimal Level of Arousal*. Hillsdale, NJ: Lawrence Erlbaum Associates.

—— (1983). Sensation seeking and sports. *Personality and Individual Differences*, 10, 391–418.

—— (1984). Sensation seeking: A comparative approach to a human trait. *Behaviour and Brain Science*, 7, 413–434.

# Index